Unquiet Souls

Unquiet Souls

*Fourteenth-Century Saints
and Their Religious Milieu*

Richard Kieckhefer

*The University of Chicago Press
Chicago and London*

RICHARD KIECKHEFER is professor of the history and literature of religions at Northwestern University. He has written two previous books, *European Witch Trials: Their Foundations in Popular and Learned Culture, 1300–1500* and *Repression of Heresy in Medieval Germany.*

The University of Chicago Press, Chicago 60637
The University of Chicago Press, Ltd., London
© 1984 by The University of Chicago
All rights reserved. Published 1984
Printed in the United States of America

93 92 91 90 89 88 87 86 85 84   5 4 3 2 1

Library of Congress Cataloging in Publication Data

Kieckhefer, Richard.
  Unquiet souls.

  Bibliography: p.
  Includes index.
  1. Spirituality—History of doctrines—Middle Ages,
600–1500. 2. Piety—History of doctrines—Middle Ages,
600–1500. 3. Christian saints—Biography.
4. Hagiography. I. Title.
BX2350.2.K47 1984   282'.092'2 [B]   84-210
ISBN 0-226-43509-1

Contents

Henry Suso in the midst of adversity, a detail from a drawing in a fifteenth-century manuscript of the *Exemplar*, Stiftsbibliothek Einsiedeln, Cod. 710(322).

Acknowledgments

*I*n working on this book I have reflected at times on Charles of Blois. The witnesses for his canonization testified that he, like other holy men and women of the fourteenth century, was thoroughly absorbed in the lives of previous saints. We are told that at mealtime he related tales of the saints with such animation that he often neglected his food altogether. He might apprehend someone passing through a room, and insist on regaling that person with the life of some saint. Certain of his listeners found these habits wearisome, and suggested he would make a better friar than secular lord, but others were moved to profound devotion.

While I cannot claim to have evoked especially pious sentiments through my own fascination with fourteenth-century saints, I have felt something of Charles's compulsion to share this fascination with others—colleagues, students, friends and family, strangers at conventions, and anyone else willing to listen. I have profited much from the ensuing discussion, and am indebted for the help I have received, ranging from penetrating observations to bibliographic tips.

I owe gratitude to many colleagues and friends. From Barbara Newman in particular I had the benefit of numerous probing discussions on the book's historical, theological, and even editorial dimensions; her insight, well known to readers of her work, has left its mark throughout. Caroline Walker Bynum also gave the manuscript her careful attention and furnished a wealth of useful suggestions. For both the general presentation and points of detail Robert E. Lerner's critical remarks proved invaluable. Mary Douglas posed challenging questions both about the general thrust of the work and about specific aspects. Lynn Laufenberg gave the manuscript a thorough reading and made many helpful suggestions. Daniel Shaw and Melanie Starr Costello helped focus the issues in a seminar discussion of the book.

Ann Johnston provided useful medical information on Dorothy of Montau. To Father Louis Cameli I am grateful for his comments on the theological aspects of the project. Elizabeth Stegner went beyond secretarial assistance in commenting on the substance of the work. My wife Margaret and my children Daniel and Christine bore patiently with my immersion in the project. My research assistant Sheryl Weiner spent hours in the Northwestern Library putting together materials that helped greatly in locating thirteenth-century precedents for fourteenth-century sanctity. Many individuals at other institutions have been valuable sources of information and insight: Alois Haas, Anneliese Triller, André Vauchez, Marcia L. Colish, Kaspar Elm, Sister Suzanne Noffke, Elizabeth Felts McKlveen, Margot King, Anne Derbes, Maureen Slattery, James Hitchcock, Paul Gehl, and others.

For supporting trips related to this work I am deeply grateful to the American Council of Learned Societies, the Northwestern University Grant Committee, and the Alumnae of Northwestern. Their generosity has been great.

I have enjoyed kind and effective service from numerous librarians—especially Marjorie Carpenter, of the Interlibrary Loan Office at Northwestern, who tracked down some of my more obscure references as far afield as Metz, and Frau Christina Becker, of the Monumenta Germaniae Historica in Munich. Other libraries that have rendered gracious service are the Regenstein Library at the University of Chicago, the Newberry Library, the library of St. Mary of the Lake Seminary, the Bayerische Staatsbibliothek, the Stadtbibliothek München, the Deutsche Bibliothek in Frankfurt, the Stadtbibliothek Bad Windsheim, the Universitätsbibliothek Tübingen, the Bibliothèque Nationale, the Bibliothèque Calvet in Avignon, the British Library, and the library of the Istituto Storico Germanico in Rome.

1
Introduction

The saints of the fourteenth century have found little sympathy among their modern interpreters. Some of these holy men and women still have circles of devotees, but the broader culture looks on with puzzled irreverence. In his *Varieties of Religious Experience,* William James devotes three pages to Henry Suso's autobiographical account of his ascetic rigors. He recounts how during one period Suso wore a nighttime garment with a hundred fifty brass nails pointed inward; how he fashioned a cross to wear on his back, with thirty nails protruding into his flesh, so that "Whenever he sat down or stood up, it was as if a hedgehog-skin were on him"; how he took to sleeping on an old, discarded door; how he subjected himself to intense cold, drove himself mad with thirst, and endured other self-torture, all to honor "the Divine and Eternal Wisdom, our Lord Jesus Christ, whose agonizing suffering he sought to imitate." At the end of this account, James dismisses Suso as "distinctly pathological," and evidently deserving no further scrutiny. Similarly, Johan Huizinga deprecates Peter of Luxembourg as having "a narrow mind, which can only live in a carefully isolated sphere of devotion." In childhood and in adolescence—he did not live into adulthood—Peter manifested a thoroughgoing spirit of devotion and austerity which Huizinga finds repugnant. "His personality as it disengages itself from the narratives of the witnesses in the proceedings for his canonization is almost pitiful." When on one occasion Peter shows genuine understanding of what is going on around him, and "the very recesses of his narrow mind seem lighted up for a moment," the event is exceptional.[1]

These reactions are by no means isolated. In fiction, too, the saints appear as alien characters. Günter Grass, in his quasi-historical work entitled *The Flounder,* draws upon historical sources to give an unflattering portrayal of Dorothy of Montau. For him she was "an unfortunate woman who suffered under the servitudes of her time—more foolish than clever, tormented by insomnia and migraine, a slovenly housekeeper, yet remarkably efficient when it came to organizing processions of flagellants, a woman of gaunt beauty and ruthlessly strong will, despite her hours of convulsive ecstasy unable to think up appealing miracles, endowed with a slight lyrical gift, sluggish in bed but energetic with the scourge, a good walker, hence adept at pilgrimages. . . ." Grass does not dismiss Dorothy as quickly as James and Huizinga dispatch their fourteenth-century saints, yet the rest of what he has to say is in the same vein. Elsewhere one finds a tone of bewilderment. When Barbara Tuchman was planning her book on the fourteenth century, *A Distant Mirror,* she sought a central figure around whom the presentation might revolve, and she ruled out the choice of a cleric or saint such as Catherine of Siena, "because they are outside my comprehension." Her attitude is not surprising: although Catherine is one of the saints with a modern following, the sources for her life show exuberant austerity and devotion similar to what the other saints displayed. One psychiatrist suggests, in a nuanced and generally sympathetic discussion of saintly mortification, that it was anorexia nervosa that led Catherine to starve herself to death at age thirty-three. At the risk of giving scandal, he ventures to say that "the entire history of Catherine of Siena is that of a partially sublimated sado-masochism." He admits being tempted to write a psychoanalysis of her: "The psychoanalyst can find there everything he is looking for."[2]

Seen as isolated personalities, these figures may indeed appear simply mad. Once one looks at them together, discerning common patterns in their spirituality and noting that these patterns occur time and again in the lives of fourteenth-century saints across much of Europe, one begins to ask: can the epidemic of madness have been so widespread? Perhaps so, but then the question is why these figures aroused reverence as well as fascination among their contemporaries. Could the entire culture have become infected? Surely the answer is not that simple.

One might seek to explain the saintly excesses of the era by setting them within the broader context of late medieval culture, which has long impressed historians as overwrought. For Huizinga, there was a sense in which Peter of Luxembourg typified his excitable era, so readily disposed toward extremes of passion, both violent and devout. Writers such as Millard Meiss have tended to see the Black Death, which claimed at least a quarter of the population in mid-century and recurred thereafter, as a main cause of the frenzied, overcharged culture that became so pronounced in fourteenth-century Europe. At most, though, the Black Death accentuated a feverish mood that was already well established. In an essay on the mental climate of the century, David Knowles characterized even the intellectual life of the period as tending to draw extreme conclusions from long-established premises: the Franciscan Spirituals pressed the demand for absolute poverty to its limits, the Nominalists took the notion of divine freedom to extremes, political theorists pursued Aristotelian premises more boldly than their predecessors, and so likewise with other leading thinkers. If even the intellectual leaders tended to such intensity, one might reflect, what could be expected of less sophisticated minds?[3]

Indeed, much the same kind of development was occurring in the piety of the era, as traditional motifs became endowed with passionate intensity, not only among the saints. Christendom had long been familiar with penitential self-affliction, patient submission to suffering, absorption in Christ's passion, and states of spiritual bliss or excitation that one might call mystical, yet the sources for the fourteenth century suggest that all these forms of spiritual life took on a feverish intensity in the fourteenth century that was more pronounced, more widespread, and (perhaps most importantly) more widely respected than before. In that regard the spirituality of the era shares in that intensification seen elsewhere in fourteenth-century culture.

To place these developments within such a broad cultural framework, however, is not in itself to explain them. It is not enough to say that fourteenth-century saints were intense because their era was intense, or that general spirituality was intense because intensity was somehow in the air. However elusive a full explanation may be, one must at least try to probe further—to describe, analyze, and then in some measure explain these trends—which is what this book will attempt to do.

Late Medieval Hagiography: The Sources

As a first step toward an explanation, let us examine briefly the sources we have at our disposal for the saints' lives. It should be a truism that when we study the saints of the fourteenth or any other century what we are in fact studying are not the saints themselves but the documents that claim to inform us about them. To be precise, we should not say that Peter of Luxembourg confessed his sins several times daily but that the sources represent him as so doing. We should not speak of Dorothy of Montau as indifferent when eight of her nine children died but should merely say that the sources convey no sense of emotional response. When the sources tell us that Catherine of Siena remained celibate, we may reasonably trust this information; to accept their version of the resulting conflict with her parents, and to build an interpretation of social dynamics on this foundation, is to place one's faith in what may be partly a literary topos. In general, what we need to explain is not the feverish intensity of the saints themselves but that of the sources. Because it would be tedious to repeat such qualifications at every turn, they will be left unsaid but understood in this study. The problem is one that arises in any historical inquiry, but saints' biographers are notoriously fond of ideal stereotypes, and saints are thus likely to be hidden behind a more than usually heavy veil of pious convention. To be sure, a saint described in stereotypical ways may actually have been living out traditional ideas of sanctity. But it is usually impossible to determine the extent of the sources' historical accuracy, so we must ultimately bracket out the question of historicity and focus on the texts themselves. The central question is not why the saints were as they appear in the sources; they may or may not in fact have been so. The fruitful question is why their biographers represented them as they did—why they recognized certain traits and not others as integral to sanctity.[4]

Apart from such general caveats, one must be aware of specific trends in the sources for any particular era—and in the thirteenth and fourteenth centuries there were important changes occurring in the documents for saints' lives, changes which have bearing on the content.

The sources for the saints of the late Middle Ages fall into two main categories. First there were vitae, or narratives of their lives (to which accounts of posthumous miracles were often appended). Usually written soon after the saint's death, a vita sought to persuade the populace that the holy man or woman was in heaven and could serve as an effective intercessor, so that people would pray for the saint's intercession and thus obtain the miracles required for canonization. At the same time, the vita endeavored to persuade the papal curia that the holy man or woman was genuinely holy and a faithful child of the church; this needed to be shown because scoundrels of all kinds might gain popular veneration as saints, as records from the fourteenth century amply testify. To appeal to their lay audience, the vitae might contain evidence of charismatic or miraculous powers; to persuade the curia, they would relate in detail the saints' virtues. Second, there are *processus canonizationis,* canonization proceedings, or records of what witnesses deposed in quasi-judicial inquiries to determine eligibility for canonization. The witnesses were generally selected because they were sympathetic, and their answers to the fixed lists of questions almost always supported the cause of canonization. None of this means that the writers of vitae or the witnesses in canonization proceedings were insincere or dishonest—only that their reverence for the saints conditioned what they saw as relevant testimony, and that in subtle or less subtle ways their devotion could color their perceptions and recollections.[5]

Apart from these explicitly hagiographic materials, there are supporting texts of various kinds that shed further light on the saints' spirituality, on their day-to-day lives, and on contemporaries' perceptions of them: treatises written or dictated by the saints can be especially helpful sources for their spirituality, and letters written by or to them lend information about daily events and their reactions to them. This book will take into account not only these materials but an even wider body of devotional literature, in an effort to place the saints within the broad context of late medieval religious culture from which they derived nourishment: sermons, poetry, drama, and many other materials. But the main repositories will be the vitae and the canonization proceedings.

One important development of the thirteenth and fourteenth centuries was a dramatic increase in the sheer volume of these materials. The increase is partly in the rate of survival: writings of almost all kinds survive in greater proportions from the later medieval centuries. There were special reasons, though, for proliferation of hagiographic texts. By the early thirteenth century the popes had established their exclusive right to canonize saints. Eager to assert this authority, they responded favorably to numerous requests for canonization: a recent study lists twenty papal canonization processes during the thirteenth century, most of them leading successfully to canonization, in contrast to a mere handful earlier. This meant that churchmen throughout Western Christendom, seeking to prove in Rome the sanctity of their local holy men and women, had to send both delegations and written materials to Rome to secure the canonizations. Vitae, canonization proceedings, and other documents were assembled at Rome in unprecedented abundance. By the fourteenth century, though, procedures for canonization had grown far more complex, and required onerous expenditure of time and money. Many candidates for sainthood, never elevated to that rank, remained *beati*, or blessed. (The distinction between *sancti* and *beati* was first articulated in the fourteenth century; a *beatus* then was merely a person venerated locally but without papal confirmation.) There are only twelve known papal canonization processes from this century. Whether successful or unsuccessful, the increasingly complex efforts on behalf of candidates now produced extraordinarily thick dossiers. The canonization proceedings for Delphina of Puimichel run in the modern edition to 548 pages, exclusive of apparatus; similar records survive for Bridget of Sweden, Peter of Luxembourg, Catherine of Siena, Dorothy of Montau, Nicholas Hermansson, and Urban V. Catherine's confessor wrote a vita for her that was uncommonly long and full. Dorothy of Montau's wrote several accounts of her life, one in German and others in Latin, the longest of which runs to 363 pages in a modern edition, again excluding scholarly apparatus. For both of these women we also have treatises or letters that they wrote or dictated. Their lives are thus better documented than that of any previous saint, excepting perhaps only Augustine of Hippo. For sheer bulk of evidence, the saints of the fourteenth century present a scholar's delight.[6]

Alongside the standard vitae, the fourteenth century produced important specimens of spiritual autobiography. The best known instance is Henry Suso's *Life of the Servant,* which William James found so distasteful, but which impresses many readers with its richly poetic expression of intense religious feeling. Here as in other works, Suso depicts himself as the faithful though sorely tested servant of Eternal Wisdom (i.e., Christ); amidst his torments he enjoys intermittent visions of angels and other celestial beings. Georg Misch has characterized this book as "a work in grand style . . . which belongs to the highest ranks of religious autobiography," and a new departure in the history of a soul, distinctive for the mystical view of human experience in which it is grounded. To this one may add Rulman Merswin's agonizing recollections of his own religious conversion, and from the early fifteenth century we have Margery Kempe's autobiography, the earliest in the English language. These works are far from containing unrelieved self-glorification, yet they present their authors as such fervently devout souls that one might speak of the genre as autohagiography. In addition there are frequent autobiographical fragments in that mystical literature which flourished in the fourteenth century; the works of Julian of Norwich and Richard Rolle, for example, present insight into their authors' lives. It is ironic that the mystics, bent on dissolving self-consciousness in their contact with the divine, should have been prone to autobiography; but to the extent that what they had to relate was mystical experience, they alone were in a position to tell of it, however haltingly.[7]

At least as important as these autobiographical materials are those that one might call quasi-autobiographical. Certain women saints of the era had biographers who had been their confessors, their devotees, even their disciples. As André Vauchez observes, relationships of this kind became increasingly common at this time: Catherine of Siena, Dorothy of Montau, and Bridget of Sweden are conspicuous examples.[8] Their biographers had spent countless hours listening to the saints tell of their spiritual lives and their treatment at the hands of fellow townspeople or family members. At times they probed the saints' attitudes toward these experiences. Essentially, what they gathered was oral autohagiography. They thus had privileged access to their subjects' own perceptions of their lives, and they shared these perceptions with their readers.

There was precedent, of course, for all such genres. There were several autobiographies by saints; the classic model for spiritual autobiography was Augustine's *Confessions*. Yet comparison with Augustine's work is instructive: whereas Augustine set forth in his autobiography a theology of Christian life, the autobiographical works of the late Middle Ages tend to contain only implicit theology; and while Augustine took his own experience as a starting-point for reflection on that grace which is integral to Christian experience, the late medieval autobiographies focus on the special graces and especially the mystical experiences of the saints. The autobiographical fragments in mystical literature, again, have precedents: Hildegard of Bingen left such fragments in her accounts of her visions, primarily in order to validate the visions themselves and place them in context, and for similar reasons Elizabeth of Schönau gives more sustained and frequently poignant testimony to the agonies she underwent. The quasi-autobiographical works were anticipated by vitae such as that of Mary of Oignies, written by her confessor and disciple James of Vitry. Even allowing for such precedents, however, the hagiographic literature of the fourteenth century is far richer in these materials: there are more examples, and the individual works tend to be longer and fuller. Perhaps most importantly, there were more saints in the fourteenth century who remained active in the world, and whose autobiographical reactions to the varied circumstances of secular life are more diverse and hold greater narrative interest than the inward lives of cloistered saints.[9]

The autobiographical and quasi-autobiographical materials, taken together, have strongly affected modern perceptions of late medieval piety. While they do not constitute the greater part of the source material, they include texts which have had wide influence and continue to be read, whether sympathetically or critically. Partly because they are distinctive, and partly because they tend to be dramatic, they have made a vivid impression on readers.

While these materials present the saints' lives from the inner perspectives of the saints themselves, this is not to say that they are marked by psychological realism. Indeed, rather than attempting to display the workings of an individual soul, the saints and their biographers drew heavily, as in preceding centuries, upon traditional types and models. Catherine of Siena's biographer, for instance, assimilated her to Anthony the Abbot, Francis of Assisi, Moses, and other figures.[10] What is distinctive is that in the process of applying these models the biographers reveal the passionate intensity with which the saints themselves sought to take upon themselves the sufferings of the martyrs, the rigors of the desert fathers, and the Franciscan modes of imitating Christ. The intensity is that of a person struggling mightily to follow a distant and romanticized ideal. Stereotypical as the struggle might be, these vitae portray it with a combination of vividness and unreality which forthrightly produces a grotesque impression. The very form of the vita thus lends itself to expression of a particular view of sanctity.

Late Medieval Hagiography: The Theological Vision

While the hagiographers were not writing formal theology, there is a theological vision of the saintly life implicit in what they wrote. The main purpose of this book is to distill that vision and show its place in late medieval religious culture. Later chapters will attempt to unfold this outlook in concrete detail; for now, a preliminary sketch may prove useful.

Explicit theological statements do often occur in the prologues to the vitae. Thus, Dorothy of Montau's biographer began one of his accounts of her life with reflections on Ephesians 5:16, in which Paul exhorts his readers to proceed circumspectly, "redeeming the time, because the days are evil."[11] Looking at the state of the church and of secular government, the biographer saw nothing but disarray. The church in particular had fallen on evil days, divided as it was in schism. Portents in the heavens declared the sorry lot of Christendom; at the sound of the fourth angel's trumpet "the third part of the sun was smitten . . . and the third part of the stars, so that the third part of them was in darkness" (Apoc. 8:12) out of contempt for the church and disobedience to its mandates. The Lord had sought to redeem these evil times by sending Dorothy and equipping her with the requisite virtues: "He washed her with the water of refreshing tears, and with desire and love for the pleasant company of the blessed. He cleansed her of blood through unheard of castigations and disciplines. He anointed her with the oil of finest mercy and fragrant piety." He placed her in Prussia, on the fringes of Christendom, so that her contemporaries might be cured of their sanguinary inclinations through her prayer and example, just as the woman with a hemorrhage was cured by touching the fringe of Christ's tunic (Mk. 5:25–34). Being a woman, she was frail; in the eyes of the learned she might appear foolish. But the Lord chooses the weak to confound the strong, and the foolish to confound the wise. More than two centuries earlier, Hildegard of Bingen had cited this inversion of strength and weakness to justify her vocation as prophet: given the weakness and womanliness of contemporary males, God had elevated a frail woman to rectify the abuses of the age. Unlike Hildegard, Dorothy of Montau seems never to have claimed a public vocation, yet her biographer saw redemptive efficacy in the public proclamation of her private life.[12]

The vita of Nicholas Hermansson opens with rather different hints at a theology of sainthood. It is dangerous, his biographer says, to praise a holy person while he is still alive; one risks the temptations of adulation and presumption. Once such a person is safely dead, though, one may and should extol his merits. Just as Gedeon and his companions hid their lamps until such time as they could stun their enemies with the blinding light, so also with saints: while alive they are despised and judged worthless by their impious contemporaries, but when they glisten with miracles after death they stun their adversaries and often bring them to repentance. More specifically, says the biographer, we celebrate and reflect on the merits of the saints for two reasons. First, that God may be praised and honored in his saints (cf. Ps. 150:1), whom he glorifies not only in heaven but also on earth by means of miracles. Second, so that others may be incited to good works in imitation of those whom they delight in celebrating, and that they too may thus obtain the grace of justification. Though we cannot commemorate all the saints, it is fitting that each region, city, or parish should honor its own patron; indeed, the command to "Honor thy father and thy mother" can be interpreted as applying to these spiritual parents. Just as France venerates Denis, England honors Thomas Becket, and Sweden generally celebrates Sigfrid, so those in the diocese of Linköping should venerate their father Nicholas.[13]

In short, while Dorothy of Montau's biographer attempted in his prologue to show her role for a specific time, Nicholas Hermansson's focused on his significance for a particular place. Yet there was nothing specific about Dorothy that made her appropriate for her time, or about Nicholas that made him uniquely fitting for his place; what was needed above all was simply a saintly figure, or someone who conveyed a sense of divine presence and efficacy, to redeem and sanctify his or her milieu.

These prologues help to clarify the authors' theological understanding of why the saints should be venerated, and why it was important to write their vitae. What they do not convey is a sense of why the vitae depicted the saints specifically as they did, or why they highlighted certain themes and left others undeveloped. It is these latter questions, though, which are vital to the theological vision of sainthood, and for answers to them we must turn not to the prologues but to the chapters that follow. What one finds there, at least in many important texts, is a fairly clear and distinctive notion of sanctity. The vitae of the fourteenth century are not uniformly and absolutely different from those of earlier periods, to be sure, but there are important differences in overall thrust.

The first such feature may be stated concisely: if earlier hagiography represented God as working *through* the saint, the tendency now was to show God as working *for* the saint.[14] The vitae of the earlier Middle Ages commonly show the saints as epic heroes, bristling with heroic outward deeds; as commanding figures, intimate with God and exercising charismatic power before society; as bearers of *virtus* in the double sense of "virtue" and "power." The hagiographers of the fourteenth century, on the other hand, often recapture an Augustinian fascination with the inner life and an equally Augustinian sense of disquietude. In many instances the saint is a tortured soul, acted upon by human and demonic adversaries, but saved ultimately by divine action. The holy life appears as a strenuous and uncertain groping toward a goal not fully perceived, let alone conceptualized. The saint is a figure overwhelmed with grace and devotion, overwhelmed with adversity, overwhelmed with feelings of guilt and penitence. The obstacles to holiness appear not only at the outset but throughout the saint's life. Both sides of the dialectic show God working for the saint: he is the one who sends or permits the suffering, and at the same time he gives the saint grace and strength to endure. This later viewpoint is in some ways more realistic than the earlier triumphal view of saintliness: the holy life is in fact one of struggle and uncertainty, and the saint's acknowledgment of dependence on God is true to Christian notions of salvation. At the same time, this vision of the saintly life is itself a cultural product, molded by its own set of conventions— which will be subject matter for the bulk of this study—and was not simply a formulation of eternal verities. Ultimately, the saints' disquietude reflects Augustine's conception of the soul as restless in its quest for God, though this Augustinian theme becomes translated into a late medieval idiom, less subtle than that of the Latin Father.

So long as God's work *through* the saints had been emphasized, it was apparent that his power extended beyond them to their society, or to the beneficiaries of their charity and miraculous powers; but now God appeared to be concentrating his efforts on the saints themselves. He could still be seen as working for Christian society, but less directly. His saints became channels for divine self-revelation mainly when his work in them was publicly proclaimed. Thus the role of hagiography was crucial, as the biographers of Dorothy of Montau and Nicholas Hermansson were keenly aware. It was the vita that not only advertised the saint's life (as had always been the case), but pro-

vided the necessary interpretation of it, calling to the reader's attention what was not obvious, that the agonies of the saint manifested
God's purging rod and his sustaining grace.

These tendencies were especially pronounced in the autobiographical and quasi-autobiographical materials. In these texts,
which present the saints' lives from their own points of view, the tri-
umphalism of most earlier hagiography is clearly replaced with an
emphasis on the strenuous and often frustrating quest for holiness.
The feverish qualities criticized by James, Grass, and others arise
from such attempts to highlight this strenuousness.

A second keynote of fourteenth-century hagiography is a tendency
to accent the darker side of earthly life. Late medieval saints and hagiographers shared with Augustine, and indeed with Christians of all
eras, a conviction that the miseries of this life are ultimately redressed
only in the afterlife. What they did not share was a sense of provisional fulfillment and provisional access to God available even here below,
not in spite of but precisely through the created order. Augustine
looked at creation and saw in it evidence of the creator. The same
recognition of the sacramental and thus sacral character of the created world appears in the Franciscan literature of the thirteenth century, including the early vitae of Francis of Assisi. Herman Joseph, a
Premonstratensian saint roughly contemporary with Francis, coped
with tribulation by contemplating the heavenly reward that he anticipated; but one night, as he immersed himself in such contemplation,
he came to an open window, beheld the heavens, and found in them a
delightful reminder of his creator. He prayed, "Oh Lord, creator of
all, while I live in this Babylon I must know you 'through a glass in a
dark manner' [1 Cor. 13:12]; yet give me knowledge of your creatures, by which my mind may be raised somewhat toward more perfect knowledge of you." At once he was caught up in rapture, in which
God granted him special knowledge of the created order. Such coun-
terthrusts to the otherworldliness of Christianity can be found elsewhere in hagiography; even the saints' miracles can serve as
reminders that the natural order is suffused with grace. Yet there is
very little of this conception in fourteenth-century saints' lives. In the
autobiographies and quasi-autobiographies there are even relatively
few cases in which the saints during their lifetimes bless the natural
world with their miraculous powers.[15]

This unrelieved otherworldliness is paralleled by other tendencies
in the hagiography of the era, and linked with them. There is an
emphasis on patience that is not balanced by a commitment to reform
the world and find remedies for its afflictions; the ultimate end and
reward for suffering could not be expected on earth, and the best
response was patient endurance. There is an absorption in the pas-

sion of Christ that is not balanced by attention to his resurrection; the individual's sharing in the resurrection was essentially a future expectation, and during the present life one remained a sufferer along with Christ. The texts convey a sense of sinfulness that is not linked to a consciousness of redemption and forgiveness; penitence was a constant need so long as one remained a *viator* here below. There is a preoccupation with exceptional, mystical states that is not balanced by recognition of the sacrality in normal life; ecstatic states during this life were foretastes of the afterlife rather than ways of sanctifying present existence. In other words, life on earth was a vale of tears that called for patience, penitence, assimilation to the suffering Christ, and fervent yearning for escape. Qualifications to this characterization could be introduced, and later chapters will attempt to refine this analysis. Essentially, however, the theological vision in fourteenth-century hagiography displays a systematic imbalance, or rather a set of related imbalances.

The piety of the era has often been described as introspective—as encouraging a fascination and concern with one's own state of soul more than an attention to outward and objective realities.[16] Something of this sort can be seen, especially in the autobiographical and quasi-autobiographical sources. This self-absorption was not an isolated phenomenon, however, but was linked with the other forms of imbalance we have discussed: brooding consciousness of guilt would inevitably encourage introspective concern with one's state of soul; labored emphasis on mystical states could again encourage such inwardness; patience meant accommodation to the external world, but seems to have directed attention mainly toward one's own response to affliction; even devotion to the passion, which in a different context could become a way of focusing on transcendent mysteries, seems instead to have encouraged self-conscious fascination with one's own anguish.

Such pervasive imbalance surely did not arise from simple inadvertence. As we shall see in subsequent chapters, there were historical reasons for asserting the value of patience at the expense of a more active spirituality, for stressing guilt more than forgiveness, and so forth. From a theological viewpoint, the important effect of the imbalance was to highlight at every juncture the sense of strenuousness and disquietude. By setting aside the sacramental conception of earthly life—or clearly subordinating it to a darker conception of this life—and by slighting along with it the assurance of forgiveness and resurrection, hagiographers were able to convey all the more effectively the saints' agonizing struggle for holiness.

It is difficult at times to know how the hagiographers expected the reader to respond to these themes in the vitae. Nicholas Hermansson's biographer spoke of the saint's exemplary role: as the saint had done, so should the reader do. There was a well-established tradition in medieval hagiography, though, which distinguished between *imitanda* and *admiranda*, the imitable deeds of the saint and those which should arouse a sense of wonder. This theme is seldom so explicitly developed as in the thirteenth-century life of Mary of Oignies. Having recounted ascetic rigors that would seem mild by fourteenth-century norms, her biographer warns the reader against imitation:

> I do not tell this to recommend her excess, but to show her fervor. The discreet reader must note, in regard to these things and many others that she did with the privilege of grace, that the privileges of a few do not constitute law for all. Her virtues should be imitated, but we are not to imitate her deeds of virtue without private privilege. For although one may force one's body to serve the spirit, and although we ought to bear in our bodies the wounds of our Lord Jesus Christ (cf. Gal. 6:17), nonetheless we know that "the king's honour loveth judgment" (Ps. 98:4), nor is sacrifice plundered from the pauper pleasing to the Lord (cf. Is. 3:14, 61:8). Necessities should not be withdrawn from the pauper flesh, but its vices should be repressed. Therefore, when we read what certain saints did on the personal counsel of the Holy Spirit, we should wonder at their deeds rather than imitate them [*admiremur potius quam imitemur*].[17]

The biographer of Herman Joseph makes the same distinction, and says that to imitate the saints' extremes (their *admiranda*) is as bad as not to imitate their virtues (their *imitanda*): if negligence in following their virtues is a sign of sluggishness, pursuit of their extremes can lead to ruin. The topos recurs in Bonaventure's life of Francis of Assisi, can be found in certain fourteenth-century vitae, and arises again, for example, in the writings of Teresa of Avila. It is essentially a way of expressing the traditional notion of vocation: some individuals have a calling to lives of exceptional rigor, but most do not, and must content themselves with thanking God for what he makes possible in his chosen few.[18]

Yet the distinction is not altogether unproblematic. It always had been one basic function of a saint, after all, to demonstrate in concrete detail what a life of virtue entails. One was to learn from the life of a saint what it meant to be charitable, penitent, and so forth. If one had to distinguish between the general virtues of the saint and their specific manifestation, how was one to disentangle the former from the latter? The biographer of Mary of Oignies clarifies the point by a specific example. Having related how Mary and her husband took a vow of chastity, and how the bond of their spiritual marriage brought him to greater love for her when he had forsworn carnal affection, the biographer continues:

> Let those unhappy persons blush and tremble, who pollute themselves outside of marriage with illicit intercourse, seeing that these blessed youth conquered the impulses of youthful ardor by the fervor of religion, and abstained even from licit embraces for the Lord's sake.[19]

The point is, so to speak, essentially an argument *a fortiori:* if a saint is able to overcome lust even to this heroic degree, then an ordinary Christian should all the more be capable of normal chastity. The same could apply to other areas of life: if the saint can subject his flesh to the harshest mortifications out of love for the crucified Savior, others should be able to bear lesser sacrifices; if those called to the heights of sanctity agonized over the slightest peccadillos, those with a greater burden of guilt should at least display the normal contrition required for sacramental penance.

As we shall see, this logic was routinely at work in the lives of four-teenth-century saints, who inclined with exceptional consistency and with dramatic intensity toward the inimitable extremes. If the lives of fourteenth-century saints aroused revulsion in readers such as James and Huizinga, this should cause no surprise. They no doubt provoked equal revulsion among fourteenth-century readers, and in all like-lihood they were intended to have just that impact. The saints' *admiranda* were evidently meant to arouse more than admiration, more even than wonderment: they were supposed to shock the reader, to provoke in him a moral reform, to suggest that the way toward per-fection was a strenuous path that required as much fervor as one could sustain.

Although the hagiography of the fourteenth century was marked with new intensity, the principles it imparted were essentially tradi-tional and monastic. The general trends seen in the saints' lives can be traced back for centuries, and these trends had been gaining in popu-larity since the eleventh century at least. Devotion to the passion of Christ and penitential spirituality had been central themes in the mon-astic writings of the high Middle Ages, and had been popularized largely through the effort of the Franciscans, Dominicans, and other mendicant orders. Visions and other mystical experiences had surged in importance with the rise of women's mysticism in the twelfth cen-tury. Much has been made of the rise, in the thirteenth and fourteenth centuries, of a distinctively lay religious culture. In fact, many of the saints of the fourteenth century were laypeople, or members of the semireligious mendicant third orders, or mendicant friars who spent their careers mingling with the laity and addressing their needs. Yet while there was a shift in the context of sanctity, there was essential continuity in its content. Rather than developing new models of saintliness, to exalt the sanctity of marriage and of work in society, the lay saints as well as the mendicants imbibed a spirituality transferred from the monastery. The harsh asceticism they took upon themselves, their thoroughgoing absorption in prayer, and their alienation from the world about them all grew out of the monastic tradition. Many of them are reported to have wept profusely, out of contrition or devotion; for centuries, it had been a standard theme that the business of the monks was to weep. The specific practices and devotions—penitential flagellation, fondness for Mary in various protective roles, devotion to the passion of Christ, and so forth—generally emerged from the monasteries. While the context of lay piety was secular, its substance was essentially that of the cloister. Not that laypeople were coerced into adopting such norms, but over the centuries it was monastic spirituality that had defined what a saint was, and monastic conceptions could not readily be superseded.[20]

The shift in context did have an impact on the content of piety, in the sense that traditional themes lost much of their subtlety; in the process of becoming popular, spirituality lost its connection with explicit and mature theology. The fourteenth century witnessed a profusion of devotional literature that made no claim to theological sophistication. Augustine and Bernard of Clairvaux might be cited in the popular literature of the late Middle Ages, but not imitated; Hildegard of Bingen might be followed, but at a distance. This was, one might argue, the inevitable result of democratization. One might still find sophisticated expression of ascetic and mystical theology in works written for elites—for example, in *The Cloud of Unknowing*.[21] One might also find works that miscalculated the sophistication of their audiences, such as the sermons of Meister Eckhart. But it was the genuinely popular literature that seems to have done most toward setting the tone for late medieval conceptions of sanctity. None of this, however, precludes the possibility of a serious theological vision implicit or partially articulated in this literature. Even in the narrative setting of the saints' lives, where one might least expect to find formal theologizing, there is an underlying theology of the ideal Christian life that is worthy of exploration.

Plan of This Book

In setting forth the theological vision of fourteenth-century hagiography, this book will—after introductory sketches of three representative saints—explore four basic themes. With some qualifications, this study may be seen as a series of essays on four major elements in fourteenth-century sanctity: the virtues of the saints, with special reference to the virtue of patience; their private devotions, specifically their devotion to the passion of Christ; their participation in the sacramental life of the Church, with the focus on penance; and their inner spirituality, as seen in their experiences of rapture and revelation. Any of these themes might be broadened. Virtues such as obedience and charity might be treated alongside patience, for example, and eucharistic as well as penitential themes might be highlighted. Yet the specific foci here selected are those that dominate in the fourteenth-century literature, particularly the hagiography.

The major qualification that must be introduced is that this schema is in many ways too tidy: as we shall see, discussion of the saints' penitence leads back to discussion of their virtues, just as unfolding of their mystical experience requires understanding of eucharistic and Marian devotions, and in other ways the categories sketched above become lost in a crisscross of interconnections. Few themes in the piety of the late Middle Ages, or of any other era, can be dealt with in isolation from other strands of religious life. Nonetheless, this simplified schema may serve as a starting point, or as an indication of the basic thrust of each chapter.

Throughout, this book will examine the ideals of holy life that the saints embodied, rather than the canonical status of sainthood. Whether an individual received the canonical rank of saint was often a matter of political circumstances, and might reflect more the developments of later centuries than the mentality of the saint's own day. For our purposes, the term "saint" must thus be used in a broad sense, to include persons officially canonized as saints, those venerated as blessed but not canonized, and even a few who are represented in hagiographic fashion in the sources for their lives despite total absence of cult. In short, the term will stand here for all those persons represented as distinctly holy figures in the biographical writings of the era.

The chronological limits of this work will be similarly loose. The individuals studied here lived in the fourteenth century, in the sense that they spent the bulk of their adult lives in that century; for the most part they died between 1320 and 1420. In a broad overview of this kind there is no problem in annexing to the fourteenth century the last years of the thirteenth and the first years of the fifteenth. More crucial is the question of when the sources were composed: an account written within a few years of a saint's death in 1420 may still give valuable testimony to fourteenth-century notions of holiness, but a vita written a century after its subject expired in 1375 is prima-facie suspect evidence, and may breathe an atmosphere different from that of its subject.

Why the fourteenth century? There is an element of arbitrariness in any periodization, particularly in an area such as the history of spirituality. It is the essence of spirituality to draw nourishment from the sources of tradition; it is by its nature conservative (except, of course, when it is reactionary), and thus one cannot expect to find clear points of departure in its evolution. To the extent that one can distinguish broad and in some ways subtle shifts, it might be argued that the natural unit for study is not the fourteenth century, but rather the thirteenth through fifteenth centuries—from the rise of the mendicant orders, and the development of curial procedures for formal canonization, to the onset of the Reformation. This suggestion would indeed be persuasive, except for two further considerations. First, by limiting ourselves to the fourteenth century we can more easily place the sanctity of the era within its broad cultural context; we can see how trends in spirituality were reflected also in general literature and in art. To do this for three centuries would make for an unwieldy survey. Second, while much that can be said about the fourteenth century can be said as well about the thirteenth and fifteenth, the fourteenth century presents the key trends in bolder relief. In the thirteenth century there were several figures who displayed a feverish spirituality; Christina the Astonishing and Mary of Oignies are textbook examples. Yet these individuals were for the most part women with little influence during their lives and limited posthumous cult. By the fourteenth century the seeds of fervor had yielded fruit in abundance, and leading figures, men as well as women, began to share in it. Catherine of Siena and Bridget of Sweden, both widely venerated by their contemporaries and canonized soon after their deaths, manifested acute spiritual sensitivity and had to overcome reputations as fanatics. A prominent preacher and writer such as Henry Suso, an influential bishop like Nicholas Hermansson, a noble and courtier as powerful as Elzear of Sabran—all these and others manifested the devotional intensity that seems to have marked the fourteenth century more consistently than other periods. To some extent there was a feminization of male piety, as men began to adopt the extreme fervor previously reserved for women. The fifteenth century saw a withdrawal from these trends, an abatement in the level of intensity, though to pursue fifteenth-century developments in detail would require another book.

The intent of this book may become clearer by comparison with two other recent books dealing with sainthood in the later Middle Ages: André Vauchez's *La Sainteté en occident aux derniers siècles du Moyen Age d'après les procès de canonisation et les documents hagiographiques* (Sainthood in the West in the last centuries of the Middle Ages, according to the processes of canonization and the hagiographic documents), and Donald Weinstein and Rudolph M. Bell's *Saints and Society: The Two Worlds of Western Christendom, 1000–1700*.[22] While both of these works are broader in chronological scope than the present study, from their rather different perspectives they cover much of the same subject matter to be examined here.

Vauchez deals primarily with the cult of saints and the ecclesiastical control of that cult in the thirteenth through fifteenth centuries. He draws mainly from the canonization proceedings and related documents, to show how popular cults emerged and how the Church responded to them; his work also cites the vitae, but they are of secondary relevance. He traces the history of papal canonization: its emergence around 1200; the thirteenth century, when popes readily canonized holy men and women upon local request; and the following period, when "the smallest town, soon the smallest village, wanted to have a patron saint of its own," but the popes, frightened by the anarchic proliferation of cults, left most of these would-be saints with the lesser dignity of *beati*. He also shows differences in the very conception of sainthood. By the fourteenth century, the popes held an elitist notion of sainthood, and preferred to canonize individuals distinguished by their noble birth and intellectual or ecclesiastical achievement. In the last quarter of that century, the popes were increasingly receptive to mystical currents of sanctity, typified by Bridget of Sweden. Yet populace and papacy were working at cross-purposes: while popes refused canonization to most of the local patrons, there was little popular support for many of the pope's choices. Elzear of Sabran aroused little enthusiasm among the populace of Christendom, and Bridget of Sweden, whose cause was promoted more by her Italian friends than by her fellow Swedes, was such a controversial figure that her canonization of 1391 had to be confirmed in 1415 and 1419. In the last quarter of the fourteenth and the first quarter of the fifteenth century, "official" sainthood underwent influence from pietist and reforming circles, yet these were again the concerns of the hierarchy more than of the people. The canonization of Catherine of Siena owed more to the efforts of reformists in her order than to the devotion of her native town. Vauchez refines these theses with further distinctions—geographical, social, and otherwise. Essentially, he is interested in ascertaining those factors of ecclesiastical politics that differentiated various models of sanctity in the late Middle Ages. It is a central contention of his book that by the fourteenth century there were divergent and competing notions of saintliness.

The present book will attempt to supplement Vauchez's by showing that amid all this diversity there were also certain constants. While it is always useful to distinguish differing types of saints, and to show which groups in society identified themselves with which types, it is likewise essential to attend to those themes which cut across all possible typologies, recur in a kaleidoscope of ever-shifting permutations, emerge in times and places where they are perhaps least expected, and when repeatedly stressed tend to define the saintly ideals of a culture. Whether it was a priest in a small German town or a cleric in the shadow of the papal curia who wrote a saint's life, in the fourteenth century the finished vita would be likely to emphasize such themes as patience and devotion to the passion, themes which were common not only in the era's hagiography but in its broader culture.

The book by Weinstein and Bell is a collective biography of saints from the high Middle Ages through the early modern era. The first part deals with the stages of life through which saints, like other human beings, passed: childhood, which from the late twelfth century on was a time in which girls especially broke away from the worldliness of their families and turned to that ascetic life which eventually would blossom in sainthood; adolescence, when more deliberate rejection of parental values became possible, in response to the call of preachers or other figures outside the family; and adulthood, when dramatic conversions to religious life were still possible but were usually seen as crucial moments in a long process of spiritual growth. Weinstein and Bell show in detail how different members of the family were likely to respond to these conversions to religious fervor; they argue that in the sixteenth century there was a tendency for familial relations to recede in significance, as conversions more often occurred away from home (for example, at universities). The central conclusion of this part of the book is that later medieval vitae show the saints living within a context of strong familial affection; even parental resistance to conversion was based on deep-set care for younger members of the family. The authors thus perceive in the Middle Ages what some historians have represented as a new development in the eighteenth century: the rise of "affective family ties." The second part of the book undertakes a typology of saints. In the eleventh century, saints were mostly male and generally held power in society; by the twelfth, reformers in the Church had called into question the link between power and holiness, so that saints were more often than before from lower social ranks, and were more frequently female. As saints came increasingly from the laity, private almsgiving and self-denial gained in importance over the institutional charity and discipline of the monasteries. This book too contains many further nuances, but the themes touched upon here are basic to the discussion.

As is no doubt clear, Weinstein and Bell rely on the hagiographic

materials as sources of accurate material more than the present book
will do; in the first part of their study, in particular, they display considerable faith in the historicity of the documents. One can prescind
from any such faith and still find merit in their conclusions: whatever
the realities of family life may have been, high and late medieval vitae
tended to represent the parents of saints as having a loving but mis-
guided concern for their children's welfare; in this and other ways,
the vitae contain an implicit sociology of saintliness. In other words,
one may see Weinstein and Bell's data as referring not to social realities but to hagiographic views of those realities. In so doing, one
brings their project closer to the present one, since here too the effort
will be to clarify the hagiographic viewpoint. Clearly the saints' biographers and the witnesses for their canonization held views on many
subjects—politics, society, and so forth—that entered into their testimony regarding the saints and made for a richness of content in the
sources. What we shall be primarily concerned with here, however, is
not so much the general view of Christian society that emerges from
the hagiographic material, but specifically the notions of what constituted a saint as a saint. Rather than looking primarily at the setting
out of which the saint emerged, we shall be looking at the saints who
emerged from that setting.

Whereas Vauchez is mainly interested in the saints from the viewpoint of ecclesiastical history, and Weinstein and Bell approach them
from the perspective of social history, we shall be concerned here
mainly with the theological assumptions of the sources. Vauchez, like
Weinstein and Bell, is mainly interested in establishing distinct categories of saints and then correlating these categories with non-
hagiographic variables; the present book focuses instead on those
shared motifs which cut across these categories and cannot be explained by reference to them. This is partly a matter of personal interest. It is also, however, a matter of conviction: the vitae and
canonization proceedings were assembled with the deliberate intent
of showing their subjects as exemplars of saintly ideals, and it is the
vision of saintliness that emerges most clearly from these texts. While
it may be useful and interesting to read behind the sources and ascertain what gave rise to them, it remains the first responsibility of an
interpreter to take seriously the mentality of the hagiographers and to
assess the meaning of their texts on that basis.

2
Three Representative Saints

*B*efore analyzing the main themes that recur in fourteenth-century hagiography, we shall take a brief look at the lives of three individual saints. The intention is threefold. First, we may thus gain basic familiarity with some of the *dramatis personae* who will appear in later, thematic chapters. Second, these sketches may show how the saints lived in their concrete historical contexts—their geographical, social, ecclesiastical milieux. An alternative would be full, systematic discussion of each of these settings, but much of this has been done elsewhere.[1] By focusing here on specific examples, and evoking a few of the possible contexts without pretending to be exhaustive, we can proceed more directly to the thematic chapters. Third, attention to the complete lives of representative saints may to some degree compensate for the abstraction, or the lifting of material from its original contexts, that inevitably occurs in thematic analysis. In other words, before studying fragments of saints' lives in the necessarily artificial setting of thematic discussion, it may be useful to examine a few saints whole and entire.

Many saints might recommend themselves for this purpose, but the three to be examined are Dorothy of Montau, Peter of Luxembourg, and Clare Gambacorta. These three are relatively unknown in the English-speaking world, though English translations of Grass and Huizinga have given the first two a kind of notoriety. All three are nonetheless interesting enough to merit attention, and the material for their lives is ample. Among them, they cover many of the possibilities seen in the lives of fourteenth-century saints. Geographically, they represent the three major centers of late medieval sainthood:

Dorothy came from the German-speaking territories, Peter was from France, and Clare lived in Italy. (England and Sweden also produced widely venerated saints, but fewer of them.) They exemplify some of the distinctive features of male and female spirituality. They display different states in life: Dorothy was a housewife for most of her life, and a recluse at the end; Peter was a cardinal; and Clare was a Dominican nun. Their social backgrounds were similarly diverse: Dorothy's parents were peasants and her husband was an urban artisan, Peter was from one of the great aristocratic families of Europe, and Clare came from the patriciate of Pisa. Most important for present purposes, though, is that these figures manifest different forms of sanctity. Dorothy, whose confessor-biographer divulged a wealth of information from her inward perspective in her quasi-autobiographical vitae, epitomizes almost all those tendencies that have given the fourteenth-century saints a reputation for idiosyncrasy and disquietude. As one might expect, we shall meet with her often in subsequent chapters. Peter, who is known mainly from the proceedings of his canonization, imbibed much of this intensity but was in some ways more conventional. He too will make fairly frequent appearances in later discussion. And Clare, for whom a fellow nun wrote a fundamentally traditional vita, serves mainly as a reminder that not all the era's saints were feverish or prone to extremes.

Dorothy of Montau: Housewife and Anchoress

Born in 1347 at Montau, in the eastern German territories, Dorothy was pious from her early years.[2] The first signs of extraordinary fervor came at age six, when a careless maid spilled scalding water on her, and she took refuge in her devotions as she recovered from this accident. Before long she had become a youthful ascetic and mystic. She married at sixteen, and bore nine children, of whom eight predeceased her when the Black Death swept across northern Europe. Her married life at Danzig was one of continuous affliction: her husband took her devotions amiss, and abused her verbally and physically, even when he consented to join her in pilgrimage to distant shrines. When the pope announced a jubilee indulgence for all who visited certain Roman churches in 1390, Dorothy went there without her husband, and returned to find him dead. Now that she was free to move about as she wished, she moved to the town of Marienwerder, and became the spiritual daughter of the theologian John Marienwerder. Under his direction she became an anchoress, walled off in a cell in the cathedral; there she spent the last year of her life, exercising rigid asceticism and enjoying an almost constant stream of mystical consolations. When she died, in 1394, her spiritual father stimulated her cult by preaching her virtues to the local populace, encouraging them to seek miracles at her tomb, and writing several vitae.

These biographies speak quite consistently from the saint's own viewpoint, whether they are relating public events or private experiences. One can easily envision Dorothy, for example, telling her confessor about the adventures she underwent on her pilgrimages; the richness of detail that he relates suggests that he spent many hours listening to her tell her stories. The vitae convey unmistakably a sense of disquietude and strenuousness. They also present Dorothy as a woman of exceptionally strong emotion, which her culture, even while ambivalent, encouraged her to channel in the direction of overwrought piety. She spent much of her life groping toward a religious identity that could satisfy her. She had difficulty finding this identity in married life. She sought it with meager resources: she had little education, and until the last few years of her life she had no competent spiritual guidance. Like other saints of her era, especially female ones, she provoked opposition. When she was a child her family resisted her tendency toward ascetic extremes, and when she was an adult her effusive public devotion left an impression of profound fanaticism on those around her. Her husband, meanwhile, seems to have been fundamentally tolerant of whatever she did until his own convenience was affected, and then he reacted vigorously.

In her strongly affective piety she resembles other German female mystics, though unlike them she never entered a convent but remained in a world to which she was always something of a stranger. The people who inhabited that world were either potential adversaries (even her husband) or distant characters with only minor roles (even—or especially—her children). The only figure her confessor-biographer portrays as a genuinely close and understanding associate is himself. (One must bear in mind that even while transmitting the saint's perspective the biographer did filter what she had said, and the possibilities for authorial bias were not negligible!) If the world found her in many ways alien, the sentiment was reciprocated. Her biographies and the other sources for her life are in large part accounts of her struggles with this world and with her own identity in it.

Three manifestations of her piety figure prominently in the vitae: her pilgrimages, her asceticism, and her mystical experiences. There were other aspects to her sanctity, such as her charity toward the poor, which the vitae mention only in passing or as minor themes at best. Let us focus, then, on the three elements that Dorothy's biographer accentuated.

Her fondness for pilgrimages was scarcely unusual in the fourteenth century; while short journeys to shrines had been common for generations, it was in the later Middle Ages that long-distance pilgrimages to Rome, Santiago, Jerusalem, and elsewhere became relatively common events.[3] Bridget of Sweden went to Jerusalem on pilgrimage, and several other saints traveled elsewhere with pious intent. While Dorothy did not travel in a jovial and motley band such as Chaucer's pilgrims to Canterbury, her journeys provided the same release from humdrum existence back home, and they proved anything but uneventful. She made a few brief pilgrimages to nearby places. More important were her journeys to the shrine of the Virgin at Aachen and to the renowned monastery at Einsiedeln in 1384, another pilgrimage to the same places in the following year, and her journey to Rome in 1390.

The hardships Dorothy and her husband encountered as pilgrims were so manifold that one vita recites the details under the heading: "Examples of her great patience."[4] They had to travel at times through snow, water, or mud, frequently in danger from robbers, and often wet, dirty, and exhausted. At times her elderly husband and young daughter (the one surviving child) would ride their horse, while she tried to keep up on foot, walking or running through the snow; when she fell into a ditch, there would be no one to help. Twice they were nearly drowned. Once they got into a quarrel with an innkeeper, and would have met their death if another traveler had not intervened. At Einsiedeln they found themselves in the midst of war, food shortages, and general commotion: bells rang out to warn of military attack, and people would hurry into church or seek shelter elsewhere.

Her husband bore all this badly, and took out his miseries on Dorothy. Incapacitated by old age and injuries, he became irritable, and beat her vigorously over minor annoyances. Once she was unable to keep their daughter from crying, so he pounded Dorothy firmly on the head; she endured the blow, we are told, "joyfully." He summarily dismissed the wagon-driver they had employed, and made Dorothy do his job: watering and feeding the horses, hitching them to the wagon, setting the wagon aright when it got mired in the mud, cleaning and greasing it, and other such tasks. People would run up and poke fun at the spectacle of an old man accompanied by a woman still youthful and attractive. Whether in jest or in derision, they would shout at them, asking if she was taking him to some fountain of youth. As usual, she bore everything with patience and even joy. Indeed, she frequently entered ecstatic states as they went along the road, and became so deeply immersed in God that she became totally oblivious to the world about her—which may explain her having to get out and free the wagon from the mud.[5]

They fell prey once to robbers, who took all their money, practically all their clothes, their horse and wagon, and seriously injured Dorothy's husband. She herself took great consolation in being thus despoiled: as the bandits were making off with their belongings, she sat rapt in contemplation of God, released from all attachment to creatures, and even hoping she would be reduced to mendicancy for the rest of her life. It was to her disappointment, clearly, that they later recovered their goods.[6]

The vitae recount many more details of the hardships she encountered on these pilgrimages. Everything else—the lure of the sacred places, the piety with which she visited them, the sense of excitement aroused by visiting new places and meeting new people—is subordinated to an overwhelming sense of that difficulty which served to cultivate in her the virtue of patience. These other themes do arise: at one of the shrines she visited, for example, she felt so attracted by the holy place that she could not bear to part from it, but kept turning back on the road and returning to its precincts.[7] Far more often, though, the focus is on her patient endurance of obstacles. If her pilgrimages indicated her liberation from the bonds of domesticity, they also removed her from the security of her home. Her biographer does not seem to have had the image of life as a journey in mind, yet he effectively portrays her as progressing in virtue largely by exposing herself to trials on these holy journeys.

The other two major themes in the vitae, Dorothy's asceticism and mysticism, went hand in hand. When she had tasted the joys of contemplation, her biographer says, she began to "hate" the world and its glory. It was more a relief than a burden for her to go without sleep, food, and bodily comforts. She perceived that divine sweetness immeasurably surpasses all human solace. It became painful for her to engage in temporal concerns, to wear extravagant clothing, or to attend worldly entertainments. These inclinations grew throughout her life, and became ever more passionate. The corollary to this repugnance for earthly things was an overpowering desire to die and enter the rewards of the afterlife, a craving she felt so strongly that it sometimes left her utterly powerless and unable to rise from her bed.[8]

One of the first kinds of asceticism to which she felt called was fasting. When she was a young girl she wanted to imitate the fasts of her mother and sisters, and would beg fervently for permission; until she was nine years old, her mother refused this permission, to Dorothy's dismay. This imitation of maternal piety was typical of a saint at this stage in her life; had her conversion to religious fervor come in adolescence, her father would more likely have been the crucial figure. In any case, as she matured she became increasingly austere in her eating habits. Sometimes she would eat stale porridge or scrawny fish, or go for long periods eating scarcely more than an occasional egg. She ate meat as seldom as possible. As an adult she preserved these practices, and did little or nothing to mitigate them even when she was pregnant, which may have contributed to the debilitation and early deaths of her children.[9]

Her ascetic bent showed itself in other ways as well. She pretended to be a beggar, putting on shabby clothing and standing in front of church to receive alms. This exercise made her joyful "beyond measure," though her fellow-beggars complained of their misery, the meagerness of their proceeds, or the excessive cold they had to endure. She went as seldom as possible to festivals and other entertainments. She deprived herself of sleep. In these and other ways she strove to purge herself of worldly attachment.[10]

Her prayer, too, was a form of asceticism. Even before she was six, she performed prostrations so vigorously and so often that even in winter she perspired freely. In her youth she would stay up as late as possible in prayer; in adulthood, her husband would try to induce her to get more sleep, but she told him she was unable to sleep and he should not blame her. For many years she spent her sleepless nights in spiritual calesthenics—shuffling about on her knees, crawling, arching her body in the air with her forehead and feet on the floor, joining her hands in front of herself in the form of a cross, falling on her face with her hands behind her back as if they were bound, and so forth. By these exercises she "forced herself to serve the Lord."[11]

After her scalding at age six, she began subjecting herself to various mortifications—as if, having sensed consolation in her spiritual life at the time of her accident, she felt a constant urge to recapture that sense of bodily anguish and the attendant inward comfort. From this time on, she would beat herself with rods, whips, thorny branches, or other objects, or burn herself with water, white-hot iron, fire, or oil. She would aggravate the wounds by rubbing into them nettles, broken nutshells, other rough objects, and bitter herbs. When she came upon a vat of saltwater that had been used to cure meat or fish, she would plunge into it. While she did not maintain all these practices with consistent rigor throughout her life, she did continue her mortification in her married years, even in pregnancy and childbirth. Her confessor-biographer remarks that such wondrous deeds "should cause the weak and dissolute to be silent, and not cast aspersions on God's works, which are accomplished in this frail sex to confound them, to console the Church, to arouse the faithful, and to stir all hearts to wonderment at a time when the world is growing old and love is growing cool."[12] Here as elsewhere, God is seen as working upon Dorothy to arouse the wonderment of her contemporaries.

As Dorothy sensed, and later learned from revelation, the Lord himself was impelling her to afflict herself; she was like a pack-animal driven to a faster pace with a whip. Driving her from one affliction to another, the Lord allowed her no rest or sleep. If at times she desired to rest, to refresh her weary body, and to let her wounds heal, the Lord drove her onward to further vigils and exercises.[13] There is perhaps a temptation, in reading these accounts, to distinguish between Dorothy's patient endurance of what was beyond her control and her willful self-torture. From Dorothy's own viewpoint, as related by her biographer, this distinction would surely be false, since even self-inflicted suffering came ultimately from divine instigation.

Still, there were some wounds that she ascribed more directly to God than others. Throughout her life, she suffered from what may have been a pemphigoid condition.[14] She had wounds on her shoulders, arms, breast, back, and armpits, as also in various places on her legs. In a fleshy part of her body they could be as deep as a single finger-joint; elsewhere they were more shallow. Remaining cheerful, she managed to conceal these afflictions from everyone, even the members of her family. Late in her life, the Lord reviewed the anguish her wounds had brought her: sometimes they caused a fierce itching, as if an ant were biting at them, or as if they were filled with gnawing worms; sometimes there was a stinging sensation, as if they were filled with sharp darts; sometimes they grew hot, as if set ablaze; at other times they festered, swelled up, then burst open; again, they sometimes bled vehemently and freely. Because these wounds were sent by God, as mementos of the Lord's own passion, Dorothy's biographer refers to them as her stigmata.[15]

Along with her ascetic bent and her physical afflictions, or "wounds from God," Dorothy manifested strong contemplative or mystical tendencies from an early age. After being scalded with water at age six, and being consoled by God, she began to experience his presence frequently. She would be raised up to heaven in desire, and sometimes would feel God drawing her so strongly that it seemed as if body and soul were being drawn upward.[16] It is not surprising that her first religious awakening came in response to a traumatic experience. In a society with meager medical resources she might naturally seek divine consolation elsewhere. Furthermore, her trauma legitimized a degree of religious fervor which otherwise might not have been allowed even in a pious family, and thus gave a first taste of how her natural sensitivity could find a religious outlet. Numerous mystics began their exceptional religious lives when afflicted with illness; for Dorothy, this childhood trauma was the equivalent.[17]

Her most important mystical experiences, though, occurred after she was married. To her husband's great dismay, she seemed to live in a perpetual state of abstraction. Her biographer tells that her spirit was so "inebriated" with divine sweetness that she went about as if drunk. When she was totally immersed in spiritual delights, and withdrawn entirely from the sensory world, she would lie down as if asleep. Her husband would sometimes call to her when she was in rapture, and when she did not respond he assumed she was being insolent; at times he would pour water on her, and even then she would be unaware that she was wet until she came out of her rapture. If her husband sent her to buy fish or meat, in her fits of abstraction she might instead buy eggs or something else. At other times she was led in her exuberance to uncontrolled movement of her feet, or was unable to move about, or could not control her effusive jubilation.[18]

Clearly she cherished her raptures. Once she stationed herself in a church in hopes of a visitation from God, and labored for some time in prayers, meditations, and sundry exercises, but did not obtain the "sweetness of consolation" that she sought. She called on the Virgin and saints, but to no effect. Still she persisted, and with confidence she "knocked on the ears of God and the glorious Virgin." Her companions had by this point fallen asleep, but there were other people milling about in the church, and one might have expected them to distract her. Yet at last she was granted inexpressible delights, jubilation, and illumination with divine light, which lasted until the following morning.[19] One might interpret this episode in Pelagian fashion: it appeared that it was by her own effort that she at last attained ecstasy. Dorothy and her biographer would surely have preferred the opposite reading: her quest for special grace could not in itself lead anywhere, since God bestowed his favors only when he desired.

Dorothy's biographer devotes a great deal of attention to the various forms of love that she experienced in her mystical encounters with God, and the effects that each type of love had upon her. He reports several distinct categories of mystical sentiment: ardent love, gushing love, boiling love, wounding love, languishing love, inebriating love, supereffluent love, maddening love, violent love, and other forms. Recognizing that the labels might seem unfamiliar, he defends them as having scriptural precedent; some, at least, are used or suggested in the Song of Songs.[20] He insists that Dorothy herself could distinguish each form of love clearly from the others. In his treatment of these phenomena, Marienwerder combines the format of biography with that of the treatise—but since neither he nor Dorothy was an especially profound mystical theologian, the discussion is of interest primarily as it bears on her own experience, and not for its theological significance.[21]

A few examples may suffice to illustrate the forms of love. When she experienced ardent love, Dorothy's entire body grew so hot that she perspired copiously all over her body. She felt as if a flame were descending upon her heart, and then bursting forth to her front, back, and sides. It was as if she were overwhelmed with heat from a well-stoked furnace—except that external heat is painful, while that of ardent love is sweet. Wounding love is similar in bringing a sense of exquisite anguish: it "wounds the soul with great desire which it has for the beloved Lord." For many years, Dorothy was afflicted with the darts and spears of this love. Once in particular she had a vision of Christ and his mother in heaven, holding in their hands lances long enough to reach from heaven to earth; with them they pierced her heart, causing ecstatic pain as they thrust them into her three times. Languishing love was associated with her periods of illness or languor. While she was thus afflicted, nothing temporal gave her any delight, and indeed the taste of worldly things was painful for her. Out of sheer desire for her Lord she was forced to lie in bed day and night. Inebriating love, she found, also leaves a person detached from transitory things but in a daze, in which the recipient adheres to God for ten hours or longer, unable to control himself. A person in this condition thinks of himself as already in eternal life. Having enjoyed this experience, though, a person may have it withdrawn later in life, whereupon he thirsts for that sweet drink which will sustain him in eternity. If one is tempted to associate these experiences with physical morbidity, the temptation is perhaps most plausible in the case of "heart-rending" love, which Dorothy experienced toward the end of her life, and which, according to her biographer, ultimately caused her death. It came about, he said, when her heart became taut in its desire for God, as the string of an instrument is stretched taut and can be broken if it is pulled too tightly.[22]

The mystical vocabulary in Dorothy's vitae includes other notions that we need not trace in detail. Closely associated with her various species of love were the infusions of the Holy Spirit into her soul; he might arrive subtly and gently, or with great inward tumult. The richest mystical imagery is eucharistic: when she received communion, Christ "held a great banquet" in her soul, or "killed a fatted calf" within her, or kissed her soul and embraced it, or bore himself within her, or else she gave birth to him. On one occasion her heart was extracted and replaced with a new one—a fulfillment in her of the promise God made in Ezekiel 36:26. Her biographer comments that "whether that extraction of her heart and the implanting of a new one was only an alteration of her nature, and not a mutation of substance, only he knows who removed her heart and who was able to do so in either way." Once the Virgin presented the Christ child to her in a vision, so that she was able to hold him in her arms. Toward the end of her life, Christ came to her repeatedly as her bridegroom. Her vitae are filled with these and many more such experiences. Yet as her biographer insists, all these accounts are a mere halting and fragmentary expression of what was revealed to her. In terms of theological profundity or power of language, Dorothy may not qualify as one of the great mystics of the century. Yet the profusion of experience that she underwent surely makes her an important example of that craving for the wonder and excitement of spiritual discovery that was so characteristic of her era.[23]

These experiences were particularly frequent during Dorothy's final year, in the cell at Marienwerder. When she became an anchorite she was following a long tradition.[24] In the late Middle Ages, though, solitary enclosure was more common in England than on the Continent; Julian of Norwich, roughly her contemporary, is a well-known example. In the fourteenth century there were 123 English anchorites of whom we have knowledge, and some of the era's devotional literature (including Richard Rolle's *Form of Living* and part of Walter Hilton's *Ladder of Perfection*) was written to guide such solitaries. On the Continent, anchorites typically clustered together in association with monasteries, and they were often indistinguishable from the monks and nuns. Following the pattern that was more typical for England, then, Dorothy obtained episcopal authorization for her enclosure, underwent a year-long period of probation, obtained funds from benefactors for construction of a cell (which has survived into the twentieth century), and at last was ceremonially enclosed. She entered her cell in a state of great excitement, as devotees gathered about and asked for her prayers. Barefoot, she took nothing in with her, and when the wall had been secured behind her she felt as if she had attained eternal life.[25]

During the months that followed, she spent her time in prayer, meditation, reading, song, and rapture. She spoke only with her counselors and with those they allowed to approach her for advice. She went to confession at least once daily, and routinely she shed tears as she confessed. If she had had to go a day without communion, the deprivation would have been unbearable. She had no appetite for food, and no need or desire for sleep; with ordinary bodily functions suspended, she went also without excretion. And although she was dedicated to cleanliness, the only bath she allowed herself was a bath of tears. When cold weather set in, someone brought her a kind of cloak, and she obligingly put it on but felt colder than before; a second cloak only aggravated the hardship, and it was only when she abandoned all such coverings and relied on God that she became comfortable. When the annual market took place, outsiders coming to Marienwerder were shown her cell, and found it amazing. Evidently she had become something of a tourist attraction.[26]

The solitude she attained in her cell remained with her at death:

she died in the middle of the night, and it was several hours later that her confessor came to her cell and found her dead. The funeral occurred three days later, and it was only then that the full impact of her enclosure upon the people of Marienwerder became clear. The general lamentation at her burial soon gave way to a sense of charismatic presence, and before long visitors from near and far were obtaining miracles at her tomb. What must have been important in stimulating this cult was the funeral sermon preached by her confessor: addressing a congregation which was familiar with the essentials of Dorothy's outer life, particularly her enclosure, he made public for the first time the details of her inner spirituality, her asceticism and her mystical experiences—those same elements of her life which, along with her pilgrimages, he emphasized in the vitae.[27]

If Dorothy had died two years earlier than she did, she would never have attained the recognition and the cult that she in fact aroused. Several factors contributed to these developments. First, in submitting herself to a respected spiritual director she obtained ecclesiastical legitimation for her austerities and her alienation from the world; no longer merely signs of eccentricity, they became marks of sanctity. Second, by moving from Danzig to Marienwerder she took on the role of an unfamiliar and potentially awe-inspiring figure. Her neighbors in Montau and Danzig had known her and her family too long and too closely to expect that she would blossom into a saint; she remained always the local eccentric, who sat in church absorbed in overwrought devotion. As a newcomer to Marienwerder, though, she could arouse unprejudiced curiosity which, properly cultivated by her director, could be transformed into veneration. In her new home she was not without honor. Third, her enclosure gave her distinctive status: so long as she remained within society, she threatened its secular values by implicitly claiming a higher life accessible to all, but when she took on a special vocation to which she had a distinctive calling, she was able to serve her society all the more effectively through her intercession. Having spent most of her life as an outsider in the midst of society, she now became a recluse with a valuable role to play for that society. It has been argued that anchorites such as Dorothy were vital in the religious life of medieval Europe, as is shown by the financial support they received: "A village with an anchorite was a holier place than the village without one. . . . A city or town with several recluses represented a concentration of spiritual power."[28] Thus, if Dorothy gained renown in the last year of her life, this was largely because she brought renown to Marienwerder. While those around her acknowledged the intrinsic merit of her state, the extrinsic lure of civic pride was an inducement to that recognition.

Her entire life, as portrayed by her confessor, was one of singular alienation. It is possible that a theological bias lies behind this picture: the ascetic ideology of the era could lead to a disparagement of friendship, and even familial affection could become a sign of worldliness. There is certainly no hint in her vitae of fondness for her husband or children; the death of most of her children was little more than an opportunity to undertake pilgrimages. We hear little about other associates. After her death, oddly, her devotees emphasized her maternity: they referred to her routinely as "mother Dorothy," and appealed to her maternal solicitude in seeking cures for their own children.[29] If she had been a normal housewife and mother throughout her life, however, she could scarcely have attained this distinctive role of mother-saint. It was in part her reputation for saintly aloofness and in part her release from domesticity that enabled her to exercise a posthumous maternal function.

With all of its diversity, Dorothy's life illustrates the richness that spiritual life in the fourteenth century might entail: immersed for much of her life in the routine of a housewife in a society of late medieval German burghers, she managed to extricate herself from the dreariness that might otherwise have characterized such life; she attained mystical experiences which many would rank at the summit of spiritual attainment. But while there is clear progression in her outer life—from young girl to young wife and mother, then to pilgrim, widow, and recluse—her inner life displays an essential consistency. Fortunately, we have fuller information about this inner life, seen from her own perspective, than for virtually any previous saint. There were changes in emphasis and in the way she manifested the basic tendencies, but throughout her life she had strongly otherworldly leanings, as seen in both her asceticism and her mysticism. Thus, domesticity and mystical phenomena do not represent stages of development in her life, but rather poles of experience, ranging from the ordinary to the most extraordinary. In certain respects she was a figure with whom contemporaries could readily identify, while in others she was a citizen of an entirely different world.

In what ways was Dorothy typical of her setting? The typical saint of the German-speaking territories in the fourteenth century was female, was inclined toward mystical experiences, came from the urban middle classes, was not particularly well educated, tended toward strongly emotional expression of religious sentiment, formed strong ties with a spiritual director, and held herself aloof from civic affairs. In all these respects Dorothy fit the general pattern. Her eucharistic devotion, linked as it was with her mystical bent, continued a form of spirituality that had long typified the female mystics of northern Europe. What distinguished her from other saintly women of her time and place—Margaret Ebner, Christina Ebner, Elizabeth Stagl, Adelheid Langmann, and others, particularly in German-speaking territories further to the south—was that she did not belong to a convent. The foremost spiritual directors of fourteenth-century Germany were Dominican friars such as Henry Suso and John Tauler; the best-known women saints were Dominican nuns to whom these friars ministered, and whose posthumous veneration they cultivated. The friars themselves were at times recognized as saintly, as in the case of Suso. In addition, there were non-Dominican mystics such as Rulman Merswin who gained renown for their exceptional piety, though Merswin's autohagiographic account of his conversion did not inspire veneration of him either during his life or after his death. It was the Dominican order, though, that had the strongest influence in the religious life of late medieval Germany. Dorothy might have come under their sway if she had lived elsewhere in the German-speaking territories; as it was, her director belonged instead to the Teutonic Knights, who were dominant in the northeast but did not command the broader influence that the Dominicans exercised.[30]

Largely, no doubt, because Dorothy had only regional support, John Marienwerder was unsuccessful in his efforts to secure her canonization. Her cult persisted among the Baltic Germans and the Poles; after the Second World War, emigrees from the eastern territories brought with them into West Germany their devotion to Dorothy, and their efforts led in 1976 to papal confirmation of her cult as a saint, on the basis of long-standing veneration. These efforts also led to Günter Grass's unflattering account of her, a sign that she remains controversial even centuries after her demise.[31]

Peter of Luxembourg: The Boy Cardinal

If a saint on the streets of Danzig was incongruous, a saint in the papal city of Avignon was even more so. During its heyday, when it was the ecclesiastical capital of Western Christendom, the city gained a reputation for venality and pomp. When it became the seat of the Avignonese rivals to the Roman papacy in 1378, at the inception of the Great Schism, the mood was no doubt more sombre. Yet the town was still notorious for laxity, and proved an uncomfortable setting for a saint such as Peter of Luxembourg.

Peter was born in 1369 to the Luxembourg family from which Charles IV and other emperors came; his father was a count, his mother was a countess in her own right, and his brother served as a knight and one of the leading men-in-arms in France.[32] Peter's parents died when he was young, and he was sent to live with his aunt, where he received his first lessons from her chaplains. When he was eight, he and his younger brother were sent to Paris for further study, accompanied by three clerics. He would gladly have entered a monastery, but his brother wanted him to train for knighthood; as a compromise, his family found a position for him as a canon at Notre Dame, in preparation for a career in the Church. He continued his studies at Paris, with ten months' interruption while he was held captive by the British as a hostage for his brother. At fourteen, he found himself suddenly immersed in high ecclesiastical politics. The bishopric was vacant at Metz, an important border town between Roman and Avignonese territories, and Peter was chosen as bishop, though only for jurisdictional purposes, without receiving ordination. The military resources of his family were at once put to use in suppressing the inevitable resistance from Roman adherents in Metz. Peter never did gain secure hold on the diocese, however, and eventually withdrew to Paris. He resumed his studies but found that he now had no taste for them, and preferred his pious exercises. At sixteen he was summoned to Avignon and installed as a cardinal; he lived for only one more year, and during that time his hatred for Avignon and its laxity grew ever more intense. He became reclusive, and gained a reputation for extreme asceticism. Thus, when he died in 1387 he was immediately recognized by the townspeople as a saint.

For all his rank and presumed power, Peter spent his brief life hedged in by constraints of all sorts. Because of the expectations and demands placed upon him, he was far less free to do what he wished than Dorothy of Montau had been. Despite his clerical status, he was more of a pawn than a bishop in the game of ecclesiastical politics that he was compelled to play. As his life proceeded, he struggled ever more desperately to extricate himself from this position, but always without effect. Perhaps if he had lived into maturity he would eventually have come into his own, but the opportunity was denied him. He found satisfaction only by withdrawing into a world of piety and asceticism in which he could exert his own will. There too he had masters who attempted to control him by restraining his ardor and his austerity, but in conscience he could appeal to a higher authority. His piety was essentially conventional; his writings are noteworthy neither for inspiration nor for any particular deficiency. Though Huizinga referred to him as "pitiful," it is rather the circumstances in which he was constrained that arouse one's sympathies.

Information about him comes mainly from the canonization proceedings that were held shortly after his death. Several manuscripts survive from the early fifteenth century, indicating great interest in his cause.[33] Yet when the schism was resolved he was left with the rank of *beatus*, and was never honored as saint. The records of the proceedings are extensive, but as one would expect they speak from the vantage point of those around him rather than from his own perspective. There are early vitae, but they add little independent information to what is already in the canonization proceedings. Since even his own writings are not autobiographical, we do not have access to the same internal viewpoint for him that we have for Dorothy of Montau and for various of their contemporaries. As a result, we are left with an image that lacks the burning sense of inner turmoil seen in Dorothy. Nonetheless, we can discern an adolescent severely challenged by his circumstances and by his own scrupulous conscience, and not untouched by the century's penchant for emotionally intense spirituality.

Unlike Dorothy of Montau, Peter associated closely with several people throughout his brief life. The clerics who accompanied him when he went as a child to his aunt's house remained with him as he proceeded to Paris, and they retained an important influence on him even in Avignon. One need not have special powers of psychological penetration to see the orphaned Peter as searching for the role models and the moral guides he would have had in a normal family. To a large extent his clerical guardians no doubt served this function. Something like a monastic oblate, he grew up in a clerical "family," and his constant fascination for the cloister is no surprise. There were other guides to whom he turned, and they also probably took on the function of surrogate parents for him—if we may venture such speculation on the basis of hagiographic materials which, for these matters at least, are probably true to history.[34]

It was when he returned from Metz to Paris that he encountered two particularly influential figures and came under their guidance. One was Peter d'Ailly, the noted theologian, whose advocacy of the doctrine of the Immaculate Conception seems to have made an impact on Peter: when certain opponents of that doctrine brought him a collection of texts (presumably scriptural and patristic) that favored their viewpoint, Peter cast the offending work into the nearest fire and refused to discuss the controversy. More significant for his religious development, though, was his friendship with Philip de Mézières, erstwhile chancellor of Cyprus, warrior against Islam, defender of pilgrims, avid partisan of the Avignonese papacy (he advocated a crusade against Rome!), and a leading figure in late medieval piety. Philip introduced the feast of the Presentation into France. In 1385 he abandoned his wealth, withdrew to a Celestinian monastery in Paris, and became known as one of the most devout men in the town. Peter met with him two or three times a week when he returned from Metz; they read Scripture and saints' lives together, and Philip communicated to his adolescent disciple a burning devotion to the Avignonese papacy.[35]

Perhaps Peter's most affectionate relationship was with his sister
Jane, six years his elder, whom he got to know during a brief in-
terlude at their ancestral estate shortly before he entered the
bishopric of Metz. She had taken a vow of virginity, and refused offers of aristocratic marriage. She and Peter conversed, prayed, read
saints' lives, and recited the office together regularly, coming to meals
only when called, and resuming their exercises in the evening until
they were reminded of the late hour. Even during the night they
would rise for two more hours of prayer. They corresponded frequently in future years. Despite her superior age, he served as her
mentor; he had taught her how to read the office, and his letters to
her were filled with advice.[36]

Peter was exceptionally devout even when he first went to Paris as a
young child. As one would expect of a fledgling saint, he showed remarkable maturity, and used the free intervals amid his studies for
pious exercises. When his fellow pupils went for recreation, he withdrew to his room and recited the little office of the Virgin, or the
penitential psalms. When they went out walking, he would go to mass,
hear a sermon, or listen attentively as the Carthusian or Celestinian
monks chanted the office. Yet there was nothing priggish about him,
if one can judge from the testimony that he was consistently pleasant,
deferential even toward younger pupils, and much liked by his fellows. His mentors curbed his devotional zeal somewhat: they thought
it unwise for so young a boy to attend the early morning office of
matins regularly. Otherwise, he was there for all the services.[37]

When he became a canon, one task that he carried out gladly was
carrying the large and heavy processional cross. Most of the younger
canons attempted to evade the responsibility, or simply failed to show
up when it was their turn. Though somewhat feeble, Peter accepted
the task with relish; he refused to ask dispensation, and merely allowed someone else to help him at times by sharing the burden.[38]

As he grew older, and as he came under the influence of Philip de
Mézières and others, his devotion intensified: he began saying not
only the full office but additional prayers, twice as long as the office
itself, so that eventually he had to relieve those servants who were
waiting up to help him prepare for bed. He prayed in honor of the
Virgin for an hour each morning, and said that he would not inter-
rupt this prayer even if the king of France came knocking on his door.
As was common in this era, he relied heavily on set formulas for
prayer: the psalms, the Pater Noster and Ave Maria, and other such
formulas. He collected new prayers avidly, and associates knew they
could please him by providing them for him. As his secretary remarked at the proceedings for his beatification, "Anyone who wanted
to provide him with a treat gave him some prayer, since he took great

delight and consolation in prayers." He jotted them down on scraps of parchment, and stuffed them into a little sack that he carried about everywhere. Eventually he had them copied into a prayerbook. This manual, which is still extant, contains prayers to the Trinity, to Christ, to the Virgin, to Saint Michael, to the angels generally, to the apostles, to various other saints, and then the psalms and certain votive masses. It also contains two miniatures, both showing Peter kneeling before the Virgin at the Annunciation. Such time as he had for prayer must have been spent largely in the company of this small prayerbook.[39]

At Avignon he allowed himself only four to six hours for sleep, mainly so he could find time for devotions. He frequently arose at midnight to resume his prayers, and on the vigil of the Assumption he did not sleep at all, so that when he was discovered still awake at the time of matins he had to plead that the night passed so quickly it had not occurred to him to go to sleep. His regular position for prayer was kneeling; when someone knocked on the door to his oratory he would arise quickly to avoid being seen in that posture. Even at table, at the beginning of a meal he would give himself over to prayer, and would count the prayers on his fingers, with his hands concealed under the table. The *Vita prima* says he was so dedicated to prayer that he could scarcely remember to go to meals; before doing so he would say a hundred Pater Nosters and Ave Marias, and at table he could scarcely be kept from talking about religious matters. In addition to prayer, he did pious reading; repeatedly the canonization proceedings allude to his fondness for the lives of the saints. His younger brother, as a witness in the canonization proceedings, summarized his piety concisely: "He was always marked by good life and praiseworthy behavior, he feared God, he recited the canonical hours devoutly, he heard masses, and he visited churches."[40]

He was eager to inculcate such piety in others, as well. When one of his associates asked him what prayers he said, Peter offered to tell him if he promised to join in saying them, but the questioner was evidently not curious enough to commit himself. He gladly shared the lives of the saints with those around him. Solicitous about the religious life of his servants, he would give them moral counsel, recommend daily mass, and read them excerpts from saints' lives.[41]

This concern for others manifested itself also in his charity, which, we are told, was great. Whenever possible, in his student days he gave away what pocket money he had to the needy, especially the lepers. If he had no money, he borrowed from his brother. When his mentors saw that he was penniless, and reproached him, he first told them it had fallen from his purse, and then he pleaded that no one is made poor by giving alms, since God takes care of the almsgiver. His preceptors tried to keep beggars from him by intercepting him at the

door where he left church, but he would slip around to another exit
and find the poor out in the street. If on a given day he could not
dispense alms in the usual fashion, he would cast money through the
window to some poor person outdoors, or have his brother do so for
him. Yet his almsgiving at this stage was meager in comparison with
what he dispensed as a cardinal. With much greater resources at his
disposal, he sent money to hospitals every week, fed ten poor people
in his own home each day, procured dowries for poor girls, and in
short gave away whatever he received. This sort of detail, like much
else that we are told about his life, is the conventional stuff of
hagiography—though, of course, it may also have been true to historical reality. Always short of money because of his liberality, he
eventually sold his episcopal ring for ten florins, and in the end he
died in debt. A single franc was found in his coffer upon his death,
presumably because he had overlooked it.[42]

He was devoted to the sacraments, especially the eucharist and
penance. He went to communion on Sundays and feast days, and received it with tears of devotion; having tasted the sweetness of that
sacrament, he despised all other forms of sweetness. In sickness and
in health, when he saw the consecrated host he reacted with such a
display of emotion that he seemed to be crying. Before going to Avignon, he confessed his sins once a week or more, depending on
whether he felt any special need; he would read his sins from slips of
paper on which he had written them down. On his arrival in Avignon
he asked the Carthusian prior there to find a spiritual director for
him, and the choice was an Augustinian hermit named Giles of Or-
leans. Peter knelt before this priest, acknowledged his youth and ig-
norance, and pleaded that he needed someone to instruct him and tell
him the truth about his state of soul. Eventually his scruples led him to
confess two or three times a day.[43]

His moral rigor shows not only in his frequent confession but also
in his systematic avoidance of sin. As a student, he was careful to avoid
light conversation or familiar discourse with women. He was keenly
embarrassed when some lord or knight engaged in lewd conversation
in his presence, and he indicated his displeasure with a gesture of his
head, while remaining silent. No servant ever dared to offend him
this way. He was not enthusiastic about games: he would play chess
for leisure if some visitor came, and in his earlier years he was willing
to dance if lords and ladies asked him to do so, but he utterly despised
playing with dice.[44]

During his brother's efforts to take possession of the diocese of
Metz by military force, Peter accompanied the troops and attempted
to prevent mayhem. He pleaded for pity toward the vanquished, and
visited the prisoners to secure their spiritual welfare. At one juncture,

when the army was camping out near Metz, they had no fire, but they noticed that a sanctuary light was burning in a nearby church. To get in and obtain fire they would have had to break either the door or a window, and Peter forbade them to do either, so they had to search far and wide for another source, and were able to obtain light and warmth only when the night was half over. At the end of this campaign, Peter was equally scrupulous about payment for it: he offered to pay out of his own patrimony and the revenues of his ecclesiastical benefices, but refused to provoke the animosity of his subjects by using funds from the church at Metz. Even as he entered Metz in solemn procession, he studiously avoided pomp: he went through the streets mounted on an ass (a contemporary chronicle makes explicit the comparison with Jesus' entry into Jerusalem), then went barefoot to the church of St. Vincent.[45]

In comparison with most of the cardinals at Avignon, he maintained a relatively small household there: two clerics with whom he had long associated, two chaplains, a secretary, and a dozen lay servants. We are told that in every way he set a perfect example of clerical life; or, as the *Vita prima* punningly states it, he shed light upon the town, *lucem in burgo*. Yet the pomp and politics to which he was exposed dismayed him. He had all too little time for prayer. Soon he was wishing he had never come, and protested that he had thought of Paris as paradise but was coming to think of Avignon in less flattering eschatological terms. Worse than the distraction from his prayer was the forced association with individuals of dubious morality. Wishing to avoid going out riding with them, he prayed for an accident that he could plead as an excuse; God obliged him by sending an injury to his right leg, the effects of which lasted until his death. Yet his relief from association with the courtly society of Avignon was only partial. He grew increasingly melancholy; he was not given to frivolity or laughter, and pointed out that the gospels record how Christ wept, but say nothing about his laughing. He devoted himself more insistently than before to such prayers as he could say. Unsure of his own salvation, he would break out in tears. His secretary encouraged him to resume his studies, suggesting that through canon law he could do much for the Church; Peter replied that only prayer and good works would set the Church aright.[46]

Thoroughly dismayed with the immorality of Avignon, Peter made efforts to escape. He thought of fleeing to become a hermit, taking only a breviary and a book of prayers, and wearing clothing made of coarse material. He was dissuaded only by the argument that if he thus abandoned Avignon he would be thought of as questioning the legitimacy of the Avignonese pope. He then conceived an elaborate plan to proceed barefoot to the sanctuaries of Europe, as a kind of pilgrim, accompanied by nine scholars who would aid him in efforts to end the schism through preaching. In England he would address the king; in Germany he would instruct "his cousin the king of the Romans" and various princes about the schism. Altogether the journey would last three years, and give him that many years of relief from Avignon. But he received so little encouragement for this project that even if he had lived long enough he could never have embarked. He could only fantasize about breaking loose from a life over which he had no control, and from immorality which he found increasingly oppressive.[47]

He found his refuge in asceticism. He fasted every Wednesday, Friday, and Saturday, all through Advent, on the vigils of five major Marian feasts, and on the vigils of the feasts of various saints (including Mary Magdalene, Nicholas, Catherine, Thomas Becket, Laurence, and Martin); on those vigils he ate only bread and drank nothing but water. His ideal, which he approximated as best he could, was to live on bread and water alone. His earliest biographer, reporting these rigors, said that he treated himself like ashes. Indeed, he eventually reached the point of sitting at table without eating anything. This regimen was difficult to maintain at Avignon, in the midst of the luxurious consumption that was common among the courtiers there. He tried putting food into his mouth and then removing it surreptitiously, but this was not a ruse that was likely to succeed. He was fond of eggs, but went an entire year without any, so as not to make his stomach his mistress. When he drank wine, he added so much water to it that it lost all taste.[48]

He engaged not only in fasting but in vigorous mortifications. He developed the habit of beating himself with sticks. The earliest known instance of this practice was on a trip from Lorraine to Paris, when he went off by himself into the woods at one juncture and beat himself to overcome a temptation to unchastity. At Avignon, flagellation was one of his regular exercises; he carried it out only in the privacy of his own room, yet it became known. An associate once saw the sticks that he used for this purpose, asked what they were for, and was told they were to chase away certain dogs that had been disturbing him. Another time, when a visitor approached his room he heard the sound of flagellation, and on peeking through the keyhole saw Peter putting his clothes back in order before answering the door. To prevent his servants from apprehending him in this flagellation, he would send them out on various errands, but it was clear to them what he was doing. Yet another form of mortification that he used was a cord, rough and knotted, which he tied tightly around himself. He seems to have adopted this penance at the time he was made a cardinal. His companions suspected that he wore such a cord; among other evidence they cited the vermin in his clothes, "generated from the uncleanliness and continual putridity of the cord," as also the occasions when Peter had to leave the dining table, clearly in pain. Yet when asked about this object he always gave elusive replies, and attempted to deflect suspicion about this form of mortification. ("Indeed, you think that I wear a cord! Why would I wear one? Who put such an idea into your head?") He did admit the fact once to his brother Andrew, in hopes of inducing emulation. Many saw the wounds caused by this cord when he was stripped for extreme unction. It was only after his death that the cord itself was found, along with rods for flagellation, underneath a rug in his room. He would also gladly have worn a hairshirt, and wanted one of his servants to purchase one for him—presumably so it would not be obvious that it was for his own use—but the servant refused.[49]

His fasting and mortifications aroused opposition from his friends and associates, but Peter continued these practices, possibly because they represented his only way of asserting independence vis-à-vis his ever-present mentors and other associates. Even during his 1385 stay in Paris, his life-long clerical companions prevailed upon Peter's confessor to induce him to moderate his rigor. The confessor raised the matter in the context of confession, hoping to use the authority of his office to force Peter to comply, but Peter insisted on discussing the matter outside of confession. Ultimately he had his way; the confessor was in fact sympathetic, and would never have raised the question except under pressure. Another companion approached Peter directly, asserting that he would kill himself, yet Peter remained unpersuaded. Again in Avignon he received such advice, and again he ignored it. He insisted that many saints had done such things, and that John the Baptist had fasted when he was still a very young man. It was only late in 1386 that the pope himself intervened, threatening excommunication if Peter did not set aside his cord, eat enough to maintain his health, and submit to the advice of his physician. To Peter, this command must have seemed the ultimate denial of his meager independence. He immediately had food brought to him, and obediently ate it—but his health was already broken, the order having come too late.[50]

It was just after Christmas of 1386 that his health became noticeably worse; he was weak, and suffered what seemed to be anemia. At his doctors' advice he moved out of Avignon to Villeneuve, where the air was cleaner. He welcomed the removal, and began spending long hours in the Carthusian monastery at Villeneuve. Yet his health declined further, he was more and more clearly consumptive, and by Eastertime he was coughing up blood. It was difficult for him to eat, drink, or even pray. Yet he lingered until July. When death was at last imminent, and he was told as much, he joined his hands slowly, and three times murmured, "Many thanks!" Soon afterward, with tears of joy, he begged, "Let it be true, oh Lord!" As he entered his final agony, he seemed to be praying; he moaned and sighed slightly as those around him prayed for his soul, then he made no more sound. There was disagreement as to whether he was dead, asleep, or in rapture. Feathers were placed up to his nostrils, and there was dispute about whether they had moved; even his pulse was uncertain. When these doubts were resolved, his body was prepared for burial.[51]

When his corpse was exposed for public display, a phenomenon emerged of which the sources give no prior hint: with all of his rigors and devotions, Peter had become the object of popular veneration. Mobs flocked to pay reverence, people knelt down to kiss his hands and feet, and parents touched their children to the body. All through the day the crowds came, so dense that it was difficult to make one's way forward. When the entry was closed in the evening, people waited outside until the next day.[52]

On the day of burial all work ceased in Avignon, and people again came in great numbers, partly just to see the exposed corpse, partly to obtain the saint's blessing, and partly in hopes of miracles. During the funeral mass at the church of St. Anthony, a merchant who had suffered from gout for ten years was suddenly cured. The corpse was carried to the cemetery where Peter had requested burial, but the place was so crowded that the pallbearers could make their way to the site of burial only with difficulty. After the formal ceremony was over, the crowds merely increased. The saint's associates withdrew for supper, but soon the captain of the papal guard and a companion rushed in, out of breath, to report that miracles were occurring and that the people were so eager for relics that they would soon exhume the body if action were not taken at once. The group sent two delegates to the tomb; they found the pall and other funeral implements divided among the relic-seekers, and discovered that in place of the mound of dirt over the grave there was a hollow where devotees had scooped out earth and carried it away in sacks or in the folds of their garments. Guards were stationed to prevent further encroachment upon the saint's final repose, and before long the site was protected by wood, then enclosed with an iron grill. The miracles that occurred were so numerous that notaries were appointed the next day to begin recording them. Peter was well established as the center of a local cult that long remained important for Avignon, even if it never led to canonization and to veneration throughout the Church.[53]

Somewhat like Dorothy of Montau, Peter became the focus of a cult partly because he was an outsider, unfamiliar to those who venerated him, coming into their world with fully formed piety only a year and a half before his death. Not surprisingly, then, it was not the members of his own household who first recognized that he was a saint. They had known him too well and dealt with him too long, whether as his masters or as his servants. They could hardly be unaware of his exceptional fervor, but some of them humored him and others tried to teach him moderation. It was the outsiders, or those for whom he was an outsider, who sensed a charismatic figure mysteriously secluded within the walls of their town.

The contrasts between Dorothy of Montau and Peter of Luxembourg are many. Apart from the obvious differences of nationality and gender, and the gap in both social rank and political stature, there is the sheer fact that Dorothy lived far longer than Peter, at least long enough to embark on a kind of second career after her husband and most of her children had died. No doubt the most significant difference in the sources is that those for Dorothy convey a far better a sense of the internal perspective; the material for Peter is ample, but essentially it reports the perceptions of external observers called to serve as witnesses in ecclesiastical proceedings. The mystical dimension was more clearly present in Dorothy's life, partly for reasons to be explored later. The materials for Peter tell more about his charitable works. As for their posthumous careers, perhaps the most significant difference is that the cult of Dorothy was initiated and vigorously promoted by her confessor, with eager response from the people, whereas Peter's cult was initiated by the citizens of Avignon, who stimulated interest among the clergy. The laywoman was first venerated by a cleric, who spread her cult among her fellow laypeople; the cleric was first recognized as saint by the laity, who induced his fellow clerics to perceive his sanctity. For all these contrasts, however, both figures displayed similar intensity and extravagance in their spiritual lives, and both met with resistance to their rigors from those around them. What they have in common will perhaps become clearer in later chapters.

Like Peter, most of the saints from fourteenth-century France came from the nobility: Elzear of Sabran held substantial lands in both France and Italy, and his wife, Delphina of Puimichel, was a countess in her own right. Jane Mary of Maillé was aristocratic by both birth and marriage, served as godmother for the duke of Anjou's son, and had access to the royal court. Charles of Blois held claim to the duchy of Brittany, though he spent much of his life attempting through warfare to secure this claim, and was killed in the effort. Urban V was son of a lord in Languedoc, served as a papal diplomat, and was then himself chosen pope. Not only did these saints come from aristocratic families; most of them were deeply involved in public life throughout their careers, as Peter of Luxembourg presumably would have been if he had lived long enough. Some of them (Jane Mary of Maillé, and supposedly also Elzear and Delphina) were members of the third order of Saint Francis, and thus technically counted as mendicants, but unlike the German Dominicans they do not seem to have practiced a distinctively mendicant spirituality. They were from the countryside, and generally lived there, unlike the German-speaking saints. They differed also in that they seldom produced devotional literature, though in this respect Peter is the exception.[54]

The aristocratic ties of these saints could be either an asset or a liability—or both—to their posthumous veneration. The canonization of Charles of Blois was a matter of intense controversy: his family and its political allies were on the verge of scoring a propaganda victory by having him sainted, but when the Great Schism began the Avignonese pope needed the support of his opponents, and thus all prospects of canonization were dashed.[55] The fate of Peter of Luxembourg was that he was too closely linked with the Avignonese papacy, and when the schism ended with the repudiation of Avignonese claims he was left in a kind of hagiographic limbo. Known as blessed by virtue of his local patronage, he has never attained the honor of sainthood.

Clare Gambacorta: Dominican Nun

In contrast to both Dorothy of Montau and Peter of Luxembourg, Clare Gambacorta is a paragon of self-determination—and, some might add, of sanity.[56] Her family was prominent in the affairs of Pisa: her father had been ruler of the town, and though he was in exile at the time of her birth, he returned to power not long thereafter. Her brother Peter followed her into religious life, and like her became a saint. Against her will, she was betrothed at the age of seven, and at twelve she was sent to live in her prospective husband's home. When he died at fifteen, her family wanted to arrange a second betrothal, but by this time she had gained in maturity and resolution and had been confirmed in her celibacy by the example of Catherine of Siena, so she escaped from familial control and joined a convent of Poor Clares. Her father was inconsolable. To alleviate his grief, her brothers took a band of armed men to the convent and threatened to burn it down if the nuns did not turn her over to them, whereupon they promptly complied. For five months she was held prisoner in her parental home, without even such basic amenities as a bed to sleep on, but she refused to bend. At length her father allowed her to join the Dominicans, and went so far as to promise he would build a new priory for her. After some delay he fulfilled the promise. She served in this new priory first as subprioress, then as prioress; even in the lower rank she was the chief source of inspiration for the new community. The remainder of her life was relatively uneventful, except insofar as external events impinged on the serenity of the convent. When her father and two brothers were assassinated by political rivals, Clare refused to open the convent gates for the protection of a third brother, partly because the excommunication he would thus incur would be worse than physical harm, and partly because she did not want to encourage others in her family to use the convent as a political refuge. She exercised patience by forgiving the assassins, sought to establish a bond of charity with them by having herself sustained from their table when she was sick, and even received the women from their family when they were in danger from later political upheavals. Having led the convent effectively through financial as well as other difficulties, she died in 1419; pious at the end as she had been through life, she referred to her deathbed as the "cross" on which she lay outstretched.

The nun who wrote her biography ascribed to Clare the asceticism that was recognized as integral to sanctity. She moritified her flesh and wore a hairshirt even as a young girl; if she had to wear fine clothing on account of her status, she would conceal a hairshirt beneath it and thus pay her duty to both Caesar and God. She was devoted to poverty, and after entering the convent she always wore ragged and mended clothes, and cast-off shoes that would irritate the other nuns with the noise they made. Similarly, she exercised rigor in her fasting.[57]

Her biographer also speaks of her devotions. As a child, she would gather a band of young girls about her in a circle and read to them from some pious book, and would have them join her in prayer and in singing of hymns. When she had her own convent, she had a small cell to which she could betake herself for solitary prayer. She was devout in the company of others as well, would talk almost always of God, and gave such inspiration to all who met her that none went away without having been transformed. Men in particular were confounded to find such virtue in a woman. Even in her youth, she did not hesitate to speak bluntly to persons of high dignity and authority. If she heard anything about a priest that deserved criticism, she would pretend to go for confession and would admonish him so sharply that he would live in dread of meriting again such castigation.[58]

Among her devotions, one in particular is of interest for this study: her fondness for Saint Bridget of Sweden, one of the most prominent saints of the fourteenth century and one of the few to gain international veneration soon after death. (Dorothy of Montau gives further witness to this following, in that she had a vision of Saint Bridget.) This Swedish woman had spent much of her adult life in Italy and was at least as well known among Italians as among her fellow Swedes. Her former confessor visited Clare during her five months of "imprisonment," encouraged her with the example of Bridget, and left a copy of Bridget's vita so she could know and imitate this saint's life more effectively. From that time on, Clare took Bridget as her special patron. Later she arranged to have Bridget's life and virtues commemorated publicly in Pisa through preaching, and she had the saint's feast day celebrated annually in her convent.[59]

More than either her asceticism or her devotion, Clare's vita emphasizes her charity. This too began in her childhood: when she was living in the home of her parents-in-law, she was so generous with their belongings that it seemed as if she would give away everything they owned. She was fond of visiting the sick and cultivated the friendship of one elderly woman in particular by serving her as she wasted away physically. Heedless of the requirements of her social rank, she gave away her own clothes to the poor, preserving only what was needed to spare her modesty. Even when she was in the "prison" of her familial house, when she heard a poor woman outdoors lamenting her need, Clare handed her a dress through the window; she asked the woman to keep this act of generosity a secret, but the woman was so overcome with joy that she made her benefactress known to all. As prioress of her convent, Clare insisted that alms be given to all who came seeking them, and she sent alms out to prisoners who needed aid. She took compassion on those undergoing tribulation and temptation, and did her best to console them; her biographer says that her face was always cheerful except when she was troubled out of compassion for someone else. When a foundling hospital was in need of support, she diverted patronage from her own convent to the maintenance of that institution.[60]

The general tone of Clare's vita is fundamentally different from that of the sources for Dorothy of Montau, even apart from its relative brevity. Clare's biographer was little interested in probing her inward spiritual life; she contented herself with describing the saint's external manifestations of virtue. There is no sense of a soul caught in turmoil or laboring in anxiety. Clare was faced with opposition from those around her and responded to it with a firm will. She seems to have been accustomed to having things work as she wished. Her vita does not suggest that she was beset by inward adversity: by a troubled conscience, by overwrought devotional tendencies, or by feverish and debilitating ecstasies. The details of her life appear conventional, as if entire sections were composed of topoi from traditional saints' lives. Her lavish generosity, her devotional life, and other elements in her sanctity, while entirely plausible, distinguish her little or not at all from numerous other saints from whose vitae the biographer might have borrowed. When we are told that she wished her generosity to remain secret, but that the recipient of her favors divulged it to all and sundry, we are reminded perhaps that Christ too tried in vain to conceal his services; indeed, we are no doubt supposed to be reminded that Clare was patterning her life after that of Christ. While the impression the vita leaves is one of relative sobriety, there is at the same time little sense of an individual personality. We can discern Clare's strength of will and her cheerful, ever-patient benevolence, but further than that we cannot go. We do not get to know her as intimately as we do Dorothy and Peter. For all these reasons—and because of the simple fact that her vita is less rich than the sources for these other saints—we need not trace her life in such detail as we have done for the others.

The salient fact about Clare from the viewpoint of ecclesiastical history is her connection with the Dominican reform movement. The Dominican order in the late fourteenth century was beset by what many of its members saw as laxity and lack of religious fervor. Clare's biographer mentions, for example, that when she first became a Dominican nun there was no disciplined observance of the order's rule; evidently the other nuns held private possessions, though Clare herself belonged to a small group that had renounced private ownership. The convent seems also to have been lax in enforcing its rule of enclosure, which is to say that it evidently allowed outsiders to enter the premises with little hindrance. Raymund of Capua, master-general of the order in the last years of the century, undertook a reform of the order so vital that he was dubbed its second founder. While he did not force the Dominicans throughout Europe to revert to earlier standards of poverty and devotion, he encouraged the formation of reformed friaries and convents, which could then act as a kind of reforming leaven within the order. He was confessor for Catherine of Siena in her later years, and wrote a quasi-autobiographical vita of her, representing her as an exemplar of Dominican reform. The movement was further supported by such influential figures as John Domenici, an archbishop and cardinal, who was inspired in part by Clare.[61]

When Clare's father delayed in building her a new convent, she went to her stepmother, embraced her, and proclaimed, "My lady, God has sent you and given you as my mother, so that through you and your husband I may obtain my convent, where we can live in common, following the rule, beyond the gaze of men and free from worldly distractions." Her stepmother replied, "I blush out of respect for you, for although I had a spiritually inclined mother, wholly dedicated to virtue, I allowed myself to be ensnared by the world's traps, while you have been able to free yourself from so many impediments.

I promise, though, that I will speak with your father, so that you may obtain your desired solace." When the convent was erected, the nuns entered it with the ardor of fugitives fleeing from a war, says Clare's biographer. A grate was installed so that the nuns could not see or be seen by outsiders. The gate was triple-locked, and no one was allowed inside, under penalty of excommunication. Even the Dominican friars who ministered to the nuns were not allowed into their living quarters, except to administer the sacraments to one who was dying. Even the master-general and provincial of the order were allowed only annual visitation rights. And these provisions were confirmed by a papal bull.[62]

At roughly the same time, a Franciscan counterpart to this reform was underway. Led by Paoluccio dei Trinci, it blossomed in the fifteenth century as the Observantine branch of the Franciscan order, and produced such saints as Bernardino of Siena and John of Capistrano. In the fourteenth century, however, the Franciscans were eclipsed by the Dominicans in the production of saints. The Franciscans had spawned the Spiritual Franciscan movement, which gained a reputation for heresy. They had been censured by John XXII for their radical insistence on poverty. Thus, they were not in an ideal position to foster the cult of their saints, most of whom at this time tended to be hermits rather than leading public figures.[63]

By far the majority of the Italian saints in this century belonged to the mendicant orders. While there were fewer Franciscans than Dominicans, the disciples of Saint Francis were not altogether unrepresented: John of Alverna, Conrad of Piacenza, and others gained renown for their sanctity. Among the Carmelites there were two saints who rose to high position in the hierarchy: Andrew Corsini, bishop of Fiesole, and Peter Thomas, titular Latin patriarch of Constantinople. The young Servite order (not yet officially recognized as mendicant) had Francis Patrizzi, Juliana Falconieri, and Joan Soderini as saintly figures in the early years of the century. While many of these saints were friars or nuns, others belonged to the mendicant third orders of lay associates. While these too might live in special houses, the alternative (seen, for example, in Catherine of Siena) was to live at home while wearing their order's habit and maintaining regular contact with other members. Having been founded only in the early thirteenth century, these mendicant orders were rivals of the long-established diocesan clergy; representing a new wave of religious fervor, the mendicants were generally more effective than the diocesan priests at ministering to the religious needs of the urban laity. Largely to prove their legitimacy, and to show themselves the spiritual equals of the earlier monastic orders, the mendicants had made great efforts since the late thirteenth century to cultivate the veneration of the saints in their midst. These propaganda measures had succeeded especially well in Italy, where the mendicant orders had been founded and where they dominated spiritual life in the later Middle Ages.[64]

The mendicant prominence in Italy gave these orders a disproportionate role in the spiritual life of Europe as a whole, since in the late Middle Ages Italy was exceptionally productive of saints. Of the officially recognized saints listed by Weinstein and Bell as dying in the fourteenth century, 69 percent were Italian; though Italy produced the largest number of saints from the thirteenth through the mid-sixteenth century, its share was never so great as in the fourteenth century. Weinstein and Bell refer to the broader period as "the era of the Italian saint, and especially the northern Italian urban saint." In this respect Clare Gambacorta was typical. She also fit the common pattern in other respects: Italian saints of this time were increasingly female, they manifested a strong tendency toward religious conversion during adolescence, and they were supported by communes where religion and civic life blended, and where each community cherished its local saints as foci of civic pride. During their lifetimes, these saints served their towns as welfare agents, counselors, and peacemakers; Clare played all these roles. After their deaths, they became centers of veneration that redounded to the honor of their fellow citizens. This was no less true of Marienwerder or Avignon than of Pisa, but the Italian towns tended to be particularly active in securing veneration for their local saints. In Italy more than elsewhere, civic authorities tended to ally themselves with ecclesiastical authorities in pursuit of municipal honor. Nonetheless, canonization was a rare honor in the fourteenth century, and Clare, like Dorothy and Peter, got no further than the rank of blessed.[65]

The spirituality that Clare represents is of special interest here because of the questions it raises. One can see in her very little of that hypersensitivity that will be examined in the remainder of this book. In surveying the religious culture of an era, however, one may take either of two approaches: one may attempt a rounded survey of all the strands that make up the religious fabric of the age, or one may single out that which is most distinctive and most clearly related to developments elsewhere in the culture. This book will take the latter approach. Following chapters will examine themes that are important for an understanding of what was most distinctive in the later Middle Ages; they will attempt to show how these themes were manifested sometimes in moderate and sometimes in exaggerated ways, and how the spectrum from the moderate to the extreme made it possible for the saints to typify their society yet stand out as extraordinary characters within it.

3
Patience

*I*n a life filled with adversity, Henry Suso paused one day to look
out the window of his cell. In the yard outdoors he saw a dog
running about with a ragged mat in its mouth and tearing the mat to
shreds. Suso at once saw the dog's treatment of this tattered rag as a
symbol of his own suffering, and an inner voice told him, "Just so will
you be torn and tugged about in the mouths of your brothers." Re-
solving to emulate the mat's patient endurance, he went out and took
it from the dog, and kept it for several years as a treasured reminder
of what he was destined to undergo.[1]

If there is a single image that captures the most distinctive emphases of fourteenth-century sanctity, it is Suso's ragged mat, his *memento
pati*. The patient endurance of suffering to which he committed himself is a motif that dominates the era's hagiography, recurs in other
forms of devotional and even secular literature, and relates in important ways to further themes at the heart of fourteenth-century piety.

Patience involved submission to evil—or, more precisely, submission to God's will, which was capable of permitting evils for some ulterior end. In any event, the virtue was one of passive submissiveness.
The very word "patience" (*patientia*) is linked with "passivity" (*passivitas*), both of which suggest being acted upon (*pati*) rather than acting (*agere*). While there were saints whose cultivation of patience did
not preclude an activist zeal to reform Church and society (e.g.,
Catherine of Siena), the hagiography emphasizes passive submission
to adversity far more than active reform of the world's evils. To be
sure, patient endurance of abuse could be a way to heap coals on the
head of one's adversary and thus bring him to repentance. But direct

assault on evil was subordinated to a submissiveness which might or might not work for the betterment of the adversary.

Yet it is only in reference to external behavior that patience implies nonperformance; inwardly it involves an active adaptation of one's will to God's. Some authors use the term "patience" with reference to both outward passivity and inward conformity of will; for them, the single word conveys both the passive and the active elements in this ideal. Others use the word specifically for outward submission, but then they will often go on to suggest that this outward patience is not enough and must be accompanied by inward receptivity, or that one must accept adversity not only patiently but "gladly." We will see evidence of both usages throughout this chapter.

The idea of suffering as an opportunity for personal growth is a commonplace both in Christian spirituality and in secular psychology. There is sharp divergence, though, regarding the proper response to suffering: rather than submitting patiently to it, many would insist on grappling actively with its causes and overcoming them. As William James observed, a culture that seeks to anesthetize pain will be baffled by one that welcomes it.[2] The approach found in fourteenth-century hagiography is not far removed from that of the Orthodox nun Mother Maria of Normanby, who accepted her years of suffering with terminal cancer as a "blessing."[3] Like this twentieth-century nun, the fourteenth-century saints viewed suffering as an opportunity not simply for "character building" but for a submission to the divine will that predisposes the sufferer for otherworldly beatitude. As we shall see, the vitae routinely represent suffering as a preparation for future reward, not necessarily in the sense that it is an arbitrarily imposed means for gaining merit, but in the deeper sense that submission to God's will during this life makes a person worthy for a state of eternal surrender in celestial contemplation of God. The presupposition is that suffering, like everything else in this life, finds its meaning in a potentially permanent relationship with the deity.

Manifestations in the Saints' Lives

As is clear from even a cursory survey of the fourteenth-century saints' lives, Suso was by no means alone in his conviction that suffering is a gift from God and that patient acceptance of it is vital to the Christian life. Peter Olafsson maintained great patience in his many tribulations, always remained joyful, and remembered the words of Paul: "the sufferings of this time are not worthy to be compared with the glory to come" (Rom. 8:18). The same text occurs in the canonization proceedings for Bridget of Sweden, who was praised more for her patience than for any other virtue. She was "wondrously patient, calm, and peaceful, never quarreled, and bore with great patience the shortcomings of her household." Whether she was despoiled of her property or assaulted with a pan of dirty water, she maintained this virtue. Likewise, whatever evil befell Pope Urban V, he saw it as permitted by God for some ulterior end, and he bore it with unshaken patience. The Christological model comes to the fore in the life of Luitgard of Wittichen: mocked by all as she collected alms for her convent, she bore the abuse with inner peace, just as Christ remained inwardly imperturbable amid outward anguish. Dorothy of Montau did whatever she was ordered to do, in childhood and in marriage, without complaint or impatience. She accepted gratefully whatever befell her and gladly repaid evil with good, though the devil tried to dissuade her from such display of patience. When Christina Ebner prayed for a person who was suffering greatly, God told her that anyone who suffers should recall the patience of Christ at his birth, in Gethsemane, and toward every sinner, and the patience of the Virgin during the flight into Egypt, at the foot of the cross, and on her son's ascension into heaven.[4]

Even when the word does not occur explicitly, the concept is present. Writing to his sister, Peter of Luxembourg encouraged her to reply humbly and respectfully to harsh words, and reminded her that those who strive to serve and honor God and to live without sin are never lacking in adversity. His earliest biography told that Peter relished sorrows more than rewards, and took greatest delight in those things which normally provoke sadness; he often told his friends that unless Christ deigned otherwise he would just as soon not enjoy prosperity.[5] Such comments pervade the hagiographic literature. Taken separately they might not arouse special attention, but their cumulative effect is striking. If one considers the evidence in its totality, patience emerges as in many ways the key virtue in fourteenth-century spirituality.

The biographer of Venturino of Bergamo comments at some length on the saint's patience, and in so doing gives a clear idea of how fourteenth-century Christians understood this virtue. Venturino cultivated patience in all adversity, following the example of Christ, who was silent and patient in his passion. The saint was undisturbed by anything that happened to him; more than that, he admonished his friends not to be disturbed either, and not to take his side in any quarrel. He said it was no surprise that people sometimes were aroused against him, since he was full of faults, and it would have been just if God corrected them in even harsher ways. Rather than answering in a haughty and querulous tone, if unjustly accused, he would lower his face and show himself repentent. He always acted like a prudent tailor, sewing a small patch onto a noble garment: he would take what came his way and turn it about until it fit well. If he met with any impediment in his travel, he would tell his companion that God was keeping them from some misfortune; if they traveled quickly, without obstacles, he would suggest that God was sending him on to work for the benefit of some soul. It seemed as if he gloried in tribulation, as a way of forestalling punishment in the afterlife. By this patience he made himself pleasant and lovable, and his love fanned the coals which he heaped on the heads of his detractors.[6]

Another figure who distinguished himself for practice of patience was Charles of Blois. The witnesses at his canonization proceedings testified that they had never seen anyone who displayed such patience. When he received news that he had lost troops, villages, or castles in his war for the duchy of Brittany, he took these reports with patient equanimity. He was patient also in protracted illnesses, and when he visited poor people in hospitals he said that patience would redound to the salvation of their souls. Captured by the enemy, he had seventeen wounds, and he spent almost nine years of captivity in England, all of which counted as "persecutions" that he "bore patiently."[7]

As these examples already suggest, the occasions for exercising patience were of various sorts. In a classic discussion of patience, his fifty-fifth homily on the gospels, Gregory the Great spoke of the provocations that gave opportunity for patience as coming from three sources: from the devil, from one's neighbor, and from God.[8] All three of these agents of affliction appear in the late medieval saints' lives.

Perhaps oddly, the devil played a relatively minor role in these matters. At times his temptations served as occasions for patience, especially when they took that vehement form which figured largely in saints' lives as far back as that of Anthony the Hermit.[9] Thus, when Gertrude of Delft was tempted by the devil, he seized her arms as if wishing to strip her of her clothing, taunted her by name, and tossed her about, but she "rejoiced in the Lord, knowing that only one thus tried in battle received the crown of life." More commonly, the devil worked in subtler fashion. Urban V's patience was tried and proven, for example, when a church he was having repaired was seriously damaged by fire; he ascribed the conflagration to the devil, yet thanked God for permitting it to blaze and for giving him occasion for further goodness.[10] James Passavanti, in his influential *Mirror of True Penitence,* devoted a lengthy section to the spiritual benefits to be reaped from ordinary temptation.[11] But this motif was not common in the saints' lives, whose authors may have found it difficult to portray the Tempter as an agent contributing to human sanctity.

The ways in which fellow human beings could provide opportunity for patience were limited only by their imagination and their capacity for malfeasance. At times the deeds that called for patience were outright crimes. Thus, when Peter Olafsson was outside Rome visiting the shrines of saints, he fell among robbers, who stripped him of his possessions, snatched his cape, and left him quite naked. His biographer, alluding to the victim in the parable of the Good Samaritan, remarked that Peter was "brought by the beast of patience to the stable of divine consolation." At other times an unfaithful spouse could try one's patience. Elizabeth of Portugal displayed this virtue by bearing her husband's extramarital affairs with equanimity, by showing no interest in them when gossip reached her, and by treating his illegitimate children generously and without rancor. Through her gracious reaction she aroused her husband to a conversion of sorts: thereafter he was more discreet in his transgressions. A further occasion for patient endurance was political infidelity. When Elzear of Sabran inherited his father's lands, he discovered some slanderous correspondence from certain nobles who had tried during his father's life to have Elzear disinherited. Yet he refused to proceed against the offenders; he declined even to mention the offense to them, because if they knew he was aware of their treachery they might fear and suspect him. When their leader came to a certain solemnity, Elzear showed him special honor and cordiality, and gave him precious robes as tokens of his favor. When the people of Ariano rebelled against him over a period of three years, he refused to extract the peremptory and sanguinary justice to which he was advised. And when he found his territories burdened with debts, he thanked God for giving him lands that kept him from terrestrial attachment. He was never known to manifest anger or impatience in any sort of tribulation; on account of his patience, he was honored by all as a true lord, and loved as a father.[12]

Jane Mary of Maillé suffered various forms of personal abuse, always gladly. At one point in her life she had managed to overcome certain diseases, with heavenly rather than earthly remedies, but "lest the virtue of patience become idle in her" God allowed her contemporaries to provide new occasions for its exercise. First her husband, the baron of Silly, was made lame for three years as a result of injury in combat. Then his castle was captured, the surrounding lands devastated, and forty-six vassals killed. At last her husband himself was captured and held for ransom, and when she was unable to raise the required amount he was placed in harsh confinement and for nine days had nothing to eat or drink except his own urine. Jane Mary herself had to endure physical abuse when she was invited to the household of the queen of France but was repulsed by a surly doorkeeper, who beat her with his staff and chased her away. Asked later if she felt disturbed amid such affliction, she said, "I was neither ter-rified by the man's harshness nor harmed by the blow of his staff, for the Lord Jesus Christ protected me sweetly." When her husband died, she was forced to leave the castle in which she had been brought up, and all her friends spurned her. For fear of her family's displeasure, her friends closed their doors and gates to her; she was unable to rent a room, and even her old landlord cast her mercilessly out of the place she had been staying. Forced to find refuge in a delapidated building where dogs and pigs sometimes lay, she remained patient and cheer-ful through all.[13]

Elizabeth of Portugal, too, was subjected to dispossession. Like Eliz-abeth of Hungary, her thirteenth-century ancestor for whom she was named, she found herself dismissed from courtly society by unsym-pathetic relatives and despoiled of her possessions. She responded with unimaginable meekness, arguing that it would be better for her to bear poverty and tolerate all the injuries inflicted on her than to consent to the warfare that would be required to assert her rights.[14]

For a married saint, abuse at the hands of a spouse could be a prime occasion for patience. Dorothy of Montau is a clear example. Considerably older than she, and suffering from the wear of his years, her husband was irritable and at times violent. He allowed her to engage in works of piety during the morning, so long as she at-tended to basic chores around the house. Eventually, however, he grew weary of her devotions and threatened to keep her at home, bound by chains, if she did not stop her "running around." Indeed, he ultimately did bind her in chains for three days. Armed with "the shield of patience," she sustained all his fury without murmuring, but he took her patient silence as insolence and struck her hard on the head with a chair. That abuse too she accepted with joy and gen-tleness, and she was rewarded with inner consolation from the Lord. At times her mystical states would distract her from her housework, and her husband would chastize her and strike her, sometimes draw-ing blood. Once he struck her so hard on the mouth that her teeth practically pierced her lips. She smiled cheerfully at him, and hastened to do his bidding. On this and other occasions, those around her marveled at her patience, joy, benevolence, and equanimity. As for her husband, he was restrained only when both their confessors went to him and reproached him for attacking her when she had no control over her actions.[15]

For every occasion when the saints had to bear hostile action, there must have been dozens of times when they were victims of derogatory thoughts and words. Insult, revilement, and slander was their com-mon lot, often because their religious lives went unappreciated. Thus,

when Andrew Corsini entered a religious order his friends and relatives derided him, but he overcame them with his silence and his patience. Urban V bore abuse patiently, even though (his biographer
reminds us) as pope he could easily have had vengeance. The rabble
of Rome pursued Peter Olafsson and his companions with insults and
unspecified snares, but with great patience they "joyfully bore these
insults for the Lord's sake." If anyone offended Elizabeth of Portugal,
she did not bear resentment or demand satisfaction, but pardoned
the offense readily. Likewise, when servants poked fun at Jane Mary
of Maillé, jeering at her with contumely, she bore all for Christ's sake,
and passed by as if she were deaf. On one occasion she met with revilement from a young man who, seeing her humble garb, failed to
recognize her nobility; although her maid was reduced to tears, she
herself knelt down and thanked God for this injury.[16]

Catherine of Sweden disliked being praised for her virtuous deeds,
and when she met with reproach or derision she bore it patiently. Her
biographer tells that, while she was noted for various virtues, those
close to her praised her especially for her patience. For she was con-
vinced that if a soul does not resist perturbation with patience, it un-
does all the good it has accomplished in its prior tranquillity, and
throws everything into disorder. It is easy to wear contemptible
clothes and go about with one's head lowered, but patient suffering of
abuse is a genuine test of virtue. Just as unguents cannot diffuse their
odor unless they are stirred up, so Catherine diffused her holy odor
by patient endurance of unjust abuse, contumely, and detraction.
Such treatment came even from her relatives and servants, whom she
thus loved as benefactors. A nun who served her for five years reported that she never heard a word of impatience or saw any sign of
indignation from her. All the more amazing, her biographer says, in
that many people are aroused to enmity at the slightest provocation,
and for several days will refuse to talk to those who have offended
them by some idle conversation or other slight abuse. The biographer
goes on to say that the life of the just is nothing but warfare on earth
(cf. Job 7:1)—but Catherine, bearing the whips of her creator with joy
and thanksgiving, refrained from murmuring.[17]

The distinction between celestial and terrestrial origins of affliction
was at times obscure: even when it was clearly human agents who
were working their mischief, the saints might thank God for allowing
this to happen. On other occasions, though, God acted independently
of human beings, sending misfortunes that we would still refer to as
"acts of God." For Nicholas Hermansson, loss of temporal goods was
an opportunity to manifest patient endurance: when fire or some
other misfortune occurred, he maintained a cheerful face and
thanked God for permitting such things to happen to him rather than

to the poor, who cannot recover their losses but are oppressed with hunger.[18]

The most common form of heaven-sent affliction was illness. About the precise diseases in question one can say little: the biographers seldom indicate the nature of the saints' illnesses, but focus instead on their reactions. Thus, James of Oldo once contracted an unspecified but serious disease, yet remained cheerful and gladly received visitors, to whom he offered pious counsel. Those who came marveled that amid such sufferings he could maintain such serenity in his countenance. By way of explanation, his biographer cited the notion of Proverbs 15:7 that a joyful heart will be reflected in a joyful face, and added that James was "wholly joyful in the Lord." At last the disease proved fatal, yet to the end he exercised "daily and wondrous patience," and never gave a sign of pain or annoyance. Likewise, Nicholas Hermansson bore ailments with perfect patience, and was never moved to words or gestures of impatience or complaint. During his final illness, though he could neither eat nor drink, he scarcely ever lay down in bed, but sat at table imparting devout counsel to others as if he were in the best of health. When Jane Mary of Maillé was ill she referred to her bodily pains as pleasures. Clare Gambacorta, after long affliction with pain in her sides and diseases which were incurable because they were "contrary to each other," approached death with a terrible swelling in her head, given to her "for the perfection of her crown of patience." Despite her anguish, she maintained a cheerful disposition which inspired those around her. Similar accounts occur in the lives of numerous other saints. The biographer of Villana de' Botti credits her with a positive attachment to the fevers and pains that she bore with "astonishing patience." She often besought her confessor not to pray for her health. When she felt herself recuperating she groaned and prayed that it might not be so, but that she might be afflicted doubly with illness; thus God inflicted such a fever that she nearly expired, for which she praised him in thanksgiving. Delphina of Puimichel went so far as to suggest that if people realized how useful diseases are for detaching the soul from earthly things, they would go out and purchase them in the market just like other necessities of life.[19]

Peter of Luxembourg astonished those who surrounded him in his final illness by remaining joyful throughout his agony. When asked about his health, he would say cheerfully that he was "very well, thank God," and his tone made it hard to believe that he was indeed suffering. When he saw his illness advance, he showed nothing but joy at his physical decline. He never prayed for a cure, only for patience to submit fully to God's will. Even as he was receiving extreme unction, he smiled and protested that he felt fine. "The more he was beset with illness," his earliest biography says, "the more he bore it with patience, saying humbly that Christ had borne much worse pain for him."[20]

Thus, if a saint's illness was fatal, he or she maintained patience to the end; whether it was lethal or not, illness was a prime occasion for exercise of that virtue. Even the disease of someone else could be an opportunity for patience, as when Francis Patrizzi was kept from becoming a hermit by the necessity of attending to his blind mother.[21]

Remarkably absent from the occasions of patience is one that might have been most expected: death. The saints do frequently show their patience in uncomplaining endurance of terminal disease, as already mentioned, but it is the ongoing affliction leading up to death, and not death itself or even the prospect of imminent death, which in this case is the cause for patience. The exceptions are very few, and are not elaborated in the texts. Elzear of Sabran's biographer tells how he brought a condemned thief to contrition before his hanging; persuaded that he deserved his punishment, the criminal went to his execution "patiently and gladly." Surely more representative of everyday experience was the patience Jane Mary of Maillé displayed when her confessor and a close companion died at roughly the same time: her patience never broke, and because she was sure of their salvation she found herself happy and unable to cry at their passing. When Urban V's parents and close friends died, he kept from inordinate expressions of grief, and reflected that our uncertainty about when we will die should inspire us to be always prepared. The saints' lives furnish only few such examples of pious stoicism in the face of death.[22]

Far more numerous are cases in which one might expect patient acceptance of death, only to find the sources silent on this point. For example, it seems likely that Richard Rolle died in mid-century of the plague, but his biographer does not speak of his death or of his attitudes toward it. Dorothy of Montau lost eight of her nine children, but their demise was not a special occasion for patience; her biographer mentions it only as her means of release from domesticity. When the plague struck Lodi, James of Oldo and his extended family did what other sensible persons did: they fled to a secluded area where they would be safe from the contagion, and waited there, somewhat fidgety because of the confinement, until they felt it safe to return. Though James himself underwent a religious conversion during this experience, it evidently had no connection with the plague, and in any event it did not involve patient anticipation of his death or anyone else's. His biographer may have missed the true motives for his change of heart, but for present purposes the important point is that the biography itself says nothing about death as a provocation to patience.[23]

Perhaps death was too much an everyday phenomenon to arouse attention. More to the point, death was not so much a form of suffering as it was a release from suffering; and while a Christian might need to be called to patient endurance of illness and ill-treatment, there was little one could do about death. Thus, although the mortality rate reached a peak during this century, there was little explicit attention to death in the saints' lives. In the literature and art of the period, likewise, although death is not absent it does not yet loom so large as in the following century. *The Ploughman from Bohemia,* with the ploughman's poignant complaint against personified Death, enters the literary scene only around the turn of the century, and it is in the fifteenth century that the *Ars moriendi* treatises gain their greatest popularity. The dance of death, the rotting corpses (*transi*), and the openly displayed skull were moral and ascetic devices of the fifteenth and sixteenth centuries. Thomas More, long before his own martyrdom, displayed a moralist's keen perception of the inevitability of death that might have seemed superfluous in the fourteenth century. It is not the *memento mori* but Suso's *memento pati,* his ragged mat reminding him of the inevitability of suffering, that typifies this earlier era, as a call to reflect not on the vanity of life and the imminence of death, but on the value of suffering one's way through a life replete with miseries.[24]

One of the biblical models not infrequently cited as a model for fourteenth-century sanctity was Job, legendary for his patience. Peter Olafsson's biographer, for example, compared him with "Blessed Job," and in the midst of adversity Henry Suso turned to reflection on Job's misfortune. It was meditation on a line from Job, "The life of man on earth is a warfare" (7:1), which brought Suso to understand the centrality of suffering in his spiritual life. Confronted with her family's deposition from power, Clare Gambacorta "knew with Blessed Job not to complain about God, with whose permission these things had happened," and along with Job she proclaimed, "Blessed be the name of the Lord." Similarly, when messengers brought Charles of Blois news that he had lost villages, castles, or soldiers to his enemy, he regularly echoed Job's response to reports of ill fortune by exclaiming, "Blessed be God." On occasion he added, "with God's help we shall recover these things," thus calling to mind the final chapter of Job, though he clearly intended to take a more aggressive role in this recovery than Job did.[25]

Patience had its rewards both in this life and in the next. At times, the fruits of patience were stated in general or vague formulas. Thus, we are told that the more infirm Catherine of Sweden was in body, the stronger she was in soul, for she knew that virtue is perfected in infirmity. Peter Olafsson, in recommending the virtue of patience, told of the tribulations he, Bridget, and others had suffered in Rome, and went on to say that all their trials had "cooperated by God's grace for their good." And Urban V endured suffering out of hope for a reward not specified by his biographer. Somewhat more specifically, some of the texts argue that trials and temptations purge the soul, whether of sin or of its effects. Thus, Peter Olafsson suffered sundry temptations so that he might come to love God more perfectly, for God purges his friends of iniquity by tribulations, as vessels of election are purged in fire. The quasi-hagiographic account of Rulman Merswin affords a parallel: after suffering great temptations, day and night, Rulman learned that they were needed for his purification, so that God could dwell in him more fully, "since he likes to dwell in a man who takes his cross upon him and follows him, especially in suffering." If suffering aids in purgation, though, it also leads to illumination and union with God: Peter Olafsson, for example, was brought by suffering to "divine consolation."[26]

The ultimate reward for patience came in heaven. In some instances the conviction that one would obtain a celestial reward for patient suffering was merely a postulate of faith. Jane Mary of Maillé affirmed that injuries and adversities patiently sustained for Christ's sake profit greatly for salvation. Catherine of Sweden, likewise, was sure that anyone wishing the rewards of the future life must bear with equanimity all the evils of this present life. And Gertrude of Delft endured the devil's molestation, knowing that only the person thus tried in battle receives the crown of life. In other cases, this conviction was reinforced by a vision, as with Villana de' Botti, to whom St. Catherine appeared, holding out a beautiful crown as a promised reward for her patience. Whether the expectation of such a prize was confirmed supernaturally or not, the high value placed upon patience was one of the great unquestioned premises of fourteenth-century spirituality.[27]

This devotion to patience was widespread in fourteenth-century Christendom, and was not the specialty of any region or any particular order. Yet two saints whose writings and biographies provide especially rich sources on this topic are the Dominicans Henry Suso and Catherine of Siena. These individuals merit separate examination for what they contribute to this theme.

Some of the most colorful tales of adversity come from the life of Suso. At one point in his travels he was burdened against his own will with a troublesome companion from his order. As Suso himself was attending to business, his companion went off and got drunk among disreputable company at a local fair. Disoriented in his intoxication, he quickly found himself accused of stealing a cheese; worse than that, a group of soldiers came up and charged that the "evil monk" was in fact a poisoner of wells. His best self-defense was that he himself was only a fool, but that the friar with whom he was traveling, namely Suso, was indeed a cunning well-poisoner, equipped with a large sack full of poisons, along with gold pieces which the Jews had given to him and to his order as payment for their crimes. A mob then took up pikes, axes, and other weapons, and went in pursuit of Suso. When they found him, some wanted to drown him in the Rhine, while others, for fear of polluting the water, preferred to burn him alive. One burly peasant threatened to impale him on a long pike, "as one does to a venomous toad," and affix him to a fence so his unclean corpse could dry in the wind and all could come and curse him as he deserved. His groaning and weeping inspired a minority of bystanders to pity, and some kindly women would have given him shelter except for the pressure of the mob. He fell down before a fence, looked toward heaven, and commended his soul to God. Ultimately a priest overheard him, rescued him, provided shelter overnight, and helped him escape early the next morning.[28]

On another occasion Suso had to bear the calumny of an unchaste woman whom he had sought to convert, but who claimed him as father of an illegitimate child she had borne. His friends offered to relieve his anxiety by pushing the woman off a bridge or by slitting the baby's throat or plunging a knife into its heart. Predictably, he refused these generous offers and preferred to bear the tribulation with patience. While thus beset with adversity, he heard a voice one day reminding him that even Christ had a traitor in his midst. He replied that he had not one but several Judases to endure. But then the answer came to him, that just as Christ called Judas a friend (Matt. 26:50), so a righteous man should view his adversaries as co-workers with God, testing him for his own sake.[29]

At another juncture, in giving counsel to a disciple, Suso emphasized that patience merits rewards during this life. He said that sufferings are sometimes deserved because of one's sins or needed to purge defects such as pride. Yet God sometimes sends them to a blameless person to test him, as in the Old Testament (e.g., Job), or to contribute toward the praise and glory of God, as in the case of the man cured of congenital blindness (John 9:1–3). At times, lesser sufferings prevent greater ones, as when torment by "devilish" human beings forestalls diabolical apparitions at the hour of death, or when sickness or poverty in this life serves as a kind of purgatory on earth and thus prevents later suffering in the literal purgatory. God draws people to himself by suffering: "Wherever they turn in an effort to escape from God, he is there with the temporal misfortunes of this world, and he holds them by their hair so they cannot escape him." Which is to say that people who seek diversion in worldly pleasures confront God and

are forced to face their own religious destinies precisely through affliction. To be sure, suffering is sometimes vain and worthless; this is
the case when people suffer in an effort to meet the world's unholy
demands, or when they inflict pain on themselves with overwrought
reaction to matters of no consequence. Suso tells of a man beset with
grief who, as he passed by a certain house, overheard a woman wailing inside; he investigated, and discovered that she had lost a mere
needle. He said to himself, "Alas, foolish woman, if you had only one
of my burdens to bear you would not weep for the sake of a needle."
Yet patient, Christ-like acceptance of suffering as something sent by
God always proves helpful.[30]

Celestial reward for patience likewise finds expression in Suso's biography. When a deceased disciple appeared to him in a snow-white
robe, surrounded by light, and told of her heavenly bliss, he concluded that God-sent sorrows will be easy to bear if God rewards them
in this fashion. Elsewhere in the book, though, suffering became for
Suso almost an end in itself, or more precisely a token of divine favor,
such that absence of suffering was for him the greatest cause of suffering. One day he was bemoaning the fact that he had gone four
weeks with no assaults on either his body or his reputation. He feared
that God had forgotten all about him. Just then, however, he learned
that a certain lord, alleging that Suso had induced his daughter to
become a kind of religious fanatic, was looking all over for him and
had sworn to "run a sword through his body." Immediately Suso took
heart and even rejoiced: God had remembered him.[31]

The same motifs of suffering and patient endurance are crucial in
the life and writings of Catherine of Siena. Her biographer also wrote
a life of Agnes of Montepulciano, an earlier Dominican saint; both
Agnes and Catherine emerge as paragons of patience.[32] One of the
greatest sources of adversity in Catherine's experience was the misun-
derstanding and abuse she suffered from her own family. When she
undertook religious practices she met with unsympathetic response
from them; they would rather have seen her marry and lead a normal
bourgeois life. Her confessor asked once how she managed to retain
her self-possession in the face of their abuse, and she replied that she
imagined her parents as Christ and Mary, and the others in her family
as the apostles and disciples. From outsiders as well she received vi-
tuperative insults. One person abused her even before her associates,
but in her patience she gave no indication of annoyance, and instructed her companions to ignore his provocation. In response to
this patience, the offender went further, and even robbed her of alms
she had been given, but she persisted in her toleration. At the end of
the biography, having recounted Catherine's life and virtues in some
detail, Raymund of Capua summed up his argument for her can-

onization with an epilogue devoted specifically to her patience, "the virtue which gives the best guarantee of charity and sanctity." He remarked that patience is exercised in response to adversities, for the word itself comes from *pati,* meaning "to suffer." And while he went on to say that the adversity in question is that directed against the body, what he meant was anything contrary to natural "carnal" inclinations: assaults to one's honor give occasion for patience, just as much as disease or bodily afflictions of other sorts. Twice in his work Raymund cited with approval Gregory the Great's dictum that patience is more valuable than miracles. And throughout the work, as well as in the epilogue, he chronicled the manifold sufferings that schooled Catherine in this essential virtue.[33]

An associate of Catherine, who was present at her deathbed and wrote an account of her terminal illness, corroborates this emphasis on patience. Whenever some new form of suffering came upon her, she would raise her eyes and heart to God, thanking him for this favor. Even at that, she berated herself for accepting these sufferings with insufficient reverence, and for failing to endure them with that same "burning desire and ardent love" with which God sent them to her. The associate who tells of this patient endurance concluded, "if I were to attempt to explain the patience which she practiced, under this terrible and unheard-of agony, I should fear to injure, by my explanations, facts which cannot be explained."[34]

Catherine's own *Dialogue,* as well as her biography, stresses that suffering is not in itself meritorious but is essential for the Christian life as an occasion for developing love of God. It is love which is the key to spiritual life and growth; patient endurance of suffering is the outward occasion for cultivation of the inward disposition. Thus, Catherine says that "the soul's love in divine charity is so joined with perfect patience that the one cannot leave without the other," and indeed, "patience is one with charity." Elsewhere she proclaims that true and perfect patience is a sure indication that one's soul loves God "perfectly and without self-interest." When one rises from imperfect to perfect love, the foremost indication of that attainment is the virtue of patience.[35] In other words, patience is the key to sanctity not in the sense that it is ultimately of highest value among the virtues, but in the sense that it is the clearest and most certain indication of that love which is in itself supreme. One might well ask why patience is the best sign of love—rather than, perhaps, active service or fidelity. Catherine's insistence on the practical primacy of love reveals her conception of God and the demands that he makes upon his creatures. What God requires of the saint is, most importantly, submission to his will, and that submission is tested most effectively in those circumstances where the divine and human wills come into conflict, requiring abandonment of one's natural will in surrender to God. Hence, as soon as a person begins to know God's truth he or she will be subjected to assaults from every quarter, not simply because the world will misunderstand and fail to sympathize but because God himself so disposes matters to test one's submission to him. Catherine has a strong sense of suffering *for God*, not in such a way as to accomplish some service on his behalf, but in the sense that in patient endurance of suffering one can demonstrate that submissive love which God requires. In the same way, Henry Suso reflected that suffering for the sake of the Beloved is integrally bound up with love.[36] In this way, for both Catherine and Suso, patience becomes linked with the mystical pursuit of God and with other elements in the Christian life.

Patience in Relation to Other Themes

The significance of patience in fourteenth-century piety can be seen not simply in the frequency with which it is emphasized in the literature of the era, but in the connections between patience and other motifs that were integral to the spirituality of the age. It was a virtue so crucial for late medieval understanding of the spiritual life that it not only occurs repeatedly as a standard theme in itself but becomes associated with other central themes. One could trace the relationship between patience and various other preoccupations of the century. It will suffice to examine the links between patience and five other phenomena: the virtue of humility, the fascination with martyrdom, devotion to the passion, the thirst for mystical union with God, and that secular form of endurance manifested in chivalry.

The connection with humility is recurrent, but its meaning is elusive. The references are usually casual and unexplained, but they are so common that the juxtaposition cannot be altogether accidental. Catherine of Siena's biographer seems almost to speak of patience and humility interchangeably. When Urban V suffered illness, he maintained his accustomed silence "with humility," which is to say with patience. It was to test Francis Patrizzi's "humility and patience" that God upset his plans of becoming a hermit by striking his mother blind and tying him to her service; when he prayed to Mary, the favors he sought were humility of heart, patience in adversity, and strength in repelling the assaults of the Adversary. Following the example of Christ, Jane Mary of Maillé became "meek and humble and patient beyond human measure," as shown in her endurance of abuse. Rejected by all, she remained patient, modest, kind, and humble, as well as cheerful. Magnanimous in her relations with her family's bitter enemies, Clare Gambacorta manifested "great patience and humility." For Catherine of Sweden, patient suffering of injury was a sign of a truly humble person. It was through humble service in his novitiate—acting as doorkeeper, cleaning the friary, helping in the kitchen, serving at table—that Andrew Corsini became "silent, prayerful, and most patient." Catherine of Siena nursed a leper-woman whom no one else would dare serve, but the ingrate began to take Catherine's aid for granted and even complained about her. Though Catherine herself began to show symptoms of the disease, it was quickly remitted when she buried the dead woman with her own hands. Thus, her biographer concludes, she manifested charity, humility, and patience, and the miracle of her recovery "was a result of this holy multitude of virtues." At times the concepts are joined even when the words are not used; when Dorothy of Montau submitted to the burdens of marriage, as an exercise in humility, it is clear that she was conflating humility with patience.[37]

If a link is to be found between these notions of patience and humility, it is perhaps best expressed in terms of that submissiveness which God requires of those who love him. The truly patient person is one who, recognizing the need for submission to God's superior will, does not protest when God sends adversity or when fellow human beings heap abuse on his or her head. Patient endurance of afflictions that would arouse unregenerate man to resistance is the clearest sign of progress in both love and humility. If one is able to submit to the afflictions that the devil, one's neighbor, and God inflict upon oneself, that fact is the best indication that one has recognized one's inferiority to God and the supremacy of God's will.

A related consideration is that patience lent itself far better to narrative presentation than did humility. Humility was a matter of inward disposition, and apart from deliberate acts of self-abasement it manifested itself outwardly in restraint rather than in performance. From an external viewpoint, the humble person was simply one who avoided acting in proud, self-exalting ways. Thus, humility was not the stuff of which exciting narrations were easily formed. The story of a man going about his daily business in meek indifference to honor is not a story that is likely to galvanize many readers. Chastity and other ascetic virtues likewise consisted mainly in nonperformance: the fact that a saint abstained from sexual contact, year after year, did not in itself make for a lively story. A biographer could, of course, dwell on the active virtues, such as charitable service. As the lives of the early desert fathers so richly demonstrate, however, it was the testing of virtue in temptation that held particular dramatic interest. The scene of Anthony battling the demons is one of the great set pieces of Christian hagiography, and heroic resistance to temptations of the flesh has always aroused fascination if not sympathy. In the less legendary, more realistic atmosphere of the late Middle Ages, it was the adversities of everyday life in hard times that presented an especially rich fund of possibilities for the biographer as storyteller. The drama of the affliction could hold the reader's attention, thus allowing the saint's patience to emerge as a steadfast response to provocation. Consisting as it did in passivity, patience in itself held no dramatic interest, but when it was pitted against hostile or merely adverse activity, the interplay could be a storyteller's delight.

There were ways to demonstrate humility, too, in a narrative context, but they were severely limited. The standard device was to recount the demeaning forms of service with which the saint displayed humility: Clare Gambacorta delighted in washing dishes and in other "mean exercises," and even though Nicholas Hermansson was a bishop he did not disdain to put on an apron and serve others, or to wash the feet of beggars. Charles of Blois humbled himself before the poor, and when his vassals saw this they ridiculed him, saying, "Look at how our duke humbles himself more before some old woman than before a good man-at-arms!" Saints and their biographers might have drawn on the tales of "Christian folly" or deliberate foolishness told of thirteenth-century Franciscans such as Brother Juniper and Jacopone da Todi, but this device seems to have been played out, perhaps because the orders were seeking dignity and respect more than renown for holy simplicity.[38]

One somewhat peculiar story from the life of Flora of Beaulieu illustrates how she cultivated humility as a "guardian of virginity and all goodness." A naive admirer, moved to excess by the fame of her sanctity, came to her with hyperbolic praise, insisting that if Christ had had two mothers he would have chosen her as the second. She remained perfectly silent. He asked why she did not answer, and he repeated his praise, but she persisted in her silence, and let him leave without so much as a greeting. Her confessor later reproved her for this inhospitable approach, but she replied that the man had clearly come out of devotion and was seeking solace; if she had treated him harshly he would have left desolate, but if she had responded gently he might have thought she took delight in such praise, and thus his words would have been harmful for them both. Farfetched as this story is, it illustrates the trouble biographers had in recounting stories of humility per se, and helps perhaps to explain why humility is more often portrayed indirectly, through the related virtue of patience.[39]

The ultimate form of submission required of a Christian is that of martyrdom, and in their readiness to be martyred the saints manifested most acutely their willingness to undertake suffering—though, to be sure, the fantasy of dying for the faith was seldom more than a fantasy except for the missionaries. A churchman such as Nicholas Hermansson might realistically anticipate martyrdom in his conflicts with secular authorities, and his biographer is not being frivolous when he says that the "tyrants" marveled at Nicholas's willingness to suffer martyrdom. Elsewhere, however, the quest for martyrdom was essentially a pious dream. Elzear of Sabran in his youth expressed a desire to go off to the land of the infidel and die as a martyr; he cherished the dream of martyrdom even in adulthood, yet he never went abroad. It is even more clearly a pious device when Catherine of Siena's biographer dubs her a "martyr of patience" because of the afflictions brought on by inept spiritual directors. Catherine was deprived of literal martyrdom, for which she prepared herself on one occasion when an unsympathetic mob approached her with sticks and daggers. Still, she attained a martyr's crown by thirteen weeks of patient suffering in her final illness. Christina Ebner shared the common yearning for martyrdom when she was thirteen years old, but feared that she might not in fact endure persecution. Thus, one Good Friday she had another nun in her convent beat her vigorously, and though she was on the verge of giving in she continued to endure the blows, so that she grew in boldness and in confidence. Rulman Merswin, too, felt great longing, if it was God's will, to go to the heathen and tell them of the Christian faith, despite the dangers to which he would have exposed himself, and he would have considered martyrdom a great privilege.[40]

Peter of Luxembourg declared himself willing to endure martyrdom for the cause of peace within the Church; his earliest biographer asserts that this willingness earned him the martyr's palm even though he did not in fact die by the sword. During his terminal illness he frequently said that he would gladly have submitted to martyrdom. One of his servants took these words as pious exaggeration, and said if he actually saw a sword hanging over his head he would be afraid, and would not speak that way. Peter insisted that he was in earnest, and would indeed bear all the pangs of martyrdom. After all, he would have to die in any event, and it would surely be no particular difficulty to do so for Christ.[41]

Jane Mary of Maillé was fond of meditating on the passions of the martyrs, and burned with desire for a like fate. One day as she reflected on the stoning of St. Stephen she wished to die in that manner, if it pleased God. Suddenly she felt blows from certain invisible assailants, and in her pain she emitted sweat rather than blood, and was on the verge of fainting. Her biographer has the martyrs in particular in mind when he says, "Rightly therefore could she rejoice with the saints, and participate in their glory, who while alive desired with all her mind to be a companion of the saints in their adversity." Yet even at that, she never stood in real danger of lapidation. For Villana de'

Botti, on the other hand, the model was St. Laurence: near his feast day she prayed that she might suffer the pains he endured on the gridiron, and when she suddenly felt a surge of unprecedented heat she obtained her coveted "martyrdom."[42]

Visions recounted in the saints' lives sometimes reveal a fascination with martyrdom and an explicit linkage between martyrdom and patience. On the vigil of St. Laurence, John of Alverna was absorbed in prayer when the martyr himself appeared three times. In the last of these visions Laurence carried the iron grill on which he was burned, and he told John, "This grill glorified me in heaven, and the heat of coals gave me a plenitude of divine sweetness. For such a reward, no torment should be too grave for a Christian. If you wish for glory and sweetness, bear the harshness of this world patiently." Having thus expressed the notion that patient endurance of tribulation counts as a kind of martyrdom, the saint stood by John for a while and then disappeared. Essentially the same message was conveyed in a dream vision that Henry Suso had, in which he was about to begin celebrating mass when unexpectedly the choir intoned the mass *Multae tribulationes justorum* ("Many the tribulations of the just") for the feast days of martyrs. He protested their selection, but they replied, "God will find his martyrs today, as he has always found them. Make yourself ready, and sing for yourself!" He flipped through his missal, seeking the mass for a confessor or some other mass, but all he found were masses for martyrs. This dream struck him as odd, but the choir reminded him that the mournful hymn of martyrs always precedes a cheerful hymn. Only after he awoke and encountered tribulations did he fully understand that he was being called to the patient endurance of figurative martyrdom. In narrating such visions, the authors of these texts felt free to express the role of patience forcefully, by linking it with the traditional ideal of submission to suffering in its ultimate form.[43]

What was here explicit can be seen implicitly in the general fascination that late medieval Christians had for martyrdom. This fascination shows in the art of the period, and also in the devotion that was then emerging to the fourteen "auxiliary saints," most of whom were in a position by virtue of their own martyrdom to sympathize with the sufferings of those who besought their aid.[44]

The ultimate model for martyrdom within Christianity was Christ himself, and the significance of patience for fourteenth-century religion becomes especially clear in its relationship with devotion to Christ's passion. In various ways the demand for patience (*patientia*, or endurance of suffering) was linked to the notion of the archetypal passion (*passio*, or act of suffering). In particular, meditation on Christ's patient response to adversity served as a model for imitation and a source of inspiration. Henry Suso, beset with revilement, charged with heresy, and afflicted with high fever and a painful abscess, pondered Christ's agony in the garden and thus identified himself with the suffering Savior. Suso's mother, treated harshly by a worldly husband, overcame her tribulation by reflecting on Christ's suffering. Catherine of Sweden gave counsel along these lines to pilgrims and to the poor: they should be patient, and should keep Christ's passion always in mind. When Elzear of Sabran showed himself incapable of anger, his less patient wife demanded to know how he could restrain himself. He admitted that sometimes he found anger welling up in his heart, but immediately he turned to meditation on Christ's injuries, and told himself that if his own adversaries were to beat him and pluck the hair from his beard he would still not suffer as much as Christ did. He would continue meditating on Christ's wounds until his mind was entirely at rest. Even in his final illness, Elzear found that reflection on Christ's passion fortified him in his patience, for he had the gospel account of the passion read aloud to him. Christ's endurance of verbal as well as physical abuse was a source of inspiration. Andrew Corsini did not respond to his relatives' revilement when he entered the religious life, because "when my Lord Jesus was cursed he did not curse, and when he suffered he did not threaten." In similar imitation of Christ, whose passion she bore in mind, Jane Mary of Maillé overlooked the aspersions cast upon her and prayed for the one who offended her. In recommending patience to others, Jane Mary told them of God's mercy and Christ's passion.[45]

Two variations occur upon this general theme. First, the passion of Christ serves not only as inspiration to bear up under suffering that one happens to encounter, but as incentive to wish for future suffering. In this vein, Rulman Merswin greatly desired to suffer in honor of Jesus' suffering and death, and was sometimes so depressed at the thought of Christ's passion that he asked God to will that he become a leper, as a sign that he no longer wished to be part of this world. Secondly, meditation on Christ's passion led some of the saints to view their own trials as something of an exchange. Christ's suffering and the saints' fit together in a relationship of reciprocity. At one point in the tribulations of Catherine of Siena, Christ appeared to her on the cross, bleeding as he did "when he entered the holy of holies through the shedding of his own blood," and he said, "Catherine, my daughter, you see how much I suffered for you? Do not be sad, then, that you must suffer for me."[46]

This link between patience and the passion arises also in writings by the saints themselves. It is a major theme, for example, in the meditations on the passion attributed to Richard Rolle. After recounting the story of Christ's trial, Rolle prays for grace to suffer accusations and all the evil words of his foes patiently. Soon afterward he repeats the motif, praying for strength to bear patiently all the assaults and temptations of his enemies, "bodily and ghostly." Again, after describing how Christ was buffeted, he asks for the ability to suffer diseases and tribulations without complaint, and to thank God always for such affliction. He requests "purgatory for my sins ere I die," and "patience and heart holy to thank thee" when suffering comes. The carrying of the cross provokes him to ask for grace "to follow thee in mind of thy passion," and to suffer somewhat along with Christ. Reflecting further, he says that all his desire is focused on the Lord's passion: "I have appetite to pain, to beseech my Lord a drop of his red blood to make my soul bloody, and a drop [of] water to wash with my soul." While the theme is thus recurrent, Rolle never explains in detail what he intends; rather, it seems to be presupposed that the suffering of human beings, like that of Christ, can be salvific, and can forestall that pain in purgatory which will otherwise postpone one's enjoyment of celestial bliss, but that suffering has this effect only if borne willingly and patiently.[47]

Like Rolle, many of the saints of the fourteenth century are referred to in retrospect as mystics, meaning essentially that they cultivated an intense consciousness of God's presence and of personal union with God, a consciousness which sometimes blossomed in ecstatic mystical experiences. Not surprisingly, there is a link between such mystical spirituality and the virtue of patience.

The biography of the Netherlandish mystic John Ruysbroeck provides a useful starting point for exploring the connection. When Gerard Groot, the founder of the Devotio Moderna, tried to impress fear of the pains of hell upon Ruysbroeck, he was unable to do so; Ruysbroeck replied that he was ready to suffer all that the Lord decrees, in life or in death, and that he could think of nothing more salutary or pleasant than to follow God's will. Ruysbroeck's biographer goes on to comment that perfect love can endure all things and does not fear losing what is pleasant or being subjected to what is unpleasant. Indeed, the quest for pleasure is a distraction from true love. Those who turn the impulse of love toward themselves may see this perversion as sweet and pleasant, but for a true lover it would be a punishment. In short, the biographer argues that true love is unconcerned with those things which most people perceive as pleasurable or displeasurable, and thus it allows the true lover to accept adversity in compliance with the will of the beloved. The Lord tests his chosen ones by occasionally allowing unspeakable bitterness of mind to befall them, but he quickly consoles them, so that they either view their affliction as negligible or else bear it willingly in anticipation of the sweetness to follow.[48]

Even the affliction of spiritual dryness can be overcome by submission to the Lord's will, as one disciple of Ruysbroeck discovered. She went to him in such a condition, and bemoaned the fact that she was a poor wretch, unable to perform works of mercy, and inwardly feeling no devotion. He consoled her by saying that she could render no sacrifice more pleasing to God than the abdication of her own will, by submitting entirely to his. In other words, if she found herself incapable of either inward piety or outward charity, simple acquiescence to God's will for her at that moment was sufficient. She was greatly consoled, and from then on, whatever deficiencies she suffered, as long as they were not culpable, she bore them "not so much patiently as willingly," for the glory of Christ. In this context the contrast between patience and willingness merely heightens the emphasis which is ordinarily expressed through recommendations of patience itself: the author stresses that merely putting up with affliction is not enough, for one must conform one's very will to God's.[49]

The two motifs that occur here—patience as a manifestation of love and conformity to God's will as the ultimate form of patience—are themes we have already seen in the life and work of Catherine of Siena. Their implications for the mystical life may seem obscure but are in fact significant. The submission to God's will that both Ruysbroeck and Catherine cultivated in themselves and others was in itself a mode of union with God. Like earlier mystics, those of the fourteenth century commonly spoke of mystical union between the soul and God as a union of wills, rather than a union of natures; the mystic was one who, having conformed his or her will totally to God's, willed everything that God willed and nothing that God did not will.[50] The consciousness of this volitional identity might be stronger or weaker, but what the mystics ultimately sought was a constant state of soul in which this union of wills would be so thorough that one would be ever attuned to God, and one's awareness of God's will and God's presence within oneself would affect everything one thought and did. To be sure, the various mystics had different ways of expressing this notion, yet whatever the variations this was a common denominator among those individuals commonly known as mystics. Some of the mystics, such as John Tauler, were fond of emphasizing the notion of passivity. The very word *passivitas* is related both etymologically and conceptually with *patientia* and *passio;* for Tauler, the force of all these terms is conveyed in the German *leiden*, "to suffer." Passivity can suggest various specific themes: the abandonment of one's will and submission to God's; acknowledgment of God's work within oneself, and cessation of one's own striving so that God's operation can come more purely to fruition; detachment from particular forms of active striving, such as favored methods of devotion; and self-surrender in contemplative or infused prayer.[51] Even those exceptional, ecstatic moments that come to some mystics are from one perspective ulti- mate manifestations of passivity, since they are experiences in which one is swept up by God into a state in which one has no control what- soever over oneself and is totally absorbed in the deity. What all these phenomena have in common with patience is the notion of abandon- ment of self and surrender to God. The patience that the saint exer- cises in confrontations with everyday misfortune thus serves as exercise in that submission to God which may lead on to higher levels of spirituality.

The themes examined so far in connection with patience are all essentially religious themes. One further area in which the virtue of patience became relevant to late medieval society was the semi- religious, semisecular notion of chivalrous endurance. The link here is suggested by a passage from one of the standard fourteenth-cen- tury treatises on chivalry, Honoré Bonet's *Tree of Battles*.[52] Bonet ex- amines the virtue of fortitude, which he takes to be the most vital of the four cardinal virtues, and "one of the principal foundations of battle." Even the fortitude of the knight is a religious virtue, "for ac- cording to the Holy Scripture, the man who is not loved by God will never be strong in battle, and it is virtue of soul to be of good counsel, and to know how to command well those who are to fight in battle." With sound counsel, even one who is physically a weakling can win a battle. Indeed, one may conquer through moral strength alone, "for it is no small thing to gain a battle by patience alone without striking a blow, or to suffer death for the truth." Here Bonet betrays an element of uncertainty: patience in battle may obviate the need for actual fighting, or God may favor the just man who is feeble in body (as he favored David in the confrontation with Goliath); but in case these idealistic strategies fail, there is always the consolation of having died for a noble cause. Classical theory of the virtues had represented pa- tience as a division of fortitude, but Bonet comes close to making it the essence of fortitude: "for by this virtue a man is strong to bear tribulations in all the trials that may fall to his lot, so that he may persevere to the end."[53] He goes further, and asks, "Which is the greater virtue and the more commendable: to attack one's enemies or to await attack?" Rephrased in moral terms, the options Bonet consid- ers are aggression and patience. In scholastic fashion he considers both sides. One of the arguments in favor of attacking is from the scriptural text that it is better to give than to receive. Against this there is the opinion of Aristotle, that fortitude "consists in waiting well, and possessing your soul in patience."[54] Bonet himself sides with Aristotle, and concludes that to wait is "more virtuous, stronger and more difficult, than to attack." Whether Bonet's theory bore any resemblance to actual battlefield practice is, of course, an entirely different question. For present purposes, it is important merely to observe that there were voices in the area of chivalric exhortation echoing those in devotional literature.

Nor was Bonet alone in taking this approach. It has been argued that Chaucer and perhaps a few of his English contemporaries were "voices crying out" for a reinterpretation of chivalric honor: instead of basing it on aggressive prowess, they too saw it as resting upon patient endurance of suffering. While it is difficult to extricate Chaucer's views from those of his sources and those ascribed to his characters, there are key texts in the Franklin's tale, in the tale of Melibee, and elsewhere suggesting this view.[55]

The borrowing could work the other way as well, from secular into religious literature: at times the saints' biographers drew upon the language of combat, as in the case of Peter Olafsson, in describing heroic patience. Peter was attacked one day by robbers, but accepted his fate patiently. John the Baptist appeared to Peter's friend Bridget of Sweden at the same hour, and reported to her what had befallen him:

> Oh daughter, you should not be disturbed about the spiritual victory of your friend. That soldier and friend of God has won a splendid victory over the enemy. The enemy has pursued him recklessly. . . . Yet he has rushed against the enemy's lance, breaking it and transfixing him with his own lance—for when they had taken all his belongings, he said to them without anger, "Friends, if you wish to drink I still have wine in my flask." Then he transfixed him with his second lance—for when they took away his cape he offered them his tunic, without impatience. He transfixed him with his third lance as well—for when they were departing and leaving him naked he joyfully thanked God for these tribulations, praying for his assailants with heartfelt charity.

Taking his path again, Peter proceeded onward without being ashamed of his nakedness, and he gave his friends cause for joy at what they styled his great victory over the infernal adversary. Here the language of the battlefield and the joust is used to convey the spiritual triumph that patience can accomplish even when one appears in the world's eyes to be vanquished. The shame of defeat is inverted, and even nakedness becomes a sign of honor. In dramatic fashion, the passivity of patience is transformed into vigorous activity: Peter "rushed against the enemy's lance," thus gaining the honor of victory.[56]

Further examples of such borrowing occur in the life of that knight of infinite patience, Henry Suso. In two classic passages, Suso draws a parallel between the saint's patient endurance of suffering and the knight's exercise of chivalrous endurance. The comparison is quite explicitly not with warfare, but with the quest for reward in the ritualized combat of the joust. In the first of these texts, Suso falls into a trance and beholds a "fair youth" clad in knightly armor and boots. The youth, presumably an angel, tells him that up to now he has been a mere squire, but now God wants him to become a knight. Suso consents, hesitantly, with the request that he should be dubbed honorably, in combat. The angel smiles and assures him that he will have enough of that: the sufferings Suso has undergone so far are mere trifles in comparison with those to come, which are countless as the stars. While he cannot specify the precise nature of these future sufferings, he makes general reference to three types: first, Suso will lose his good repute through the slander of strangers; second, he will lose the comfort and friendship of his loyal associates; and third, he will have to forgo those spiritual consolations that God has been sending him. In connection with this third threat, the angel chides, "you have been a pampered, spoiled weakling, and have swum in divine joy like a fish in the sea." Trembling, Suso falls to the floor with his arms outstretched in the form of a cross, and cries out for God either to give him relief if that is his will or else to reveal to him "the heavenly will of his eternal order." In other words, he asks either that his sufferings be remitted or that their purpose be explained to him. A voice inside him replies that he should take comfort, for "I myself will be with you, and will help you to overcome all these calamities by my grace." Thus fortified, Suso resolves to embrace the combat by which he will become a true knight.[57]

In the second passage, Suso is on a ship with a gallant squire, who tells him that in a tournament a knight must endure continuous blows without flinching if he wishes honor and a prize: "if he is struck so hard that the sparks are struck from his eyes, and the blood bursts from his mouth and nose, he must suffer all this, if he is to win praise." Though depressed, Suso reflects that it is fitting for an eternal prize to require even greater suffering. Soon afterward, however, God sends him such great suffering that he forgets his "spiritual chivalry" and rebelliously asks the point of his misfortunes. In response, he hears a voice ask what has happened to his vows of chivalrous endurance; when he protests that his tournament is too arduous, he is reminded that his reward is, after all, eternal. He asks permission to weep by himself, but God says he is disgraced before the heavenly court at such womanly weeping. With a mixture of tears and laughter, Suso promises that he will weep no more.[58]

These comparisons between saintly patience and chivalrous endurance may seem strained: despite Bonet's exhortations to patient waiting, the obvious point of both combat and jousting was to inflict real or symbolic harm on one's opponent, and to that end action was better suited than passivity. Coming as he did from the nobility of southwest Germany, Suso presumably knew from eyewitness experience that it was not patient submission to suffering but skill in breaking the enemy's lance and unseating the enemy himself that was rewarded in tournaments. His romantic conception of the lady who awards a prize to the knight who suffers most heroically owed more to literature than to the practice of the joust. (One classic text was the thirteenth-century *Service of Ladies* by Ulrich of Liechtenstein, who told how he had endeavored to impress his lady with the loss of his finger, but such glorification of suffering does not seem to have been common in actual practice.[59]) Again, though, what is ultimately important is not whether such ideals were widely carried out in reality. What is essential is that the borrowing of ideology in both directions suggests a fluidity in the ideology itself. Merely to entertain a correspondence between patience and chivalrous endurance indicates both a sacralization of the secular ideal and an extension of the religious motif into areas where one might not expect to find it. The pervasiveness of patience in fourteenth-century culture becomes clear from such examples.

Manifestations in General Religious Literature

When a society becomes so preoccupied with a concept that it begins to take for granted its relevance to all sorts of circumstances, one may expect to find applications of the concept that would never occur to an outsider. Thus, toward the end of Petrarch's letter describing the ascent of Mount Ventoux—a document sometimes taken as the birth certificate of the Renaissance, yet in the main a testimonial to pious medieval morality—the author for one brief moment suggests that the meaning of the entire day's outing can be found in the duty to accept affliction: "With every downward step I asked myself this: If we are ready to endure so much sweat and labour in order that we may bring our bodies a little nearer heaven, how can a soul struggling toward God, up the steeps of human pride and human destiny, fear any cross or prison or sting of fortune? How few, I thought, but are diverted from their path by the fear of difficulties or the love of ease!"[60] The connection seems inexact, since the crosses and stings of fortune that one patiently endures are not self-inflicted. Perhaps, at the end of an arduous journey, Petrarch could have imagined that the

mountain had somehow imposed itself upon him. In any case, the
motif of patient endurance, arising here where it seems less than fully
in place, is one that lies at the heart of fourteenth-century spirituality
even outside the hagiographic context.

There were other genres of literature in which one might expect
patience to appear. The consolation literature of the Middle Ages,
directly or indirectly inspired by Boethius's *Consolation of Philosophy*,
remained popular in the fourteenth century, and authors such as
Meister Eckhart contributed new specimens of such consolatory reflections.[61] It has been suggested that this literature draws more from
philosophical ideals of Stoic indifference than from religious conceptions of patience,[62] yet the border was surely a weak one, and Eckhart
was able to use the genre to express ascetic-mystical notions of suffering. John of Dambach, whose clerical career in the stormy climate of
the fourteenth century brought him under ecclesiastical censure and
caused him other afflictions, emphasized scriptural and patristic
rather than philosophical grounds for comfort in his influential *Consolation of Theology*. In this compilation he marshaled forth consolations for people undergoing academic difficulties, suffering disease,
losing their teeth, fearful of being struck by lightning, or otherwise
disturbed. He even gave counsel for people who were too short: apart
from consoling references to short people of the bible (David,
Zacheus, and so forth), he provided scriptural proof (Matt. 6:27)
that one cannot do anything to affect one's stature, which suggests
that God meant for short people to be that way. Another work popular in the later Middle Ages, *On the Twelve Uses of Tribulation*, discussed
broader issues: adversity can be useful by purging the soul, arousing
self-knowldge, repaying debts to God, giving incentive for heavenly
solace, and so forth.[63]

Discussion of Job, which had likewise been popular throughout the
Middle Ages, enjoyed a heyday in the fourteenth and fifteenth centuries.[64] One example is Marquard of Lindau's treatise on Job, which
breaks the book into a series of "considerations" and then gives a moral interpretation of each, showing how the reader should become
"like the patient Job" (*dem gedultigen Job gelich*). Even the reference to
Job's livestock becomes a moralizing allegory: for a person to be rich
and have 3,000 camels means submitting patiently to all one's burdens
and allowing oneself to be laden down with creaturely afflictions.
Drawing upon various texts from Job, Marquard says that a person
undergoing suffering should rejoice in past virtue, think back upon
good days, reflect on how one enters and exits from the world naked,
and recognize that suffering is a noble robe, in which Christ and all
his friends are clothed. The slightest suffering does more good for a
person than if all the angels were to weep bloody tears. Every part of

one's body that suffers is eternally illumined, and the more one suffers the more one sinks into the groundless eternal source of all sweetness. If one is patient, God will take one's sufferings upon himself and will grant manifold reward, as he did to Job. The ultimate reward for patience is passage from disquietude (*vnrüge*, equated with the Latin *inquietas*) to peace, from suffering to joy, and from this vale of tears to perpetual bliss.[65]

Patience was addressed more or less systematically in various forms of religious literature: collections of preachers' *exempla* or anecdotes, handbooks on the virtues and vices, manuals for confessors, and other genres. Ralph Hanna has provided a convenient synthesis of this literature.[66] Almost invariably, these works include one or more of the classic definitions of patience: Cicero's definition, "the willed and continuous endurance of laborious and difficult things for the sake of virtue or benefit" (*honestatis aut utilitatis causa rerum arduarum ac difficilium voluntaria ac diuturna perpessio*); Augustine's definition of patience as "enduring evils with an even mind" (*aequo animo mala tolerare*); and Gregory the Great's notion of it as "enduring external evils with equanimity" (*aliena mala aequanimiter perpeti*). The literature occasionally speaks of patience as proper acceptance of both misfortune and fortune. Thus expanded, patience is pitted against the temptations to pride and cupidity that come with good fortune. (Charles of Blois provides a hagiographic instance of this formulation: witnesses for his canonization reported that he was always patient, in the face of both prosperity and adversity—*sive prospera, sive adversa*.)[67] Most commonly, however, in accordance with the classic definitions, patience is seen as a safeguard against acedia (melancholy, lethargy, and even despair) and anger (with its attendant dangers of contumely and vengeance) in times of hardship. Not all patient endurance of suffering, however, was virtuous. Following the eighth beatitude, which specified those who are persecuted "for justice' sake" (Matt. 5:10) as among the blessed, Augustine and others distinguished between endurance for worthwhile causes and suffering out of negligence, perverse insensitivity, or worldly craving for wealth or honor.[68]

Discussions of patience commonly indicated various types of affliction which can serve as occasions for exercise of this virtue. The *locus classicus* on this subject was Gregory the Great's homily cited above, in which he speaks of adversity as coming from God, from the devil, and from one's neighbor. The "divine discipline" (*flagellum divinum*) could be seen in illness, loss of loved ones, and poverty. Sufferings of this kind are corrective prods, which God uses to induce his erring children to return to the right path. One should accept this correction gratefully, without complaining against God. The second source of provocation is diabolical; usually the devil assaults human beings by

tempting them to do evil, and the experience of prolonged and serious temptation can try the patience of a person who wants to live
well. At times the devil can tempt a person by overt apparitions and
even physical attack, as in the classic case of Anthony the Hermit, with
the intent of leading that individual to despair and give up all efforts
at holiness. Affliction at the hands of one's neighbor, the third form,
is often subdivided into verbal abuse, loss of goods, and torment of
the body.[69]

In discussing the mental disposition that underlies patience, medieval writers relied heavily on classical discussions of equanimity and
apatheia, or indifference. The Stoics had exalted indifference to both
pleasure and pain, and held out as a moral ideal the total elimination
of passions from one's mind, so that one could be in total control of
oneself at all times. Christian authors differed from their classical
sources mainly in recognizing the doctrine of original sin: because
human beings are fallen, and can never wholly extirpate baser passions from their souls, patience becomes a constant struggle against
these passions. Furthermore, Christian patience is both "hard" and
"soft": hard in the sense that it can endure affliction, soft in its association with love and compassion. While the Stoics exalted autono-
mous human reason as the basis for moral norms and conduct,
Christian moralists required submission to God in charity, and in the
fourteenth century this commonly means submission to affliction. Patience reaches its height when the patient person is able to show active
charity even in the face of persecution (for example, by turning the
other cheek). The extreme patience of the martyr is motivated by this
sort of consideration, since martyrdom becomes a way of reaching out
to other souls by providing a model. The obvious exemplar of this
patience-cum-charity, in the Christian tradition, is Christ himself.[70]

Ludolph of Saxony, in his *Life of Christ,* developed the notion of
Christ as a teacher and exemplar of patience, and in the process he
provided a highly systematic fourteenth-century compendium of
much reflection that had been developed earlier. In discussing the
Sermon on the Mount, Ludolph speaks of four "steps toward peace":
the first (found already in the Old Testament) consists in extracting
no more in retaliation than one has had inflicted on oneself, the second (also in the Old Testament) involves extracting less than one has
been given, the third (the beginning of the gospel) entails total restraint from retaliation, and the fourth (the fulfillment of the gospel)
is a readiness to suffer further. At the end of his section on the Sermon on the Mount, as at the end of each section, Ludolph appends a
prayer:

Lord Jesus Christ most meek, and teacher of all humility

and patience, grant that I, the last and simplest of your servants, making myself humble and inferior to others, may wish to be contemned by all, and trodden underfoot, and, patiently sustaining injury in body or in goods, may be prepared in my soul to bear more, and to aid everyone as much as possible who asks for corporal aid. Grant also that I may not only love my friends but also my enemies, who persecute me by thought, word, or deed, and that I may be able to do good for them and bless them and pray for them, that by your grace I may merit to be numbered among your sons and chosen ones. Amen.[71]

In his commentary on Christ's missionary instructions in Matthew 10, Ludolph suggests (following Gregory the Great) that patience is particularly appropriate for a preacher, who is sent like a sheep among wolves to give an example of meekness and thus restrain the violence of others: "The Lord is a wondrous hunter, who by means of his lambs or sheep captures and conquers wolves; through patience he overcomes power [*per patientiam vincit potestatem*]." Christ himself gives a sublime example of patient endurance, which we should follow not only patiently but even gladly (*gaudenter*), recognizing that as servants we are not superior to our master.[72]

In a different context Ludolph sets forth an eloquent "praise of patience" (*laus patientiae*).[73] When tribulation comes, one should go out to meet this guest and receive him kindly, saying with a joyful heart, "Welcome be to my friend, tribulation!" For whoever suffers adversity gladly for God's sake is assimilated to the suffering Christ. "Therefore let us suffer gladly and voluntarily, for our true salvation lies in the cross, and apart from it no salvation is to be found." If a soul has no cross within it, which is to say it encounters no tribulation, then it develops no patience, and where there is no patience there is no true salvation. A patient heart is one to which being despised is occasion for joy. One should rejoice in such adversity, and take pleasure from being able to add something to the passion and humility of Christ. If one adds one's pains and adversities to those of Christ, they become sweet from this association, and God will receive them as signs of the highest patience.[74] One should in any case be confident that all that happens to one, whether joyful or sad, is given from God's great love, and thus one should praise and thank God for all, never wishing a different fate from that which befalls one. Indeed, as Ludolph says elsewhere, not being able to manifest patience in adversity should be a source of great disturbance. One should pray that one will be able to imitate Christ's example of patience and humility, a conjunction of virtues repeated in Ludolph's work, as elsewhere in late medieval literature.[75]

This theme of patience was taken up in the later fourteenth and early fifteenth century in the writings of the Devotio Moderna. Thomas à Kempis celebrated this virtue as an important key to the spiritual life.[76] When he referred to the Christian life as an "imitation of Christ" in his writing which has come down with that title, he was following a trend that fourteenth-century writers had evolved: that of imitating Christ primarily through patient acceptance of suffering. Repeatedly, but especially in chapter 12 of his second book, Thomas represents the imitation of Christ as consisting mainly in emulation of Christ's passion: "See how in the cross all things consist, and in dying on it all things depend." No matter what a person does in life, suffering will always be at hand, whether bodily or mental: "The cross always stands ready, and everywhere awaits you." It is inescapable; if borne unwillingly it will be a burden, but if accepted it will lead a person to heavenly reward. In keeping with this emphasis, Thomas speaks at every juncture of the need for patience. Chapters 18 and 19 of his third book are devoted specifically to this virtue, but the words "patient," "patiently," and "patience" recur throughout, as key words in the treatise. Patience contributes to growth in virtue, gives a sense of peace, serves as a shield, tests and purges an individual, brings reward in heaven, and protects one from the fires of hell. Repeatedly, patience is linked with humility: "My son, patience and humility in adversity are more pleasing to Me than great devotion and comfort in times of ease." If one expects special graces and consolations in the spiritual life, one will have occasion for patience here too; one will encounter times of spiritual dryness in which one obtains no consolation. In short, *The Imitation of Christ* serves among other things as a compendium of late medieval notions regarding patience.[77]

The theme of patience arises several times in the extant letters of Gerard Groote, commonly thought of as founder of the Devotio Moderna. One letter in particular, which the manuscripts entitle a "Noteworthy letter, inducing patience and imitation of Christ," was written in 1384 to an unspecified member of a religious community.[78] The recipient had been suffering tribulation at the hands of another person; the precise issue remains obscure, but the editor of the letters suggests that the person causing the difficulty had attempted to enter the recipient's monastery by means of simony, and in the ensuing strife the recipient had considered moving to a different community.

Much of this letter is essentially a tissue of scriptural allusions bearing on the theme of patience; indeed, the letter serves as a useful illustration of how Scripture was brought to bear on this theme. These references are chosen mainly to convey three essential points. First and foremost is the notion of patience as imitation of Christ, as expressed in Matthew 16:24 ("If any man will come after me, let him

deny himself, and take up his cross, and follow me"), John 15:20
("The servant is not greater than his master. If they have persecuted
me, they will also persecute you"), 2 Corinthians 4:10f. ("Always bearing about in our body the mortification of Jesus, that the life also of
Jesus may be made manifest in our mortal flesh"), Galatians 6:14
("But God forbid that I should glory, save in the cross of our Lord
Jesus Christ; by whom the world is crucified to me, and I to the
world"), and other such texts. Second, patience is exalted as leading to
a reward; this motif is linked with the first, in that the patient person
is promised a sharing in Christ's glory. There is an allusion to Psalm
125:5 ("They that sow in tears shall reap in joy"), linked with James
5:7 ("Be patient therefore, brethren, until the coming of the Lord.
Behold, the husbandman waiteth for the precious fruit of the earth:
patiently bearing till he receive the early and latter rain"). James 1:12
is cited as well, in somewhat altered form: "Rejoice, rejoice, my beloved, when you fall into various temptations and tribulations, for
when you have been tested you will receive the crown of life." The
Christological allusion is brought out, for example, in quotation of
Romans 8:17 ("And if sons, heirs also; heirs indeed of God, and joint
heirs with Christ: yet so, if we suffer with him, that we may be also
glorified with him"). The sequel to this last passage, Romans 8:18
("For I reckon that the sufferings of this time are not worthy to be
compared with the glory to come, that shall be revealed in us"), is a
key text, cited as worthy of frequent rumination. To the same general
effect, the letter quotes Acts 14:21 ("through many tribulations we
must enter into the kingdom of God"). Finally, there are a few quotations suggesting that God will support a person in suffering: Psalm
45:2 ("Our God is a refuge and strength: a helper in troubles"), Job
5:18 ("For he woundeth, and cureth: he striketh, and his hands shall
heal"), and similar texts.

Interspersed with these allusions is Groote's own commentary on
the virtue of patience. At one point he advises that the reader should
accept insults, derision, injuries, and suffering patiently, for three
reasons. First, they are fitting ways of honoring and conforming
oneself to Christ, especially when one undertakes them not in "merce-
nary" fashion, with an eye to the rewards one will gain for one's merits, but with humble willingness to ascribe them to the merits of
Christ. Nonetheless, a second reason for patience is that rewards do in
fact flow so richly from the acceptance of tribulations and temptations; presumably one should not make this one's primary motive for
patience, but Groote is willing to cite it as a supporting factor. And
third, one should consent to suffering to satisfy God's justice, which
we have offended so often and so grievously, and which leaves no evil
unpunished. The moderate pain that God sends us in this life can

prevent far greater punishment in purgatory, though we should undertake suffering more to fulfill the divine will and justice than to
work off our punishment. Patience in adversity leads to peace of heart
and inward meekness. Indeed, no one can have peace except by being
in accord with the adversities that surround oneself and bearing them
patiently. To this end one should keep the passion of Christ constantly in one's consciousness, so that every adversity which befalls
one can be borne with an even mind (*equo animo toleretur*). Yet it does
no good merely to keep the passion before oneself in meditation without striving to imitate it by being crucified with Christ: "This is the
final and principal end of meditation on Christ's passion, and mere
memory of the passion is of little value if it is not accompanied by a
fervent desire to imitate Christ." Alas, however, many people gladly
take up that cross which they make for themselves—whether by wearing hairshirts, by private prayers, or by fasting—but they cast off in
abhorrence that cross which God makes for them, which is most truly
theirs and which they should bear and embrace. Whatever afflictions
befall a person, whether they come from superiors or equals or in-
feriors, and whether they are just or unjust as far as the intention of
the inflicting person is concerned, one should accept them as sent
with kindness and justice by God.[79]

Similar themes arise in other letters by Groote. It is worth noting in
particular the contexts in which the theme of patience here arises. In
a letter of 1381 to a new recruit for a monastery, he warned of the
temptations that are likely to afflict a new monk, such as the temptation to think the monastic life is deleterious to one's spiritual growth.
One may profit from all such temptation, for "Blessed is the man that
endureth temptation" (James 1:12). "In all things let God be your
strength, your virtue, your refuge in tribulations, and your superior.
For those whom God loves, God corrects, and God wills for the strong
fighters to undergo combat and exercise that they may become more
tested." Whatever God permits to befall one, it should be suffered
willingly for his sake, for "the sufferings of this time are not worthy to
be compared with the glory to come, that shall be revealed in us"
(Rom. 8:18). The last quotation occurs again in a letter of 1382, to a
cleric who had become embroiled in an elaborate conflict and been
expelled from a certain town for his convictions. Groote says here that
it is characteristic of the saints to suffer loss of external goods with
equanimity, and that testing is necessary for them so that their superi-
or strength may merit greater rewards.

In a letter to a Carthusian disgruntled with the monastic life, he
asks what has happened to his former patience. To leave the monastery and put aside the cross he has borne thus far would be comparable to Christ's wishing to come down alive from the cross. Yet another

letter bears the cumbersome title, "Letter sent to a certain Carthusian brother, infirm in his head from birth, and somewhat melancholic in complexion, and disturbed and aggrieved by the newness of [the monastic] life and the solitude and by attacks of the devil, who was trying to induce him to desperation and to engulfing sadness."[80] The letter contains practical advice—to get enough sleep, for example, and not to be unduly scrupulous about minor faults such as imperfect reading of the canonical hours—but begins with standard counsel about the crown of life which will be given to one who bears temptations successfully.

It is not only in the explicitly religious literature of the century that patience has a major role but in the secular narrative literature as well. One theme that arises in those writings is that of patience as triumphing over adversity. In the thirteenth century, William Peraldus in his *Summa of Virtues and Vices* had spoken of patience as conquering over one's persecutors (he cites examples of martyrs whose power was heightened at the time of their martyrdom), over oneself, and over demons.[81] What Peraldus did not make clear was why patience should have such power of conquest any more than other virtues; temperance too represents a conquest of oneself, and the victory attained over external forces could presumably be obtained by means of chastity, poverty, or any other form of spiritual excellence. What emerges clearly in the narrative literature of the fourteenth century is that patience in particular has such power because the renunciation of force eventually shames one's adversary.

The tale of patient Griselda, first set down in literary form by Boccaccio and soon taken up by Petrarch and Chaucer, is a classic example of patience triumphant. The marquess Gualtieri of Saluzzo, under pressure from his vassals to marry, chooses a common girl named Griselda as his wife. She is well received by all, but to test her patient faithfulness to him Gualtieri contrives a series of tests. First he pretends to have both of their children killed, though in fact he sends them off to Bologna to be brought up. Then he obtains counterfeit papal letters allowing him to put her aside and wed another wife. To compound the injury, after he has sent her to her parental home he calls her back to help with arrangements for his new wedding. All of this she bears with unfaltering patience, at least outwardly, and on seeing that she is perfectly virtuous Gualtieri returns her to her previous position as an honest wife and mother.[82]

When Petrarch read this story, he was at once moved to memorize it, to tell it to all his friends, and to translate it into Latin. His purpose was moral: though Griselda's patience seemed "almost beyond imitation," her example might induce others to emulate her, "and to submit themselves to God with the same courage as did this woman to her husband." He continued, "Anyone . . . amply deserves to be reckoned among the heroes of mankind who suffers without a murmur for God, what this poor peasant woman bore for her mortal husband." When a friend of Petrarch read the story for the first time, he got halfway through, burst into tears, and was unable to resume, so he handed the story to a companion to finish the reading. Another friend, less impressed, found the tale wildly implausible; Petrarch said he might have replied that what seems impossible to some may be easy for another, and someone who can undergo death for another person should be able to put up with any trial or suffering.[83] Surely Petrarch was not confusing fiction and reality, but in defending the plausibility of the story he was upholding that verisimilitude which lent moral force to the tale. (Authors of saints' lives frequently proceeded on similar assumptions: they were less interested in historicity than in the moral force lent by the saints' recorded deeds.)[84]

Chaucer, telling the same story with further variations in "The Clerk's Tale," referred to Petrarch as his source. Repeatedly in his version Griselda is praised for her patience, with the suggestion that she is not altogether unusual for her sex: "married men too often use no measure,/ That have some patient creature at their pleasure." Here too Griselda's patience is given moral force by analogy with the patience that one should a fortiori maintain before God: "For since a woman showed such patience to/ A mortal man, how much the more we ought/ To take in patience all that God may do!" And Griselda is indirectly compared with Job, who is praised here for his humility—another example of the link between humility and patience.[85]

It was not only major literary figures who made use of the story of Griselda but minor ones as well. By the late fourteenth century there was a dramatic version in French, and a prose rendition came from the pen of Philip of Mézières, one of the closest friends of Peter of Luxembourg.[86]

What Griselda has in common with Job, above all, is that by means of her patience she triumphs in the end. To be sure, it is not as if she is attempting throughout the story to shame her husband into reforming his behavior; her patience is more than merely tactical. Yet as specimens of moral literature both the book of Job and the story of Griselda lead to the conclusion that a clever person can attain ultimate victory—can win over a brutal husband or obtain the grace of a God whose providence leads him to impose trials—through patience. In this respect these stories differ from the saints' lives, in which patience seldom leads to anything but further misery.[87] The interpretations of this virtue are not, however, necessarily incompatible. Through her patient endurance Griselda manages to overcome her husband, or to persuade him of her worth, but she can do so only because both of them, along with the storyteller and his audience, recognize patience as *inherently* good. A different culture might construe patience as a sign of weakness, and an invitation to further abuse. It is only because late medieval Christendom recognized this virtue as a mark of strength and an appropriate response to adversity that a patient sufferer could persuade, overcome, or shame the person causing the affliction. In other words, patience could not have had instrumental value if it had not been recognized first as having inherent value. And it is to the inherent value in particular that the saints' lives point.

One could proceed indefinitely citing literature of the century in which patience is a major theme, or even the explicit subject, as in the poem on patience by the *Pearl* poet.[88] The works already adduced may suffice, however, to illustrate the ways in which this virtue might arise in fourteenth-century culture.

Patience and Its Provocations

The fourteenth century did not invent the virtue of patience: literature extolling this virtue can be traced back without interruption to the Bible, and similar motifs can be found in the Stoic and other traditions of Graeco-Roman antiquity. Indeed, there is little in fourteenth-century treatments of the subject that qualifies as original. Even Benedict of Nursia in his *Rule for Monks,* for example, had suggested that "by patience we may partake in Christ's passion."[89] Saints' lives in earlier periods were not devoid of reference to this virtue; Hildegard of Bingen was praised especially for her patience, Richard of Chichester bore the afflictions of episcopal office patiently, and patience was often an important element in the Franciscan vitae of the thirteenth century.[90] Nor is the theme uniformly to be found in the fourteenth century. There are saints' lives and other texts where one might expect to find it but where it is not to be found. Nonetheless, one cannot help being impressed with how often the motif does arise, how fervently so many of the key figures of the century were devoted to it, and how integrally it related to other concerns of the era. In the fourteenth century more than before, patience tended to become a sustained theme, explicitly given central importance, and worked out with reference to all the quotidian details of the saints' lives. The question that arises is why this century in particular should have displayed such a fascination with this virtue.

The obvious and no doubt partially correct answer is that the age was one of unaccustomed suffering. There is evidence of a general shift in climate around 1300 which disrupted long-established modes of life: rivers that had never before in memory frozen over now did so, and recurrent flooding wrought widespread damage to the fields (indeed, an especially severe deluge of 1315 aroused comparison with Noah's flood). Population had expanded in preceding centuries, to the point that it was becoming difficult to feed all the mouths that required sustenance. Frequent famine left the population weakened and susceptible to a series of epidemics. The worst harm was done by the Black Death, which swept across the continent in mid-century and recurred sporadically thereafter. During the summer of 1348, this plague claimed half the population of Florence and Siena; while the impact varied from place to place, estimates suggest that at least a quarter of Europe's population died of the affliction during the initial onslaught. There were depressions in industry, and both urban workers and peasants rose in revolt against the upper classes. As if these misfortunes were not enough, there was war. In the words of Robert Lerner:

> Some of the most famous conflicts of history—from the Hundred Years' War between England and France to the family war between the Montagues and the Capulets—belong to this period. In fact, taking these together with the even more numerous struggles lost in the confusion of its history, the fourteenth century suffered from more, bloodier, and longer wars than any since the tenth.

Nor was the violence of war contained within formal combat: soldiers looted towns and villages, and devastated the countryside. As Lerner continues: "Only the arms industry thrived, while peaceful enterprise languished in the ruined towns and desolated countryside." No wonder, then, that Christians of this century kept reminding themselves that they could gain merit by patiently enduring their afflictions, and that their best way of imitating Christ was to submit to those crosses that God sent them. When the saints bore their diseases patiently, or accepted meekly the effects of warfare, they were offering the Christian response to adversity, which was more brutally constant in their century than in most.[91]

Yet the actual occasions for saintly patience were seldom directly linked with these developments. When Dorothy of Montau bore the insults and blows of her unsympathetic husband, or when Henry Suso endured slander and threats to his life, or when Elizabeth of Portugal graciously put up with her husband's infidelities, these individuals were not responding to the distinctive hardships of their century. As already mentioned, Dorothy lost all but one of her children to disease, presumably the Black Death, yet that fact was one of few in her life that her biographer does *not* cite as occasion for patience. Likewise, the letters of Gerard Groote seem to have addressed classic difficulties that religious in any century might have with their vows and with cantankerous fellow religious.

Many of the examples we have looked at (though certainly not all) can be better understood if one bears in mind that the saints in question were either lay or semireligious, far more than would have been the case in the Christian society of any previous century. Catherine of Siena was a Dominican tertiary, and thus affiliated with the Dominican order, but lived at home and mingled with members of lay society as well as with her highly unsympathetic family. Dorothy of Montau became an officially recognized recluse only in the last year of her life; until then, the role in which most of her contemporaries seem to have cast her was that of crackpot, and they treated her accordingly. These and other saints of the era were pious lambs surrounded by irreverent wolves. Even those who did enjoy clerical status commonly exposed themselves to the provocations of the laity among whom they lived and served, or to those of clerics who were more worldly than religious: Henry Suso's responsibilities as a mendicant friar took him out amid hostile populations, and Peter of Luxembourg would gladly have removed himself from the courtly society he so disdained in Paris, Metz, and Avignon. Earlier saints came predominantly from institutions that were relatively isolated and enclosed: the monasteries, where throughout the Middle Ages ideals of saintliness had been forged and perpetuated. It was specifically in the later Middle Ages that the mendicant orders, experiments in semireligious organization, and growing lay piety made for new saints who were no longer protected from the mockery and assaults of the general population. In many instances it was this fact that made it necessary to exercise patience.

Such tensions, rife as they no doubt were in the towns, could spill over into the monasteries and convents. Thus, the nuns at Engelthal, many of whom came from prominent Nuremberg families, found it difficult to accept the extremes of devotion that Christina Ebner brought into their midst. Because they dealt with her harshly, she had reason to exercise patience.[92] More often, though, problems arose through contact with the broader society.

Lay or semireligious sainthood *within* Christian society was relatively new, but there was one earlier period, roughly the fourth and fifth centuries, when large numbers of lay saints emerged in that monastic movement which deliberately isolated itself from society. To the extent that they succeeded in that isolation, the monks of late antiquity distanced themselves from those potentially unsympathetic and hostile forces that might have given them cause for patience. In fact, however, the isolation was often incomplete, and in classic cases

the incipient monastic movement aroused fierce adversity and opposition. The example of Jerome and his associates comes to mind,
though when Jerome fled from hostile forces in Rome he did so without that gentle meekness that late medieval saints extolled and exemplified.[93] Whereas the monks of late antiquity were confronted by
a corrupt society from which they fled, most of the saints of the fourteenth century made it their business to stay in that society, serve it in
various capacities, and bear the inevitable afflictions patiently.

It was evidently a combination of circumstances that led to the
fourteenth-century fascination with patience. The distinctive calamities of the age, combined with the special status of many spiritual leaders, gave ample occasion to practice this virtue. Furthermore, like any
cultural motif this one gained a momentum of its own: once Christians had been sufficiently reminded that endurance of suffering can
be meritorious, just as Christ's own suffering was salvific, this theme
would naturally be repeated in the widest variety of circumstances. A
phenomenon of this sort can never be wholly explained by reference
to social developments or to natural cataclysms.

It surely made little difference to the hagiographers whether their
readers underwent suffering of the same kind as the saints. Whatever
the specific provocation, the saintly patience that was elicited could
inspire an attitude of submission within the devout reader. Nor did
the hagiographer need to worry about the dangers of exaggerated
passivity: vigorous attack on the sources of adversity was the natural
human inclination, and it was this that needed to be counterbalanced.
Towns bloodied with civil strife and family feuds did not need a call to
active redress of evil as urgently as they needed a reminder that patient endurance is noble and meritorious. Those afflicted with diseases for which there was no effective cure might despair of God's aid
and lose sight of the meaning in their lives unless reminded that active
response was not called for, and that they could win merit precisely by
patient submission.

The spirituality to which these considerations gave rise is effectively epitomized in a legend regarding the mystic Meister Eckhart. After
his death, Eckhart is supposed to have appeared once to his disciple
Henry Suso, who asked him the best way to ensure his eternal bliss.
The master replied: "To die to self in perfect detachment, to receive
everything as from God, and to maintain unruffled patience with all
men, however brutal or churlish they may be."[94] Fourteenth-century
Christians may not have been consistently brutal or churlish toward
the saints in their midst, and the saints themselves may or may not
have preserved that unruffled patience that they are supposed to
have fostered, but the ideal itself was vital to the spirituality of this era
as seldom before or since.

4
Devotion to the Passion

*I*f patient submission to God's will was an essential foundation for
fourteenth-century piety, devotion to the passion went one
important step further. Taking Christ's submission to his Father's will
as the archetypal manifestation of patience, the saints and their devotees found in it the key to an understanding of God's will. In their
patience, the saints submitted to whatever God willed, whether adversity or good fortune, though it was especially in the face of adversity
that this submission was tried and proven. In their devotion to the
passion, the saints bowed to the recognition that what God demands
in particular is suffering. They viewed suffering as the specific means
God has chosen both for Christ's redemptive work and for the sanctification of those who imitate Christ. Atonement came not from charitable works, nor from prayer, nor from enlightenment, but from
pain. If God's wrath was appeased by suffering, this meant that suffering was somehow pleasing to God, and that God saw value in it
which one must acknowledge even if one did not understand it.
Catherine of Siena might insist that it is not suffering per se that God
delights in but rather the love revealed by suffering.[1] Nonetheless,
God seemed to attach more weight to love manifested in suffering
than to love displayed in other ways. Suffering was the means par
excellence for demonstrating love: this was the rule for Christ, and
consequently for his saints as well. The devotion to which this outlook
led might be brutal, yet it seemed to follow inexorably from the logic
of Christian belief.

Examples of such devotion abound in the saints' lives, but the example of Flora of Beaulieu suggests as well as any the intensity of the
saints' absorption in the passion. One Holy Thursday, Flora contem-

plated the anguish that Christ underwent in the garden of Gethsemane. Her biographer says that the sword of sorrow pierced her
heart, and she cried out, weeping, "Alas! Alas! They have bound my
Lord and are leading him away! Shall I not follow my Lord wherever
he is led?" The next day, Good Friday, she was inconsolable. In her
anguish she ran about the convent, driven into fury by her sorrow,
and the sisters could not restrain her. This agony occupied her totally
in her prayers, as if Christ's nails had transfixed her hands and feet
and the lance had pierced her side. Wailing in pain brought on by
recollection of the passion, she expressed in sobs what she could not
in words.[2] True, her frenzied devotion is extreme even for her age,
but it is not unparalleled, and in its intensity it epitomizes a general
tendency that few of her pious contemporaries can have escaped altogether. One is reminded of the devout nun who, according to
Ludolph of Saxony, was so deeply affected by Christ's passion that
whenever she beheld an image of Christ crucified she would lose control of herself and fall to the ground.[3]

These tendencies were not altogether new to the fourteenth century. Throughout the high and late Middle Ages there was increasing
attention and devotion to the humanity of Jesus, particularly to those
moments in his life that aroused sentiments of love and compassion:
his infancy and his passion. With major stimulus from the writings of
Bernard of Clairvaux, and with strong support from Francis of Assisi,
the humanity of Jesus became central in medieval spirituality. The art
and the general literature of the era manifest these concerns. The
theology reinforced them: ever since Anselm's influential work on
Why God Became Man was disseminated in the late eleventh century,
Christ's work of redemption was seen as consisting in his sacrificial
death; his incarnation, his active ministry, and his resurrection were
all subordinated to his supererogatory self-sacrifice, by which he took
upon himself the burden of human sin and made vicarious satisfaction for that sin. Not surprisingly, the hagiography of the later Middle
Ages shows the saints as heirs to this tradition, obsessed with feverish
intensity by the passion.[4]

The primary context of this devotion was the meditative practice of
the late Middle Ages. Modern literature has given considerable attention to the contemplative prayer of fourteenth-century mystics: the
intuitive, nondiscursive prayer, in which one discards all images and
concepts and surrenders oneself to the flow of spontaneous illumination. Yet contemplative prayer was the privilege of a spiritual elite, as
works such as The Cloud of Unknowing made clear.[5] Meditative prayer,
though, with its discursive reflection on images and events (drawn
largely from the life of Christ), was accessible in principle to all. Much
of the devotional literature of the era was written as an aid to such

prayer, and artwork was generally intended to stimulate meditation on its subject matter. As lay piety became more common, and the market for such art and literature expanded, meditation loomed ever larger. The monasteries too had cultivated meditation, but its role in the burgeoning lay religious culture was greater, simply because most laypeople were assumed incapable of contemplation.

Meditation appealed to both the intellect and the emotions. When the subject was Christ's passion, there was ample food both for thought and for emotional response. Even without delving into the theology of atonement, one could exercise one's cognitive faculties by setting forth the complex details of the passion narrative; what often seems an exercise in idle curiosity served to engage the mind in sustained attention to the sufferings of Christ. The same purpose could be attained through rich allegorical comparisons (e.g., between Christ's wounded body and a book inscribed in red) and through consideration of Old Testament typology (e.g., the "many dogs" of Psalm 21:17 as a type for those who reviled Christ). The possibilities for emotional reaction were equally rich, as we shall see.

Here as in other areas, the saints' devotion manifested both continuity and discontinuity with the general religious culture of their era. The saints carried to extremes that devotion to which their contemporaries were urged. By means of their uncommon fervor, they gave extraordinary provocation to ordinary piety. To explore their place in the religious culture of the late Middle Ages, let us look first at the devotion to the passion in their vitae, then at the same theme in the broader devotional literature and art of the fourteenth century, and finally at certain specific ways in which saints and some of their contemporaries sought assimilation to Christ crucified.

Manifestations in the Saints' Lives

As we shall see shortly, the general passion literature of the fourteenth century gave four reactions that meditation on the passion was supposed to evoke: gratitude, penance, compassion, and imitation. The first two are not altogether lacking in the saints' lives, but the main themes in this literature are compassionate beholding of Christ's agony and such total identification with Christ that the saint not only imitates him but becomes assimilated to him—not only becomes like Christ but becomes an embodiment of Christ himself.

The compassion aroused by such devotion was intensely emotional. Nicholas Hermansson was so moved by compassion when he spoke of Christ's sufferings that tears ran down his cheeks. Catherine of Sweden would pray for hours every night, weeping and beating her breast, in honor of the passion, and she exhorted others to keep Christ's "most bitter passion" constantly in mind. Her mother Bridget could scarcely recall the passion without tears.[6] Judging from what we know of Nicholas's position in the Church and from Bridget's fondness for elaborate allegorizing theology, it is reasonable to assume that these saints did not indulge in utterly mindless sentimentality; when Catherine of Sweden spent hours in meditative prayer, one may suppose that she was engaged in that point-by-point effort of mental attention in which meditation consisted. Yet what the hagiographers chose to stress was not the effort of mind but the emotional results. Whatever the saints' own practice may have been, the effect of the vitae must have been to encourage a predominantly emotional cult of the passion.

The nature of that emotion could be remarkably complex. At practically every juncture there are reminders that the passion was a terrifying event which reduced its beholders to tears. At the same time there was an element of beauty and consolation in it. One distinctively hagiographic manifestation of this ambivalence is found in the life of Ademar of Felsinio, who, when he said mass, was so rapt in meditation on the passion that he could scarcely keep from sighing and weeping. At times it would be discovered after mass that the corporals he had used bore stains from his tears, beautifully patterned in the shape of many crosses, and certain churches retained these items as relics. Similar yet significantly different is a passage in the life of Catherine of Siena. Christ once showed her his wounded side from afar, and she cried with desire to press her lips to the wound itself, whereupon her soul "entered right into that wound, and found such sweetness and such knowledge of the divinity there that if you could ever appreciate it you would marvel that my heart did not break." The common theme here is the beauty that underlies the passion and arouses a sense of awe. In the case of Ademar, this beauty is recognized not so much in the passion itself but in the emblematic forms miraculously produced through his devotion. With Catherine, on the other hand, ecstasy arises from her sense of extraordinary intimacy with the Savior through entry into his wounded side. In the one case it is a physical but highly abstract symbol of the passion that is found to be beautiful; in the other it is a spiritual but decidedly concrete experience of contact with Christ's flesh.[7]

At times the saints' compassionate meditation on Christ's suffering comes in a liturgical setting, as an outgrowth of extreme liturgical realism—a vivid awareness that the events acted out in the liturgy are so fully reenacted that sensitive individuals can perceive them physically. For Flora of Beaulieu, as we have seen, Holy Week was no mere commemoration of the passion; exceptionally sensitive to the events transpiring at that time, she was as deeply moved as if they were occurring for the first time before her eyes. Such liturgical realism did not have to be seasonal: John of Alverna was saying mass once when, after the consecration, he saw the crucified Christ with blood flowing freely from all his wounds into the chalice. The saint was on the verge of fainting when the apparition vanished, and all he saw in its place was the form of bread. Jane Mary of Maillé once saw the elevated host transformed into Christ as a small child with blood flowing from his wounds. These incidents show that not only the specific feasts of the liturgical cycle but even the daily reenactment of Christ's sacrifice could engender a keen sense of liturgical realism.[8]

The saints' meditation on the passion was not bound, however, to any special occasion or ritual, but could become habitual and pervade their lives. Figures such as Bridget of Sweden and Jane Mary of Maillé, seem to have done what Catherine of Sweden recommended: they bore the passion in mind constantly, or at least made it a recurrent motif in their thought. This pervasive character of reflection on the passion is given dramatic expression in certain visions, where the image of Christ seems to have been etched on the saint's consciousness. When Christ appeared once to Flora of Beaulieu, he made such a vivid impression that it did not recede for about three months: wherever she went, she saw Christ pierced with wounds, covered with blood and spittle, and looking at her mournfully. Much the same happened to Jane Mary of Maillé. One classic problem in Christian spirituality is how to interpret the biblical injunction to pray without ceasing (1 Thess. 5:17); visions of this kind, while tormenting, furnished an effective solution to that difficulty.[9]

The saints' compassion extended not only to Christ but to his mother as well. As we shall see, Mary's position at the foot of the cross gave her a double role in the spirituality of the passion: on the one hand she was a model for others to imitate in her compassion for her dying son; on the other, she was herself a fitting subject for compassion, since her identification with him caused her suffering comparable to his. The second theme in particular found interesting expression in the lives of the saints. It was not Henry Suso but his mother of whom it is said that she never attended mass without weeping bitterly out of compassion for Christ and Mary. One Lent she went into a church and saw a carving of the descent from the cross; she was transfixed with the vicarious experience of Mary's pain, fell to the ground, could not see or speak, and lay sick at home until her death on Good Friday. In light of the profound effect that Suso's mother had on his religious development, this story holds special interest: his mother becomes a sort of Mary-figure, yet another mediator, imparting to him a sense of compassion for Christ's mother, who in turn inspires compassion for her son. Different but no less interesting psychological motives can be glimpsed in a vision that Jane Mary of Maillé had at age six: she was with the body of her deceased mother, at night, evidently over-wrought, when Mary appeared to her with a thurifer containing in-cense made from drops of Christ's blood, and from then on her heart was fixed on the passion. The possibilities for interpretation are intri-cate: the celestial mother appeared perhaps in lieu of Jane Mary's natural mother, but rather than merely substituting for the deceased parent she gave religious significance to her death through the act of ritual benediction. At the same time she called to mind that even the sacred mother-child relationship had to be severed by death. Yet whatever its specific psychological underpinnings in any particular instance, the ensuing devotion to the passion was a general phe-nomenon of the culture, not reducible to psychological idiosyn-cracies.[10]

Visions of the passion held a central role in the hagiography. It would clearly be futile to seek out any factual basis for these inci-dents, but at times one suspects that the vision-narrative was a hagiographic device for describing less exceptional meditative experi-ence. We are told that Peter of Luxembourg enjoyed at least one vi-sion, and that was of Christ crucified—an incident that became important in fifteenth-century artistic representations of Peter. Rou-tinely, though, he is supposed to have prostrated himself in such fer-vent prayer before the crucified Christ that he could practically behold him. We have here an explicit distinction between the virtual beholding of meditation and the actual beholding of visionary experi-ence. On other occasions it is less clear whether meditation was the occasion for what the biographer is claiming as a genuine vision or whether the vision-narrative is (as one might suspect) a way of talking about the meditation. Thus, Jane Mary of Maillé awoke one night and began meditating on the passion, and in that context she "beheld" him with wounds in his hands and feet, and indeed all over his body; suddenly she found herself drawn to the wound in his right side. Per-haps neither the saint nor the hagiographer would have felt com-pelled to distinguish rigidly between humanly induced meditation and divinely bestowed vision, especially since even the former would be seen as ultimately aroused by grace.[11]

The standard way in which the saints found themselves assimilated to Christ crucified—or perhaps one should speak here too of stan-dard hagiographic ways of expressing such assimilation—was by shar-ing in the stigmata or wounds of Christ. The saints' wounds might be visible or invisible; in either event, the infliction was usually described in graphic physical terms—as had not been the case in the famous stigmatization of Francis of Assisi. At one point in her life Catherine of Siena asked "one little request" of Christ: that she be allowed to share in all his sufferings, and that she be united with him on earth through his passion, since she could not yet be united with him in heaven. Christ appeared to her and told her to stretch out her hand. She did so; he took a nail and pressed it into her hand so hard that it felt as if it went straight through, and she felt as much pain as if it had been struck by a hammer. The wound caused her continual pain thereafter, though it was invisible to others. Later she received the full stigmata, which came to her from Christ's body "in the form of pure light" and caused her such pain that she felt she would die within a few days unless the Lord worked another miracle to sustain her. Whereas Francis of Assisi had been so enrapt in the vision of Christ that he only noticed his wounds incidentally, Catherine was acutely conscious of the physical pain she endured. Similarly, when Christ impressed on Margaret of Faenza not his actual wounds but merely the pain associated with them, she felt the fullness of his agony and marveled that her soul was not severed from her body. He told her, "Daughter, do not be afraid, for I am with you, and have given you strength to bear these things." In an approximation to such experience, Flora of Beaulieu suffered great pain in her right side, as if it had been opened with a lance, and if she heard reference to the passion or saw artistic reminders of it she suffered great pain. She seemed to bear the crucified Lord within her own body, as if she herself were affixed to the cross. When Gertrude of Delft received stigmata that were quite visible, though, her experience was closer to that of Francis. It was an occasion for wonder and praise rather than anguish. When blood flowed from the wounds, the blood itself was "beautiful" and the flow caused her a kind of consoling sweetness. Perhaps the biographers felt it particularly necessary to emphasize the physicality of the infliction when the effect was invisible, simply to impress upon the reader the reality of the stigmata, while in a case such as Gertrude's this point could be made by referring to the wounds that were there for all to see. In any event, the same ambiguity can be seen here that we noted in connection with compassionate meditation: while incidents of stigmatization tend to be more agonizing in the fourteenth century than they had been with Francis, and while God's testing and sustaining work for (rather than through) the saints thus received poignant expression, the experience could still give rise to pleasure as well as to pain.[12]

Meditation on the passion could furthermore have comforting effect by taking one's mind off one's own sorrows. Accused of heresy and afflicted with serious illness, Henry Suso lay sleepless and meditated on Christ's agony in Gethsemane. Rulman Merswin at times was comforted by meditation on the passion, though at other times it made him disconsolate or even ill. When Villana de' Botti was sick she beheld the crucified Christ before her, and in compassion for him she became oblivious to her own pains. In these cases the passion itself remains a gruesome event, but it is precisely because of its compelling horror that awareness of it takes the edge off one's own suffering.[13]

It is only rarely that the passion becomes a source of consolation in what might have seemed the most obvious way: by pointing to the resurrection. One episode from the life of Margaret of Faenza illustrates the peripheral role that the resurrection could play in these matters. As the solemnity of Christ's passion was about to be celebrated in her convent, she prayed for some sign that her love was acceptable to Christ. At once she was struck with intense pain in every cell (*particula*) and every joint of her body; there was nothing in her that was not transfixed with this pain. Languishing, she groaned feebly, and her abbess and fellow nuns came running. They feared she was about to die, and she could not reveal to them the true source of her infirmity. By Sunday at dawn, though, she turned her thoughts to the resurrection, and at once she regained all her strength. One of her associates, coming to bring her food from the infirmary, found her totally and to all appearances miraculously recovered, and ran to tell the abbess and all the other nuns this news, at which they rejoiced greatly. Even here, though, the release from infirmity is also a release from that mystical approbation of her love that she had requested. This example of liturgical realism, therefore, does not so much point to the resurrection as the momentous event giving meaning to the antecedent suffering; instead, the suffering has meaning of its own, and the "resurrection" signals little more than that the mystical ordeal is over.[14]

One might suggest that the resurrection is implicitly suggested in any reference to the passion—that the cross always pointed beyond itself to Easter—yet for lack of textual evidence it would be hazardous to assume that the saints and hagiographers intended this. Perhaps the resurrection was deemphasized because it could not be imitated, whereas the saints could readily share in the passion. Saints could and did take upon themselves sufferings modeled after those of Christ, but they could not rise from the dead. Yet the saints and their biographers could have taken any experiences of healing, conversion, or relief from affliction as occasion for reflection on how Christians share in the grace of Christ's resurrection even during earthly life, if their theology had inclined them toward this interpretation. For reasons we have discussed, though, it did not so incline them. The typical assumption is that of Catherine of Siena, who requested a sharing in Christ's passion while she was still on earth specifically because that was the best and perhaps ultimately the only way to be united with Christ while still on earth.

If taken as referring to literal visions, these episodes in the saints' lives could suggest that Christ remained the Man of Sorrows even after the resurrection, and that even now the sins of humankind were causing him pain. The effect would be to deny altogether the glorification of Christ associated with the resurrection. When Bridget of Sweden was a girl, the crucified Christ appeared to her in a dream and called attention to his afflictions. She asked, "Oh Lord, who has done this to you?" He responded, "Those who despise me and neglect my love—they have done this to me." The effect of such a vision was highly significant for the religious culture of the late Middle Ages. Early Christian visionaries such as Paul had seen "the risen Lord," and their visions of him had been the earliest attested evidence of his resurrection. What Bridget and her contemporaries gave witness to was—or seemed to be—the ongoing passion of Christ. In popular Christianity, at least, the implication was that Christ not only had suffered for human sin but was still doing so.[15]

The passion took precedence over Christ's incarnation, as well as his resurrection. A few of the women saints manifested a tender, maternal fondness for the infant Jesus, but they were the exceptions. The norm is clear from the life of Margaret of Faenza. For a long time she preoccupied herself with the infancy of Jesus, and from this devotion she derived a sense of wondrous sweetness; she did not care about ascending to higher things, her biographer says. One day, though, Christ spoke to her and said it was not right for her to taste only his honey and not his gall. If she wished to be perfectly united with him, she should meditate on the mockery, opprobrium, scourging, torments, and death that he suffered for her sake. Thus admonished, she "embraced the cross of the Lord's passion," meditating on it day and night. She seems not to have added this as a new devotion alongside her earlier meditations; instead, it evidently replaced the earlier devotion to Christ's infancy. Either motif could have stimulated feelings of compassion, but it was by meditation on the passion alone that she could begin to unite herself with Christ and to share in that work of redemption that he accomplished specifically by his passion and death.[16]

By the same token, devotion to the passion tended to overshadow attention to Christ's active ministry. To be sure, most of the saints at least dabbled in charitable works, and some of them were seriously committed to such service. When miracles occurred they were almost always on behalf of the needy. Yet imitation of Christ's works of service was at best a subsidiary motif in fourteenth-century hagiography.[17] Imitation of Christ meant essentially identification with his passion. It was the passion that dominated all else.

Manifestations in General Literature and Art

This single-minded focus on the passion can be seen not only in the hagiography but also in the broader religious culture of the century, though the further one looks the more qualifications one must introduce in making such a generalization. Before continuing with this analysis of the saints' devotion to the passion, it may be useful to consider some of those works from the wider culture which directly or indirectly must have influenced the saints' perceptions.

The importance that late medieval Christians attached to meditation on the passion is clear from an anonymous German poem of the late fourteenth century called *The Forest Brother*.[18] This work tells of a hermit who lived in the woods, serving God unceasingly with prayer, fasting, vigils, and virtuous works. He asked God in his prayer how he could best serve him. One day he heard a great, pitiable groaning outside his door, and he opened the door quickly to see what he could do to help. What he saw there was a naked man, covered with wounds and caked with blood, and carrying a cross on his shoulder. Terrified, the hermit asked who had done this to the stranger; the latter answered that it was his enemies who had inflicted this suffering upon him. The hermit asked what had happened to his clothes, and the visitor said they had taken them away. He asked why he bore such an enormous cross, and the sufferer replied that his enemies had compelled him to take it up, to his considerable grief. What had he done to provoke such treatment? Only teaching the truth. Taking pity on this figure, the hermit invited him to lay down his cross, come into his hut, and clean himself. He brought some warm water, and washed the visitor's body. Noting that the man had deep and wide wounds in his head, hands, feet, and side, he recognized (at last!) an unmistakable likeness to Christ—but as he pondered this similarity the guest vanished. God then enlightened the brother: the man was indeed Christ himself, who had come in response to his prayer for guidance as to the best form of service. He could best honor God, he now learned, by thoroughly absorbing himself in meditation on the sufferings he had been blessed to behold, and by bearing in mind the love for us that God thus manifested.

This story is based on earlier Latin versions, which take the form of brief sermon *exempla*. One such version, also from the fourteenth century, represents Christ as acknowledging at once who he is, and saying that he has come to tell the hermit that he should serve God by helping him to bear the cross, a task he should accomplish by keeping the passion before his mind. The longer, verse adaptation of the story not only adds further details but provides for a kind of suspense by leaving the hermit unsure of his visitor's identity until after he has disappeared. The theme of delayed recognition suggests, perhaps, that one should be constantly on guard for manifestations of the Lord, who may at any time appear incognito. This theme had long been known in Christian literature; it occurs in the Bible, in the story of the men of Emmaus, though it is the risen Christ whom they recognize belatedly and not the persistent *Christus patiens*. In any case, both the long and short versions of the present *exemplum* testify to the centrality of the passion in late medieval piety. More importantly, they suggest that meditation was itself seen as a vitally important way of sharing the burden of the passion and uniting oneself to Christ through one's compassion.[19]

Another German story tells that a certain learned Dominican was meditating one day on the passion, and prayed to God to make him worthy to be a true cosufferer with Christ, nailed with him to the cross, however much pain he might have to endure.[20] After he had thus invited suffering, through divine dispensation he came upon a booklet which described in great detail the sufferings of Christ, as related in a vision to a nun. He became aware that, while the gospels give only meager accounts of the passion, Christ now wanted to reveal his sufferings more fully to his chosen friends. Soon afterward he fell ill, and those about him feared he would die. As he lay alone and sleepless one night, he begged to know when he would have suffered enough, and he felt the same anguish that Christ had felt with bloody sweat in the garden of Gethsemane. He anointed his body with blood, in imitation of Christ, and promised that if he recovered he would publicize, by means of the booklet he had discovered, those sufferings of Christ in which he was now sharing—though if he did not recover soon he would cast the booklet into a fire. He then got up from his bed and went to a chair, where he beheld an angelic vision of great comfort (a detail borrowed from the writings of Henry Suso), and was cured. Having emerged from his own passion, he proceeded to revise and publish the booklet recounting the nun's vision. Here again one can see a sense of urgency: through special dispensation of providence, the Dominican became keenly aware how important it was that Christians learn the details of the passion as an aid to sharing in its agony. Through an unfolding of all these details, the mind as well as the emotions could be engaged in consideration of the passion, albeit in an unsophisticated manner.

The urge to supplement the gospel accounts of the passion goes back to antiquity, when the apocryphal gospel according to Nicodemus supplied details (such as the harrowing of hell) not contained in the canonical gospels.[21] There had been other such works over the centuries. What emerged in and around the fourteenth century, though, was an unprecedented torrent of such materials, in Latin and in the vernacular: treatises, meditations, sermons, and poems of all descriptions, relating the story of the passion in minute detail and unfolding its significance for religion and morals. Only a fraction of these works have been published. Germany was particularly rich in such writings, but England and other countries produced their share as well. Two major works which had widespread influence were the *Meditations on the Life of Christ,* written in Italy in the late thirteenth or early fourteenth century, and highly popular throughout late medieval Europe partly because they were falsely ascribed to St. Bonaventure, and Ludolph of Saxony's encyclopedic *Life of Christ* from the middle of the century. While both of these works cover more than the passion, the sections in them dealing with the passion are important because they typify late medieval thought on this topic and because they exerted great influence on subsequent writings.[22]

The method of pseudo-Bonaventure is essentially hypothetical: the author acknowledges that when he goes beyond the gospel accounts of Christ's life he is in effect inviting the reader to follow him in pious conjecture as to how things might have been. Ten of the book's hundred chapters are devoted to the passion, from Gethsemane through Calvary: first comes a "meditation on the passion of the Lord in general," then a series of meditations for the canonical hours (in which the events of the passion are divided and distributed throughout these meditations), with a special chapter on the piercing of Christ's side, and an extra one for after compline. The introductory chapter, on the passion in general, is essentially an invitation and a preview; the reader is told that to glory in the passion one must keep it in mind with "continued meditation," and is asked to reflect that throughout the passion Christ "was in a continuous battle, in great pain, injury, scorn, and torment," and was never allowed even the slightest rest. Before morning (presumably at matins), the reader is to reflect on the events in the garden of Gethsemane: "Consider how anguished He is now in His soul. Also note here, in contrast to our impatience, that the Lord Jesus prayed three times before He received any answer." Here as elsewhere, meditation bred reform. The following meditations deal with Christ's appearance before Pilate (prime), the carrying of the cross (terce), the crucifixion and the compassion felt by the Virgin (sext), the "seven words" and death of Christ (none), the piercing of his side (an interpolation), the deposition (vespers), the burial (compline), and the withdrawal of the disciples from the tomb (after compline). Throughout, the emphasis on Christ's patience is sustained: he "bore everything most patiently," sat patiently while being mocked as king, and in praying for his enemies displayed patience and love. The author exclaims, "Your patience, Lord, is indescribable." The account is at times graphic, as for example in the account of the scourging: "The Flower of all flesh and of all human nature is covered with bruises and cut. The royal blood flows all about, from all parts of His body. Again and again, repeatedly, closer and closer, it is done, bruise upon bruise, and cut upon cut, until not only the torturers but also the spectators are tired; then He is ordered untied." The author provides alternative versions of how Christ was nailed to the cross: it may have been before the cross itself was stationed erect, or it may have been afterward. In either event, one has occasion to reflect on the pain and ignominy to which he was subjected.[23]

Ludolph of Saxony's *Life of Christ* is far more conspicuously learned than the pseudo-Bonaventuran *Meditations*, partly by virtue of its numerous patristic quotations, and partly because of the tendency to schematize and enumerate everything. It is a far longer book, and a much greater portion of it, roughly a quarter, is devoted to the passion. The general plan is similar to that of the *Meditations,* with events divided according to the canonical hours, after which there is an epilogue and a "praise of the cross." Much of the content is devoted to description, but the interpretation of each incident is what looms particularly large. One format that Ludolph employs repeatedly is a list of the various teachings (*documenta*) to be derived from a particular aspect of or incident in Christ's passion, followed by a suggestion for conforming oneself to him (*actus conformationis*) and applying the lessons of the passion to one's own life, and then by a prayer. Various data are interpreted "mystically" as well as literally: the number of wounds, the form of the cross, the nature of Christ's tunic, the two thieves, and the burial. Old Testament "figures" are cited, which were supposed to have anticipated one or another episode in the passion. At times Ludolf pondered which types of person could be compared to the participants in the passion—who, for example, could be likened to those who mocked Jesus on Calvary. Several sections are devoted to explanation of some problem: in what sense Christ's kingdom is not of this world; why Christ chose to suffer his death outside of the city; why he chose to die on a cross; why the inscription on the cross was in three languages; why he did not come down from the cross; and what one should seek "in the wounds of Christ." Ludolph also gave geographical information, in particular on Calvary and its church and on the form and location of the sepulcher. With a fondness for drawing up lists, he discussed the four kinds of solace to be derived from the passion, the three causes of the Lord's sadness, the fourfold way in which one can be buried with Christ, and so forth. And he worked in other kinds of lore, such as the story of the "forest brother." Essentially, then, what he composed was a *summa* replete with historical, theological, moral, legendary, and geographical information and reflection.[24]

When devotional writers described the passion, they used two general devices: narrative elaboration and systematic description. Frequently they combined the two, by interrupting the narrative sequence to ponder in detail one or another scene, in particular the crucifixion itself.

In embellishing the narrative account, writers could use various sources. They could draw upon scriptural and apocryphal texts, they could extrapolate from these texts what was likely to have happened, and they could use their imaginations. Apocryphal literature, for example, told how the centurion Longinus had been blind until the water from Christ's side splattered on his eyes and healed them; this story was repeated in late medieval accounts.[25] Extrapolation and imaginative detail are exemplified in one German writer's fascination with the raging, devilish crowd that apprehended Jesus in Gethsemane and dragged him from place to place during the night. Arriving with Judas, they proved themselves the meanest people on earth, possessed by nine devils who were Lucifer's closest companions. They cried out with a raucous voice, "We are seeking Jesus of Nazareth." When he replied, "I am he," his words stripped them and the devils of their power, and they fell down to the ground as if dead, until God revived them so the passion could continue. They dragged Christ forth in wild disarray, hitting him all over his body and yanking his hair out so that locks lay about on the ground. One of them pulled him by his hair, another by his beard, and yet another by his ears, as if he were an ape or a fool. They tugged on his clothes, attached ropes to him and dragged him along, and frequently thrust him down and jumped on him. In their wild raging, they acted as if they had a wolf in tow. (Details of this sort would eventually find graphic expression in the paintings of Hieronymous Bosch and his followers.) The same account tells how the soldiers who flagellated Jesus beat him so hard that his flesh was torn from his bones, and one could see the bones with blood flowing over them. It relates how those who mocked him as a king spewed into his mouth and over his face the filth from their own mouths and nostrils.[26] No doubt this account was intended to arouse revulsion, and no doubt it succeeded.

If Richard Rolle was less grotesque in his meditations on the passion, he was pursuing the same imaginative form of narration when he emphasized how the "armed knights" led Jesus forth, "naked as a worm," amid great throngs of people, and kicked him along as if he were a dog. Likewise, Rolle tells how strong men were chosen for the flagellation, and it took a long time for them to grow exhausted, so that with their strokes they made of Christ's body nothing but wounds that eventually merged into one great wound.[27]

The possibilities for systematic description of isolated, fixed scenes are illustrated by an extended but digressive meditation addressed to the crucified Christ by "the monk of Farne," identified by modern scholars as John Whiterig.[28] At one point his focus is on the contrasts presented by the crucified Savior: in himself most beautiful and good, he has become accounted as a leper and a wicked man; though strong and powerful, he allowed himself to be executed like a thief; supremely wise, he allowed himself to be the butt of mockery; his head, an object of awe for the angels, is pierced with thorns; his face, which gives delight to the heavenly hosts (1 Pet. 1:12), is "spat upon by vile mouths"; his hands, which "fashioned heaven and earth," are pierced by nails; his belly, "from which flow living waters" (John 7:38), is "contracted with hunger and pain"; and so forth. In the following chapter, the monk considers how each of Christ's five senses was afflicted on Calvary. With his sense of sight he beheld himself and the thieves crucified, his friends deserting him, his enemies clustering around, his sorrowing mother, and "corpses of condemned criminals strewn around about." With his hearing he was subjected to "threats, murmuring, sarcasm and taunts from the bystanders." His sense of taste exposed him to the bitterness of gall and vinegar. Nor was his sense of smell protected, since his nostrils "breathed in the stench of the corrupting corpses of executed criminals lying round about." As for touch, the possibilities were numerous, but the monk cites in particular the sensation of the thorns in Christ's head. In a later passage in this meditation he insists that it is important to study the crucified Christ, whose body, "hanging on the cross, is a book, open for your perusal"; indeed, "without knowledge of this book, both general and particular, it is impossible for you to be saved."

Richard Rolle, while discussing the various scenes in the passion seriatim, frequently draws back from the narrative context to focus on a particular scene.[29] In the course of discussing Christ's carrying of the cross, he inserts one such passage: "Ah, ah, this is a rueful sight. Thy head is full of thorns, thine ear full of blood, thy face all wan, thy looking is all mournful, thy cheeks and head all bruised with buffets. Thy visage is befouled with spitting. . . . The flesh where the cross sits is skinless and overrun with bloody rows; the pain of thy bearing grieveth thee so sore that each foot that thou goest striketh to thy heart." Again in depicting the body of Christ after his death, Rolle paints a graphic picture with all the essential details: the five "great floods of blood," the chin hanging down on his breast, the eyes turned up to show the whites, the shrunken lips, the white teeth showing, the face pale, the hair clotted with blood. In one extended passage he gives a metaphorical account of the wounds, which were like the stars of heaven by virtue of their multitude (though they shone far brighter, by day as well as night, and could not be covered by clouds). His body was like a net, full of holes and able to draw human beings as a net draws fish. Again, his body was like a dovecote, or like a honeycomb, or a book with red ink, or a meadow abloom with "sweet flowers and wholesome herbs." Farfetched and arbitrary as these images may seem, they served as ways of reflecting upon the significance of the passion through a richness of poetic images.

Henry Suso, in his highly popular and influential *Little Book of Eternal Wisdom*, gives an almost clinical description of Christ's state on the cross. Christ himself is speaking to his servant:

> See, My right hand was pierced by a nail, My left hand was transfixed, My right arm was stretched out, and My left most painfully twisted, My right foot was cut, and My left cruelly hacked through. I hung impotently, and My Divine legs were most weary. All my tender limbs were immovably riveted to the narrow halter. My hot blood burst out copiously through many a wound, in My anguish, so that My dying body was covered with blood, which was a distressful sight. Behold, a lamentable thing: My young, fair healthy body began to grow grey, to dry up and wither. The gentle weary back leant painfully on the rough cross, My heavy body sank down, My whole frame was bruised, wounded and cut through and through—and yet My loving heart bore all this lovingly.[30]

One recent writer suggests that such passages were not meant to display or elicit a "morbid sentimentality," but rather to arouse a sense of delight in the triumphant love that Jesus manifested on Calvary. In the same vein, another author speaks of late medieval Christians as deriving "spiritual refreshment" from contemplation of Christ's tortures.[31] This may sound like special pleading, yet it is not without support from the sources. When fourteenth-century authors indicated how they expected their readers to react to their accounts, they spoke of four main types of response: gratitude, penitence, compassion, and imitation. At times they also spoke of joy, and certain authors conceived reflection on the passion as a means to mystical delights.

The sentiments of gratitude and penitence were reactions which left the reading or meditating person at a distance from Christ: one beheld from that distance the objective work that the suffering Savior accomplished on one's behalf. The motif of gratitude is one that *The Forest Brother* stresses: one can best serve God by keeping the passion ever in mind and by responding gratefully to that act of love that God performed for humankind. Rolle, too, was moved to thank Jesus for undergoing his suffering. Profoundly impressed with the significance of Christ's deed, Rolle reflected also on the implications of his own complicity in that sin which made the passion necessary, and thus he was moved to penitence. Protesting that he himself was "cause and guilty of all thy painful death," he proposed to embrace the foot of the cross (as tradition represented Mary Magdalene as having done), to lie down flat on the earth "among the stinking bones," and out of a sense of his unworthiness to keep from casting his eyes on "that glorious sight of thy wounds."[32]

Compassion and imitation were responses that closed the distance between oneself and the suffering Christ: identifying oneself with him, one suffered along with him and strove to partake of his sufferings. As has been suggested by modern authors, compassion was essentially an inner response, while imitation was an outer one, a distinction paralleled at times by that between *affectus* and *effectus*.[33] Pseudo-Bonaventure repeatedly exhorted his readers to compassion; at one point he wrote, "Look at Him well, then, as He goes along bowed down by the cross and gasping aloud. Feel as much compassion for Him as you can, placed in such anguish, in renewed derision." Through "com-passion" one became a sharer in Christ's passion. Imitation was essentially accomplished through emulation of Christ's patience, a motif already discussed. To some extent, willingness to imitate Christ became an index of one's sincerity; compassion was easy enough, but it was more difficult to take upon oneself the sufferings of Christ, and only the truly dedicated would do so. Thus, Henry Suso suggested that "loving imitation" was preferable to "tearful lamentation," though both were good and desirable.[34]

Ludolph of Saxony sums up many of these themes when he says, "We must bear Christ's cross, and help him to bear it, in our heart, by recollection and compassion; in our mouth, through frequent and devout thanksgiving; and in our body, by flagellation and castigation—so that we give thanks to our Savior by our heart, our mouth, and our deeds." The mortification that Ludolph speaks of is an expression of penitence, but it is simultaneously a statement of desire to imitate the sufferings of Jesus in his passion. Elsewhere, Ludolf says that if one is moved neither by feelings of compassion nor by desire for rejoicing, but feels oppressed by a hardness of emotion, one should nonetheless praise God in whatever way one can, and "commit to his most kind hands what by yourself you are unable to supply." In other words, one will not always be able to arouse in oneself subjective feelings in response to the passion, yet this emotional dryness does not absolve one of responsibility for willing the proper response, and if one's will is properly disposed one may entrust oneself safely to God.[35]

The ultimate model of compassion for the suffering Christ was his mother, who saw him carry his cross, stood at the foot of the cross on Calvary, received her son's body into her arms at the deposition, and was separated from him only with great reluctance. Medieval theology portrayed her as a "co-redemptrix" largely because of her compassion for her dying son. Her participation in his sufferings plays a dominant role in the pseudo-Bonaventuran *Meditations:* her compassion added to his passion, "and conversely" (that is, the two of them grieved because of each other's grief); she "wished to die with Him rather than live any longer"; while she prayed to the Father for him, he likewise prayed for her, protesting, "I ought to be crucified, not she, but she is with me on the cross"; she remained faithful even after his death, and remained at the foot of the cross, persuading the soldiers not to break his legs; Simeon's prophecy that her soul would be pierced by a sword (Luke 2:35) was fulfilled; at his burial, she said she would gladly be buried with him, and would in any event bury her soul in the tomb with his body. A German version is more emphatic: embracing her dead son tightly before his burial, she was filled with such anguish that she could not say a single word, but merely held him in her arms as if bound to him with iron bonds. There is no sense here of Mary as the one who maintains faith in Christ's resurrection even when others lose this confidence; instead of the serenity of faith, what one sees is a shock bordering on desperation. Essentially, however, she was not serving in an entirely distinctive role but was enacting in its purest form that compassion which is incumbent on all Christians. Richard Rolle even sees her as a mediatrix of compassion, and prays to her to obtain for him one of the "wounds and pains" that she suffered, as a "prick" for his own heart, and to secure for him "a drop of that ruth that thou had to follow him with as thou did." As the ultimate exemplar of compassion, Mary is the source as well as the model of compassion for others who wish to share in the suffering of Christ.[36]

Further extending the theme of Mary's compassion, both the art and the literature of the later Middle Ages attempted to link the nativity and the passion of Christ by foreshadowing Christ's death even at the moment of his conception or birth. In art this was done either through juxtaposition or by symbolism: for example, by setting the madonna alongside the Man of Sorrows or the crucifixion in a diptych, or by showing the infant Jesus reaching out for a thorny rose.[37] The connection could be evoked in more detail in literature.

Bridget of Sweden, for instance, suggested that "when the Virgin had borne God's son and began to touch him with her hands, suddenly it occurred to her how he was to fulfill the writings of the prophets." As she wrapped him in swaddling clothes, she considered those blows that would lacerate his entire body and render it seemingly leprous. She reflected in detail on the specific assaults her infant son would ultimately encounter: how the impious would stain his lovely face with their spittle, how his own blood would clot and darken his eyes, how his nerves and veins would be extended unmercifully on the cross, and so forth—in short, how "all of his glorious body, as it were, inwardly and outwardly, would be tormented with bitterness and anguish even to death." Thus, while she took keen delight to give birth to God's son, her joy was mixed with the most grievous sorrow.[38]

The sense of identification with Christ that meditation on the passion fostered has led some authors to speak of a "passion mysticism" of the later Middle Ages.[39] The mystical element in this devotion to the passion is especially pronounced in those authors who speak of the humanity of Jesus, and especially his suffering humanity, as the proper means of access to his divinity. By meditating on the anguish of the crucified Savior, one comes eventually to a sense of profound contact with the deity that was joined with his humanity. This link can be traced back to Augustine, and was particularly important for Bernard of Clairvaux.[40] One of the leading representatives of this spirituality in the fourteenth century was Henry Suso, especially in his *Little Book of Eternal Wisdom*. At one juncture in this dialogue the servant protests to Eternal Wisdom that he has sought his divinity everywhere, but only his humanity was revealed to him; he has looked for sweetness and found only bitterness. Linking the typical language of passion mysticism with Suso's distinctive language of chivalrous service, Eternal Wisdom responds:

> No one can attain to Divine heights or to unusual sweetness, unless he be first drawn through the example of My human bitterness. The higher one climbs without passing through My humanity, the deeper one falls. My humanity is the way by which one must go, My sufferings are the gate through which one must pass, if one would attain what thou seekest. Therefore, put away the timidity of thy heart, and enter the lists of knightly courage, where I am, for weakness befits not the knight in the place where his lord stands in valiant courage. I will clothe thee with My armour, for all My sufferings must be experienced by thee, according to thy strength.

Eternal Wisdom then indicates the sufferings that the servant must undergo, especially scorn from his fellow human beings.[41]

If meditation on the passion is a means toward higher mystical consciousness, is it a temporary phase through which the mystic passes? For some contemplative writers this is clearly the case. Thus, *The Cloud of Unknowing* envisions discursive meditation on the passion (or on anything else) as a technique for beginners; ultimately one abandons such discursive prayer for the nondiscursive prayer of contemplation. For other writers the situation is more complex. Thus, John Tauler thinks of step-by-step reflection on the life of Christ as a method for beginners, yet even in the higher stages of spiritual life there is place for a kind of nondiscursive view of Christ's life in which one grasps it totally in a single glimpse. Furthermore, one's life always remains conformed to that of Christ. This last point is one with which all the mystics would surely have agreed, though some, such as Suso, were more emphatic than others in their stress on the need for perpetual conformity to the suffering and patient Savior.[42]

So far we have examined only the meditative literature on the passion. There were numerous other genres of religious literature which presented the same themes we have encountered, sometimes with distinctive elaborations. Closely related to discursive meditative works, for example, were prayer formulas such as the rhythmic *Ave caput Christi gratum*, the stanzas of which directly addressed the wounded head of Christ, then each of the wounds in his body, then his body in its entirety; falsely attributed to Gregory the Great, the prayer was highly popular in the fourteenth and fifteenth centuries, and one scholar has ascribed it to Gregory XI. English vernacular lyrics often took the form of prayers devoted to the passion; one of the more tender of these centers on the tears that Christ shed on the cross:

> Lovely tear from lovely eye,
> Why do you give me woe?
> Sorrowful tear from sorrowful eye,
> You break my heart in two. . . .

Lyrics of this sort, alongside longer narrative poems of the passion, form an important part of the century's poetic composition. The same devotion showed in the drama of the century: the French *Palatine Passion*, the German *Passion of St. Gall*, and other such vernacular works led toward the elaborate passion plays of the fifteenth and sixteenth centuries. Even the relatively simple plays of the fourteenth century helped to spark popular interest in the passion, particularly by developing minor characters such as Malchus and the centurion Longinus. For example, the St. Gall play represents Longinus as piercing Christ's side not to end his suffering but to punish Christ's "sorcery."[43]

Apart from works devoted entirely or in large part to explicit discussion of the passion, this devotion arose frequently in an incidental manner. The letters of Catherine of Siena give some idea how a fourteenth-century writer might weave images of the passion into diverse contexts.[44] Repeatedly she speaks of doing things "for love of Christ crucified," or the like. She begins her letters by saying that she is writing "in the precious blood," and she speaks of Christians as plunged, drowned, bathed, clothed, and lost in that "sweet blood." Not quite so frequently she mentions the cross, and describes it as a standard, a baton, a tree, a table, or even a chair, or as an object on which one loses or finds oneself. At times she refers to the wounds of Christ, and encourages her readers to lock or hide themselves in Christ's wounds. With all these images she urges her readers to immerse themselves in consciousness of the sufferings of Christ and to share in them. Thus she writes to Raymund of Capua:

> Rest in the cross——with Christ crucified. Delight—in Christ crucified; delight in suffering. Be a glutton for abuse—for Christ crucified. Let your heart and soul be grafted into the tree of the most holy cross—with Christ crucified. Make his wounds your home.[45]

In another letter she says first that "in the blood of Christ we are made strong," and then she addresses the blood itself:

> O pity-full Blood, channel of pity-full mercy! You are that glorious Blood wherein ignorant man can know and see the truth of the eternal Father. . . . O Blood, scattering the darkness and giving man light that he might know. . . . O tender Blood, you strip off the self-love which weakens any soul. . . .[46]

The cumulative effect of such passages depends not on any logical sense of the specific texts, many of which seem weak in rational meaning, but rather on the fervor with which Catherine commits herself in devotion to the suffering Christ who is the source of grace and of saving knowledge.

If the passion literature of the fourteenth century represented the sufferings of Christ in particularly great and graphic detail, giving rise to charges of "morbid sentimentality," much the same can be said of the depiction of Christ's sufferings in painting and sculpture. Here too, as elsewhere in late medieval religious culture, the passion overshadows both Christ's resurrection and his active ministry (though the incarnation does find its place, especially in portrayals of the madonna). In the art of the century one can observe two fundamental developments: on the one hand there was an acute evocation of anguish in representations of the passion, more than in earlier art; on the other, there was a blossoming of new motifs which, particularly in northern Europe, multiplied the ways in which the suffering of Christ might be expressed.[47]

The transition from the figure of "Christ triumphant" to that of "Christ suffering" is well known. Early medieval crucifixes tended to show Christ in majesty, dressed in royal attire, conquering over sin and death; from roughly the turn of the millennium, there was a gradual shift in style, with a growing tendency to portray Christ as slumped in agony and stripped to his loincloth. To be sure, the transformation was never simple or complete. One recent author contrasts two crucifixes erected in England in the mid-fourteenth century: one at Meaux Abbey, carved from a nude model to ensure realism, and another at Durham Cathedral, wrought in silver and showing Christ with all the accoutrements of regal glory, including even a detachable crown of gold. The general lines of development, however, are clear enough.[48]

In Germany, the striving for realism reached a high point with the crucifixion group done at Naumburg in the middle of the thirteenth century. The naturalism here is adapted to convey a vivid sense of agony on the part of the Virgin, John the Evangelist, and the dying Christ, and an equally striking impression of intimate contact among these figures. By the beginning of the fourteenth century, then, artists were prepared to go beyond such realism to a distortion of both the cross and the Crucified, in an effort to suggest all the more powerfully the wrenching anguish of the passion. German folk-artists fashioned crosses from rough-hewn wood, Y-shaped rather than in the traditional cruciform pattern, and portrayed Christ himself with legs and head twisted, eyes staring blankly, mouth gaping open, ribs protruding, and blood gushing from open wounds. While this tendency long preceded the mid-century plague, crosses of this sort took on new meaning as they were set up to induce penitence and devotion so that God's wrath would not require illness and death as a scourge.[49]

There were parallel developments in Italian painting. Giotto's painted crucifix of around 1290 for Santa Maria Novella in Florence has been spoken of as a revolutionary work, which broke through the stylized forms of earlier painting and for the first time depicted "the pathetic dead Christ in a straightforward, highly realistic manner."[50] In the early years of the fourteenth century, though, a master such as Pietro Lorenzetti was able to go beyond realism to intentional distortion in an effort once again to convey an intense feeling of anguish. A painted crucifix of his from the late 1320s portrays Christ with a greenish hue that evokes a sense of terror: "The twisted body, contorted face and slack abdomen leave no doubt that the Crucifixion has taken a horrible toll."[51] By no means every crucifix shows this sort of distortion, yet the general range of emotion had clearly been extended to include images of a more grotesque kind than had earlier been known.

Enhanced devotion to the passion led also the invention of new artistic motifs. Thus, the pietà, or representation of Mary holding her dead son on her lap, arose around the turn of the century in German convents. The notion had received vivid expression late in the thirteenth century, when Mechtild of Hackeborn cultivated meditation on the scene of mother and child. The first known representation in art comes from 1298; throughout the fourteenth century it remained a popular motif in German wood carving. Typically the Virgin is shown transfixed with grief, and at times she appears to be so absorbed in the awesome sacrifice of her son that her expression becomes impersonal, perhaps even stunned. In the following century the motif became increasingly popular in other media (such as painting) and other countries; through the addition of attendant figures, the pietà evolved into the full-fledged lamentation scene.[52]

At roughly the same time as the pietà, representations of the instruments of the passion came into vogue: the nails, hammer, pincers, crown of thorns, and so on. These implements were known as the "arms of Christ" (*arma Christi*), in the double sense of the weapons that he used against death and Satan and also his coat of arms or emblem. Numerous items that were not actually instruments came to be included: trees (standing for the garden of Gethsemane), dots (for the sweat of Christ), hands (for the smiting of Christ's face), the stigmata (sometimes symbolized by such items as roses), and even Christ's head. The earliest extant representations are in manuscript illuminations of the late thirteenth and early fourteenth centuries. Numerous examples from the fourteenth century survive.[53]

Another motif in art of the passion, the "Man of Sorrows," dates back at least to the twelfth century, but gained much in popularity and in richness of variation during the fourteenth. It displayed Christ alive again after his crucifixion, but revealing himself as the wounded and suffering Savior rather than as risen in glory. He shows his wounds to the viewer to arouse devotion, while at the same time presenting himself as an intercessor. Around 1300, large wall-paintings of this motif were painted in South German churches. Before long there were statues as well as paintings showing the theme. Here too, as in the visions of *Christus patiens*, the resurrection seems to be not merely ignored but by implication denied.[54]

In paintings of the crucifixion itself, a major development of the fourteenth century was the growing tendency toward elaborate representation of Calvary. Not merely the Virgin and Saint John were included, but the two thieves, soldiers, Mary Magdalene, and a large crowd of bystanders, while angels and sometimes demons hover in the sky above the mountain. This proliferation of characters heightened the drama, added a sense of momentousness, and perhaps even gave the viewer a feeling of participating in the event as a vicarious member of the crowd below the cross.[55]

For the most part the art of the passion in the fourteenth century was iconic or symbolic rather than narrative: it focused on the major scene or object rather than on the sequence of events. Thus, there was little interest in the episodes leading toward Calvary (Gethsemane, the trial of Christ, the flagellation and crowning with thorns, the carrying of the cross) or in his deposition and burial. The same tendencies may be found in fourteenth-century depictions of Christ's infancy or in representations of the saints. Only in the fifteenth century was there major growth in fascination for the story as such, with a corresponding eagerness to depict its various episodes in art.[56]

What relevance do these works from the broader culture have for an understanding of the saints' lives? In the case of the passion literature, there is an obvious answer: the saints themselves took a role in writing such works. Henry Suso made the passion a central concern in his literary output; if the attribution is correct, so did Richard Rolle. While Catherine of Siena and Bridget of Sweden did not write works specifically on the passion, they were likewise virtually obsessed with its significance, and their obsession emerged clearly in their writings. While there is seldom direct evidence, it is reasonable to assume that the other saints were familiar with such works. They lived in an age of growing literacy, and even if they could not read these writings themselves they were exposed regularly to individuals who could read or summarize them. Furthermore, one may suppose that they would have obtained much of the content of these works through sermons. At times there is evidence that the saints used the prayer formulas that were disseminated so widely in the fourteenth century: the prayerbook of Peter of Luxembourg contains a long rhythmic prayer, analogous to *Ave caput Christi gratum,* in which each of the streams of blood flowing from Christ's members is compared to one of the four rivers of the Earthly Paradise. At least as readily, the saints would have had access to the works of art that were on public display in churches and chapels everywhere they went, and often in homes and along roadsides as well. (When Peter of Luxembourg is said to have venerated crucifixes that he encountered in his travels, the reference is presumably to roadside shrines.) At least two saints' lives echoed the motif of the *arma Christi.* Jane Mary of Maillé not only kept Christ's wounds, death, cross, crown of thorns, gall, and implements of execution "before the eyes of her mind," but had the symbols of the passion depicted on parchment as a way of inducing others to recall Christ's fate, and had the insignia of the passion portrayed on her personal seal. And in one of Margaret of Faenza's visions Christ appeared to her with the implements of the passion round about him. One might reasonably expect that artistic representations had an influence on the visions the saints beheld, and that they reported having seen what art had conditioned them to expect. At the very least, the heightened fervor found in literature and art of the passion encouraged the saints in their own devotion.[57]

Identification with Christ through Devotion

Integral to much of the saints' devotion was their liturgical realism—their consciousness that the liturgy genuinely made present the sufferings of Christ, and that full sensitivity would make this presence apparent. It was not only in public liturgy that the saints' attained this consciousness but in private devotions as well. In their own rooms, along roadsides, or virtually anywhere, the saints immersed themselves in devotional ceremony which gave them a sense of identification with the suffering Christ. To be sure, there was a further dimension to the public liturgical enactment: theology guaranteed that when mass was celebrated the sacrifice of Calvary was made fully present. This was not the case with private ritual. Yet the subjective sense of assimilation to *Christus patiens* could nonetheless be attained in private devotions as well.

The central object around which these devotions revolved was the crucifix. Sculpted, painted, or drawn, it was a valued memento. Numerous simple, unrefined crucifixes from this century have survived, and no doubt there were countless others which were later discarded for lack of aesthetic appeal. It would be difficult to exaggerate their significance in the saints' lives. Catherine of Siena, Clare Gambacorta, and Andrew Corsini are casually mentioned as having prayed before crucifixes, and the custom was presumably routine. Peter of Luxembourg wore one at all times over his heart, and delighted in praying before one. Every day he prostrated himself before the cross in prayer, preferably in a secluded spot. From youth, whenever he came upon a cross in his journeys he venerated it with utmost piety. As a canon at Paris he took pride in bearing the processional cross. With similar devotion, Peter of Fulgineo embraced a crucifix at his death. After undergoing a religious conversion, James Oldo spent much time in the church of St. Mark of Lodi, where he turned his artistic

talents to painting a crucifixion scene with Mary and John at the foot
of the cross. Robert of Salentino wore a small wooden cross on his
breast. Jane Mary of Maillé had a representation of the crucifixion on
parchment, which she carried beneath her tunic, "that the memory of
the Lord's passion might be implanted on her heart"; she handled it
every now and then, as an exercise in devotion. Henry Suso encountered two remarkable crucifixes in the course of his travels: one of
wood, in a shrine at a small town, where people deposited wax ex-
votos in return for miracles, and a life-size stone image in a monastery, which allegedly exuded blood from the wound in the side during
one Lent. (Suso himself was accused of concocting this miracle to obtain donations from those who came to behold it, and when sentiments were arouses against him he had to flee for his life.)[58]

An episode from the life of Clare Gambacorta underscores the significance ascribed to crucifixes. When Galeazzo of Siena was out traveling one day toward the end of the century, he passed by a church
half-ruined in war, and at a distance he saw a small crucifix within a
niche in a walled-up window. As he beheld this crucifix, he heard a
voice say to him, "Take me to the convent of St. Dominic which has
recently been built at Pisa, where I shall be preserved with great devotion." He took the crucifix and proceeded to that convent, along with
a great throng of people; all who saw the crucifix were moved to compassion for the suffering of Christ. When he arrived, Clare, who had
recently been made prioress of the convent, was praying in the
church; she was interrupted by a voice telling her to rise and go to the
entrance, where her celestial bridegroom awaited her. She was astonished, but continued in prayer until she heard the same message
again, and knew that the voice was angelic. She went to the entrance,
where Galeazzo presented his discovery. The nuns received it with
copious tears, and in great solemnity they placed it on their high altar,
and covered it with veils. Displayed to visitors through a grate, the
crucifix was renowned for the miracles it worked. The narrator who
tells all this adds piously that it is hoped the nuns in that convent will
follow Clare's footsteps and instructions and conform themselves to
Christ by suffering on the cross along with him.[59]

Apart from crucifixes, the fourteenth century saw a renewed fascination for relics of the passion. Devotion to such relics had been part
of popular piety for centuries: fragments of the cross were venerated
in the East even in the fourth century, and eventually the nails, the
tablet from above Christ's head, the column from the flagellation, the
crown of thorns, and other items became centers of veneration. The
Crusades brought renewed fascination for such objects in the West,
and those who had been to the Holy Land during the age of the
Crusades brought back implements of the passion such as the soldiers'

pincers, hammer, ladder, and even dice. Again in the fourteenth century there was a surge of interest in such objects, and once again an
increase in their range: the bandage used to cover Christ's eyes, tufts
of hair yanked from his head, the loin-cloth that had preserved his
modesty, pieces of Judas's silver, the torn curtain from the Temple,
and other such mementos of the passion, having long since disappeared, were alleged to have made their return. In 1354, a special
feast commemorating the lance and nails was introduced into the
Western liturgy. Likewise, it was during this century that the shroud
now preserved in Turin was first recorded as being known in Western
Europe. Where relics directly related to the passion were not available, relics indirectly reminiscent of it could be miraculously produced. Thus, miraculous bleeding hosts became common in this
century; numerous churches had such hosts in their possession.[60]

Devotion to such relics, while not omnipresent in the saints' lives,
can at times be found. Jane Mary of Maillé, for example, managed to
obtain several fragments of the cross from aristocratic friends; "for
the praise and glory of the Lord's passion" she had them enshrined in
silver gilt crosses and donated to various churches. One witness in her
canonization proceedings testified that she had great reverence for
the passion and for the "mystery of the holy cross." His best evidence
for this devotion was her having obtained a fragment of the "true
cross," which she proposed to divide in two and deposit in two gilded
silver crosses she had had made for different churches. She had a
Franciscan friar cut the fragment with a small knife, and at once
blood flowed out; she collected the liquid, and deposited it along with
the wood in each of the metal crosses. In presenting one of the reliquaries to the church of St. Martin, she asked that each time a priest
went to the altar to celebrate mass he should carry this cross in memory of the passion; the canons of the church readily consented. Later
she was curious whether the blood was still in the cross, and she asked
the witness several times to ascertain whether it was. He replied that
he would be happy to inquire, though the result of any such inquiry
remains unspecified.[61]

Devotion to the *Via dolorosa* in Jerusalem, with its "stations" representing scenes from Christ's way of the cross, blossomed in the fourteenth century as never before, but the custom had not yet arisen of
erecting a series of statues representing these "stations of the cross" so
that pious Christians could reenact Christ's progression in their home
countries. Nonetheless, Henry Suso devised a system of devotions
which anticipated this development. He worked out a system of
streets, along which he passed as he reflected on the various stages in
Christ's path. On the first street he desired to leave friends and possessions behind, and to suffer grief and poverty; in the second he

resolved to repudiate honor, since Christ had become a worm; and so he proceeded through four streets, and onward through further stages of the passion.[62]

A different way of replicating a pilgrimage to the Holy City was to visit a church where a sepulcher representing that of Christ had been erected, as Jane Mary of Maillé did; Peter of Luxembourg, we are told, desired ardently to visit the sepulcher itself. A more vivid re-enactment of Christ's experience was James Oldo's actually lying down in a sepulcher representing that of Christ. He did so at first out of idle curiosity, to see "which of us is taller, Christ or I." No sooner did he lie down, though, than the the Holy Spirit worked a transformation in his soul, "like white-hot iron in frigid water." He lost all his taste for the vanities of the world, and converted at once to a life of piety. This incident is a perfect example of the effect that devotional reenactment was meant to have: it transformed a sinner into a saint, or made the saint a more perfect one, precisely through subjective assimilation to Christ.[63]

Reading the gospel accounts of the passion appears to have been popular. Rulman Merswin read the passion story in an unsuccessful effort to quell his temptations. Jane Mary of Maillé read the passion according to John daily; when she was seriously ill she had someone else read it to her as she sighed and groaned out of sorrow for Christ's death. She began reading it late one Holy Thursday evening, but was almost immediately interrupted by what she referred to as rapture, and thus was unable to continue until the next morning. And Elzear of Sabran, Villana de' Botti, and Henry Suso's mother all had the passion narrative read to them as their own deaths approached.[64]

Ludolph of Saxony recommended various forms of devotional practice related to the passion, especially in his "acts of conformation." One should not merely meditate passively on how Christ was slapped on the face but should conform oneself to Christ by giving oneself a mild slap (*alapam moderatam*). Recalling Judas's false kiss, one should exert oneself to action contrary to the betrayer's: one should take a crucifix and kiss the feet of Christ with sincere faith and devotion, deeming oneself unworthy to kiss his mouth as Judas presumed to do. If one does not have a crucifix handy, one should substitute the ground or some other object, as one feels inspired. One saint who observed such practices was Bridget of Sweden, who every Friday would burn herself with candle wax as a reminder of Christ's wounds, and would eat bitter herbs in memory of the gall that Christ was made to taste on Good Friday. Another was Clare of Rimini, who on Good Friday would have herself bound to a stone column in the piazza and beaten severely.[65]

Robert of Salentino was more extreme than most saints in his imitation of the passion. He found a tree that had grown in the shape of a cross, presumably a Y-shaped cross such as was popular in four-teenth-century art; he cut it down and carried it to his cell. Then he cultivated the practice of suspending himself from it while saying the Pater Noster. As he died, too, he observed such devotion by holding his arms outstretched in the form of a cross, inspiring his biographer to comment, "Oh truly blessed man, who began from the cross, pro-ceeded in the cross, and at last died on the cross!"[66]

The saint who commemorated the passion most systematically in her own devotions was Dorothy of Montau. Her confessor tells at some length of the exercises she put herself through; they amount to a kind of Christian yoga, in which bodily postures were correlated with meditations on Christ's sufferings. At night she would extend her arms in the form of a cross and stand until she was worn out. Then she would stand against a wall, with her arms sometimes sup-ported by nails (which she seems to have held with her fingers), while at other times she would insert her fingers into holes in the wall to help bear the weight. In memory of Christ's threefold prayer in Geth-semane, she had her own threefold devotion: first she would kneel with her hands stretched out in the form of a cross, then she would kneel with her hands joined and raised to heaven, the way images of Christ showed him praying on Mount Olivet, and finally she would fall onto her face with her hands extended cross-wise. In memory of Christ's arrest, she stood sorrowing, with her hands raised on high and held rigid above her head. Recalling how Christ's hands were bound with merciless tightness, sometimes in front of him and some-times behind, she stood for an hour with her hands crossed in front of herself, then she would stand with her hands behind her, then with her hands still thus held she would fall backward. Reflecting on how Christ was led to Annas, Caiaphas, Pilate, and Herod, she would bal-ance herself on her toes and hands, move her hands forward as far as she could, remain thus poised in meditation or prayer, then move her hands back to where she started. At this point her confessor and biog-rapher says that if anyone finds this exercise too difficult it will suffice to proceed with head bowed, mourning and sorrowful, in memory of this phase of the passion. In observance of the flagellation, she first went through a pantomime of being disrobed, then stood as if em-bracing a pillar, then pretended to be clothed again. And so forth, through the remaining stages in the passion.[67]

In conclusion, Dorothy's biographer comments that exercises of this kind, if done with proper Christian devotion and accompanied by meditation on the passion, can arouse the fire of divine love, so that outer motions may prompt inward betterment of soul.[68] As already suggested, though, these techniques are more reminiscent of certain

forms of yoga than they are of standard Christian meditation. Such
elaborate interaction of mind and body in prayer is not typical of medieval devotion. What is distinctively Christian is the ideal of acting
out the salvific suffering of Christ; thus, while the outward obser-
vances are strikingly unfamiliar in their context, the intention is entirely traditional.

Johan Huizinga wrote with dismay about the multiplication of devotional forms in late medieval Christianity.[69] One can indeed discern
a proliferation of devotions in many areas: devotions to the saints,
devotions to Mary, and not the least devotions to the passion. What
this development signals more than anything else is the rise of piety
among the urban laity, seeking to share in the richness of the Christian tradition without benefit of the training and discipline available
to the clergy. Dorothy of Montau is merely the extreme case of a tendency more widely observed; many others in her age were endeavor-
ing to identify themselves through homegrown rituals with the
suffering Savior, and the devices that they put together for themselves varied from the simple and easy to the exceptionally rigorous.
Anyone could venerate a roadside crucifix with a few prayers, but
only a few would be inclined to reproduce Dorothy's elaborate exercises—even when her confessor provided helpful advice for substitu-
tion. What all these devotions provided was a sense that one was
bringing oneself within the inner circle of devotees. As Christ told
Bridget of Sweden, those who despise him and neglect his love are the
ones responsible for his sufferings; failure to venerate the crucified
Christ could be represented as culpable and contemptuous neglect. As
he told the forest brother, one must help him bear his cross by carrying it in one's mind. Neglect of the passion was tantamount in some
measure to responsibility for it, but by meditating on it, and by making use of those devotional aids to meditation that late medieval
culture was so fond of, one could assure oneself that one was doing
what one must to absolve oneself of guilt. The alternative was to recognize oneself in that throng of unruly ruffians who dragged Christ
through the streets, and fourteenth-century authors labored to make
that identification uncomfortable.

Identification with Christ through Asceticism

As the case of Dorothy of Montau makes abundantly clear, there is at
best a thin line of demarcation betwen devotional and ascetic practices. Those seeking to identify themselves with the suffering Christ
might do so by means of ritual devotions or by means of rigorous
mortification, but the distinction is not always easy to draw. Yet there

were some who more clearly than others strove to imitate Christ by actually inflicting pain upon themselves. At least implicitly, the model of the suffering Christ had always been a main source of inspiration for Christian asceticism; in the late Middle Ages, the obsession with the cross led to a widespread, overwhelming, and quite explicit desire to share in Christ's agony through self-imposed ascetic practices. Not content merely to bear up patiently under sufferings sent to them by God and their fellow human beings (a motif we have already discussed), they took matters into their own hands.

The lives of the saints are replete with examples. Thus, Jane Mary of Maillé was struck with "great compassion" one year during Passion Week, and desired to "suffer something for Christ." She took a long, sharp thorn, and stuck it into her own head, where it remained until Holy Thursday, when it fell out spontaneously without even leaving a scar. Much the same tendency can be seen in the lives of Catherine of Siena, James Oldo, and Villana de' Botti. The classic instance of deliberate assimilation to the crucified Christ is Henry Suso, who "felt an ardent desire to bear on his body some sign of the sympathy he felt for the painful sufferings of his crucified Lord," and who thus proceeded to wear a nail-studden cross, flagellate himself, and in other ways reenact Christ's passion. He engraved the monogram "IHS" on his chest with a stylus: "From the sharp stabs the blood flowed copiously out of the flesh and ran down over his body and down his chest. It was such a lovely sight that in the glow of his love he did not heed the pain much." Then he went, still bleeding, to pray beneath a crucifix. One is tempted to diagnose severe masochism, but the reason for Suso's exhilaration was surely not that he enjoyed the pain in itself, but that he found in it a mystical sense of identification with his Savior. The saints' could even cite scriptural basis for these practices: James Oldo's biographer explained that by his mortification the saint was crucified along with Christ, as Paul had enjoined (Gal. 2:29).[70]

Peter Olafsson strove to participate in Christ's sufferings, and to this end he bound hair-cords so tightly around his loins and chest that his flesh was bruised and wounded. He further wounded himself with briars and brambles, strewing them on the floor of his room and then rolling about on the floor. He flagellated himself. Night and day he wore an iron breastplate which was "more harsh than any hairshirt." He immersed himself up to his navel in cold water during the winter. His biographer suggests two explanations for such conduct: on the one hand it was intended to purge himself in time of temptation; on the other it was that he might be "inebriated with the sweetness of the Savior's wounds, for it was sweet for him, and the highest consolation, to be wounded with Jesus Christ." It is clear that to the biographer, and probably also to the ascetic himself, these motives were complementary rather than mutually exclusive: it was by identification with the suffering Christ that one kept oneself from the temptations of the world.[71]

If a psychiatrist would suggest masochism, an anthropologist might seek to explain these practices in terms of status gained within the saint's society.[72] Again, one must keep in mind that the sources do not provide or intend to provide the information we would need to discern the saints' motives. The sources are not much more helpful as guides to the saints' actual reception in their society, but what they do say suggests that mortification did little to enhance the saints' renown among their contemporaries. Taking the vitae as implicitly theological documents, though, we can specify confidently the message their authors meant to convey: by means of these rituals of identification, the saints aroused in themselves and in those about them a keener awareness than Christendom customarily held of that anguish which Christ himself wanted to make known. One might go further and suggest that, like the Virgin, the saints were mediators of compassion: aroused to pity by the accounts of their suffering, and made aware that the passion of the saints followed from their compassion for Christ, fourteenth-century Christians might be led thus indirectly to a more vivid sympathy for their Savior. By making the anguish of Christ contemporary and graphic, the saints could serve as aids to the devotion of their society.

It has been suggested that it is the function of saints in any era to go beyond the bounds of what is normally expected, to engage in extravagant, demonstrative, sensational deeds, which challenge people's common sense and provoke their response.[73] Indeed, it is part of medieval and Catholic tradition that the saints are individuals who go beyond the commandments of God and accept the fullness of the counsels. Thus, John Marienwerder, Dorothy of Montau's confessor and biographer, says that it was not enough for Dorothy to accept sufferings patiently, or even to welcome them gladly (*gaudenter*); going further, in accordance with that fortitude which is not merely a cardinal virtue but a gift of the Holy Spirit, she inflicted sufferings upon herself, thus gaining the merit for supererogatory compliance with God's counsels.[74]

What was important to the contemporaries of these fourteenth-century saints was that by living such wildly abnormal lives they were setting themselves apart from the rest of humankind, and thus making themselves useful to others as intercessors. A figure such as Peter of Luxembourg might arouse suspicion during his lifetime among his pious associates, most of whom seem to have thought his piety extreme. Yet no sooner did he die than the people of Avignon began to capitalize on his efficacy as a miracle-working intercessor, and his associates then cooperated with the populace by testifying at his beatification proceedings that he had indeed been a saint. The voice of the people remained very much the voice of God, and what the people wanted was a figure who stood effectively before God's throne and served there as their patron. From the viewpoint of late medieval society, *that* was the point of the extravagant supererogation. And in an age when suffering was a daily experience, it took a great deal to impress others with the extraordinary character of one's suffering.

But why did the extravagance have to take the form of suffering? Why not superabundant charity, or prayer? The saints of the era did engage in these activities as well, but for many if not most of them suffering played a more crucial role. To explain that fact, it is not enough to appeal to the Anselmian satisfaction theory of atonement; that theology remained a constant in Christian culture long before and long after the fourteenth century, while emphases in the notion of saintliness shifted. Is it possible that people in an age which demanded so much suffering were looking for exemplars who could show them the proper way to suffer? More plausibly one might argue the opposite: that in an age that was trying its best to cope with suffering, those who gladly embraced pain and inflicted it on themselves were utterly incomprehensible, and thus were the most obviously distinctive of heroes, and the most logical candidates for intercessors.

In any event, the saints' strongly positive evaluation of suffering is clear. Suffering was for them the key to holiness. As John Marienwerder explained, Dorothy of Montau afflicted herself with mortifications so that she might be a perfect imitator of Christ, for "it is more perfect to imitate Christ in sufferings than in actions."[75] In this claim, the central themes of passivity, patience, and passion once again converge.

5
Penitence

*A*rroused to keen awareness of their responsibilities before the Savior who had redeemed them and would one day come to judge them, the saints of the fourteenth century often developed exceptionally sensitive consciences. In this respect John of Caramola was typical. Hired at one stage in his life to stand watch over a vineyard, he was utterly scrupulous in his performance of the task. Even when assured that it would be permissible, he refused to take a single bunch of grapes for himself. Marveling at such a strict conscience, his biographer concluded that "it is a trait of holy minds to acknowledge guilt where there is no guilt." The theme is not original: almost the identical words occur in the life of Mary of Oignies. Yet here too the fourteenth century heightened the fervor attached to inherited norms.[1]

The penitential fervor of the century is perhaps more difficult to comprehend than the patience or even the devotion to the passion. Unjust suffering can arouse sympathy no matter how it is borne, and it is not difficult to see how an event so brutal as Christ's passion might excite strong emotions. The saints' extraordinary penitence, though, seems to have been simply misconceived: they attributed to themselves guilt when their actions were innocent even by contemporary standards. If their patience and their devotion to the passion entailed exceptional reactions to correctly perceived states of affairs, their penitence suggests they were venerated in part for having cultivated erroneous notions about themselves.

Problematic as this aspect of fourteenth-century sanctity was, it nonetheless lay at the heart of the era's conception of sainthood. In some respects it was even more central than the motifs we have already examined. More directly than these other themes, the penitential zeal of the saints focused their attention inward, subjecting them to that discomforting scrutiny that was a prerequisite for any moral reform. If the extreme patience and the extreme devotion of the saints were supposed to arouse their devotees to heighten their own religious consciousness, that intention was all the more explicit in the saints' penitence. Similarly, if the saints' constant submission to adversity and their assimilation to Christ underscored their vulnerability and their need for divine aid, their consciousness of sin manifested a far more central weakness and made the work of God on their behalf all the more clearly a pressing need.

The great saints of all ages have accused themselves of being the greatest of sinners. Teresa of Avila testified eloquently to this mentality. In earlier times John Cassian had given a parable of two men entering a room to take inventory of its furnishings—one a man with dim vision, who could make out only the largest items of furniture, and the other a man with keen eyesight, who could discern even the smallest trinkets. So likewise, a person with refined moral sensitivity could detect the minute defects of his soul that would escape the attention of a less discerning person.[2] Such discernment is not always easy to distinguish from mere scrupulosity, a theme that claimed greater attention in the theology of the fifteenth century than it did in that of the fourteenth century.[3] If scrupulosity is taken to involve a kind of spiritual hypochondria, though, or a tendency to see flaws where there clearly and simply are none, this is not what the saints' biographers meant to describe. What they attributed to the saints was a sensitivity to worldly attachments which are the common lot of unregenerate humankind, and which linger, albeit weakened, even in the saintly individual. As we shall see, there is at times evidence that the saints may in fact have been scrupulous, and that this condition may have driven their associates to desperation. What the hagiographers praise, though, is not so much this tendency as the willingness to undertake radical purgation of one's soul, to strip away from it all attachment to creaturely delights. Not that this form of spirituality is unproblematic, but the problems are different from those of mere scrupulosity.

In this area as in others, it is easy to convict the hagiographers of imbalance: their emphasis on guilt tends to obscure the assurance of forgiveness that plays an important role in the New Testament and in much of Christian theology. One might argue that the rhythm of spiritual life requires a moment of compunction that leads spontaneously to a conviction of grace; one might further suggest that compunction can be induced by example, while its release must arise from one's own experience. Yet readers schooled in consciousness of their guilt

without being led to expect forgiveness would be more likely to devel-
op lasting scrupulosity than to come spontaneously to a sense of release from their guilt, whatever the hagiographers' intention. Perhaps
the best defense of the hagiographers against the charge of leading
their readers into neurosis is that their saints' exceptional moral sensitivity was a counterbalance to the natural insensitivity presupposed
in their readers. Townspeople who were just being coaxed to undertake frequent confession did not need assurance of forgiveness as
much as they needed reminders of the sins that required forgiveness. The theological assumption of universal proclivity toward
worldliness had a practical corollary: it was more dangerous to leave
the reader's conscience insufficiently challenged than to risk arousing
excessive sensitivity.

Manifestations in the Saints' Lives

In her penitential ardor Catherine of Siena was a paradigm of
saintliness. At the age of six she was out walking down the street when
she beheld a vision of Christ, Peter, Paul, and John, but was distracted
momentarily when her brother came and tugged at her, calling her to
move along. When she lifted her eyes back to the vision, it was gone.
She burst into tears, "upbraiding herself bitterly for having allowed
her eyes to stop looking up towards heaven." Later she had a similar
experience when her brother distracted her from a vision of St. Dominic; although she turned her head only slightly, and immediately
turned back, she wept and castigated herself for this "terrible sin." In
early adolescence, encouraged by her mother and sister, she began
paying attention to her personal appearance. She did nothing else to
attract male attention, and in fact she fled from men as if they were
serpents. Yet she had spent time adorning her "putrid flesh" to "de-
ceive some poor mortal," and that was in itself a cause for later grief.
In confession she would berate herself for this offense "with so many
sobs and tears that one would have thought she had committed heav-
en knows what sin." Her confessor protested that there was no sin at
all in what she had done—perhaps some slight excess, but no violation
of God's law. In response, she lifted her eyes to God and bewailed his
having sent her a confessor who found excuses for her sins. In this
and in other matters she was so severe with herself that if her confessor had not known better he "would have believed her to be at fault
where there was no fault, and where indeed there was if anything
merit in what she had done." To frustrate her family's efforts at finding her a husband, she shaved her hair off, "hating it as the cause of
her grievous sin." She undertook severe mortification in payment for

the pains she knew her sins deserved. When critics murmured against her in her later life, she took their detraction as punishment for her sins: "All the evil that happened to her she attributed to her sins, and all the good to God." Once when two friars were going to visit a certain hermit they asked her if she wanted to go along; because she was in rapture and not entirely aware of what she was saying, she falsely said yes. Immediately she felt remorse for this "lie," and weeping continuously she refused all food and drink for three days and nights to expiate the offense.[4]

The offenses of which Catherine accused herself unquestionably seem trivial; so, for that matter, does Augustine's youthful theft of pears, for which he upbraided himself no less vigorously than Catherine, and for similar reasons. The essential question is not whether the particular offense is momentous, but whether a soul that is properly disposed is capable of such an offense at all. Like an act of minor rudeness that is in itself insignificant but calls into question one's attitudes toward other persons, Catherine's vanity and lapses from full devotion to God seem to have troubled her not so much because they were objectively grievous but because they raised for her serious doubts about the orientation of her will. If she intended to set aside worldly attachments and direct herself wholly toward matters spiritual, her lapses were not mere temporary setbacks but signals of imperfect resolution. In Augustinian terms, she was forced to recognize her own divided will, and that awareness seemed radically incompatible with the goals she had set for herself.[5]

Peter of Luxembourg, too, was known to have an exceptionally sensitive conscience, though in his case we know all too little about the nature of his offenses and his attitudes toward them. The witnesses for his canonization proceedings were less interested in such matters than in the outward signs of his penitence, especially his penitential devotions. Daily he prayed for pardon of his sins. When he was a student at Paris he confessed once a week ordinarily, purging himself of the most trifling offenses. When his conscience was in any way uneasy, he went to confession more often. Daily he examined his conscience, and even asked his associates to help him recall what he had done: where he had gone, with whom he had spoken, and what offenses he had committed. One day he neglected to jot down his sins, and the next day he asked his brother Andrew to help him recall them. Andrew could remember none. Peter asked if he had not had something to drink between dinner and supper, and his brother said yes, but did not think that was sinful. Peter went off to a room by himself and spent the next two hours or so listing his peccadillos. When he traveled, one of his servants carried the folded scraps of paper detailing all these offenses, but discreetly avoided reading any of them. Later, in Avignon, Peter continued his practice of writing down his sins; he would do so anywhere and anytime, before a hearth, while in his oratory, or during his studies. His confessor told him to discontinue this practice, and if necessary merely confess more often. The result was that Peter would go to his regular confessor at least three times a week—and three or four times a week, if not more, he would rise at night to beat on the doors of his chaplains' quarters. (His chaplains, unlike his normal confessor, lived in the same building with Peter.) If one of them refused to answer and hear his confession, he would go to the other, though eventually they both became deaf to these nightly pangs of conscience, and he had to withdraw to his room. The next day he would greet them cheerfully, with no sign of displeasure. (The *Vita prima* does, however, quote him as reminding his confessor that the job of a judge of souls is to sit and listen, while the penitent's role is to kneel before him.) Ultimately he resumed his earlier practice of writing out lists, though he tried to conceal the fact. Others testified that he never committed more than minor sins, but he himself "was unable in confession to weigh the gravity of his own sins." Thus he bemoaned these peccadillos with heartfelt contrition and confessed them, often barefoot as a sign of humility, with saddened voice and copious tears. His confessor at Avignon testified that whenever Peter confessed he sobbed profusely, and would be unable to speak for the space of a "Miserere mei Deus"; sometimes he would shed so many tears that he would leave a puddle where he had knelt, as if someone had poured water in front of him. Immersed in the immoral environment of Avignon, he had serious doubts about his own salvation. His confessor often found him afflicted with torment on this question, and frequently in tears; sometimes it was only with difficulty that he could be pacified.[6]

Peter's penitential solicitude extended to others, as well as to himself. His reading of Scripture (it is not clear which passages) caused him to wonder if anyone could be saved. He encouraged his servants to confess frequently; so that they could not plead that they were unable to afford the offering that it was customary to give the confessor, he provided a small amount of money for them each week for that purpose. One of them nonetheless protested that he did not know what to say in confession, to which Peter replied, "If you never confess you will never know how to confess, but if you become accustomed to it you will soon know what to say." This exhortation worked.[7]

A small treatise attributed to Peter, *The Way to Salvation*, focuses specifically on the need for penitence and sacramental confession. One portion discusses the four "advocates," sent by the devil, who attempt to dissuade a Christian from confessing. The first of these advocates is shame at admitting one's sins; it suggests that one should not tell one's offenses for fear of being disgraced. The second is hypocrisy, which advises that one should not risk the good reputation that one enjoys with one's confessor. The third is the expectation of a long life, which will protest, "My friend, you are still young, and can confess a long time from now." The fourth is fear of doing penance. Each of these opponents must be overcome, in turn.[8]

Peter's penitential spirit manifested itself also in the stringent recommendations that he made in correspondence with his sister. She should not give way to feminine vanity, such as provocative hairdos: "Alas, if young women knew the evils of which they are the cause, they would rather have their hair be burned on their heads before the whole world than to wear it in this manner." She should be constantly on guard against careless words, and should keep herself busy with prayer, reading, writing, chanting psalms, or other pious employment, to keep herself safe from diabolical assaults. "There are so many occasions to fall: the Enemy, the world, and the flesh have such great power at the present time that few can resist them."[9]

Many of Catherine's and Peter's contemporaries shared their proclivities, troubling themselves greatly over minor sins if not imagined offenses. Andrew Corsini's conscience was distraught over every small offense he had committed. Francis Patrizzi wiped away with tears and sighs those venial sins which sometimes steal secretly into one's soul; he was not aware of ever having committed a mortal sin, and he prayed every night that he might die sooner than commit a genuinely grievous offense, yet he remained upset about venial sins, and when he committed any he atoned for them with daily penance, morning and evening. Henry Suso once found himself holding the hands of two young girls, in public, and punished himself for the offense with vigorous flagellation and other punishments. Elzear of Sabran repented and confessed the smallest misdeeds with great sorrow and tears, viewing himself as the greatest of sinners (though his wife, Dauphine of Puimichel, rivaled him for that title). Bridget of Sweden confessed her sins frequently. Her confessor testified that she lamented over light offenses as others do over the most grievous, and she examined carefully everything she did or said. Whenever she said anything that was displeasing to God, she immediately felt a bitter taste in her mouth, like that of sulphur, so she would commit the offending words to memory and rush to confess them with great sorrow and tears. When anyone else said things that were improper, she manifested equal sensitivity to their offense: her nose was suffused with the odor of sulphur. She feared greatly for the sins of her sons, and wept for them daily.[10]

Dorothy of Montau was not outdone in penitence by any of her fellows. From age six she hastened eagerly to confession, putting her older sisters and the family maids to shame and arousing their irritation. After marriage she went more often than she had earlier—daily, and sometimes even several times a day—as her conscience was stricken by even the lightest offenses. She bewailed her own sins and those of others, shedding a veritable torrent of tears on account of her own deficiency. After the mystical extraction of her heart, she became troubled if she passed a single day without hearing the Lord's voice, and if this happened she would conclude that she had committed some sin that day, at least the sin of acedia or sloth. The Lord instructed her to review her entire life and repent of whatever needed correction. She did so, and the closer she looked the more clearly she perceived what was displeasing to the Lord. Increasingly she resembled the man in Cassian's parable who, having keen eyesight, could discern the smallest items in his household inventory. From that time on, she confessed not only her recent sins but those of her entire life, more systematically than ever before, with the aid of divine illumination regarding her past sins. Whatever activities she was engaged in, the Lord would recall offenses to her mind; even as she was washing a bowl, she might suddenly think of some present or past sin, which the Lord then taught her to confess properly. After five years of this, the Holy Spirit finally gave her assurance that all these sins were mercifully forgiven. Yet she continued to sin anew and give herself fresh occasion for penitence. The Lord called to her attention that she was not pure and holy in her behavior, that she lacked absolute attention in prayer, that there was some flaw in her obedience, or that she was insufficiently circumspect in speech. Her words sometimes were or appeared to be false, injurious, frivolous, fawning, disparaging, or proud. Or the Lord would reproach her for insufficient fervor in imitating him. Thus reproached, she sat grieving and overcome with tears, and would cry out to the Lord for mercy and for aid in amending her life. Having had ample divine aid in the heightening of her consciousness of guilt, she sought divine support in its release.[11]

One occasion in particular illustrates the extent of Dorothy's sensitivity. On the vigil of All Saints' Day, when she was in her cell toward the end of her life, a young scholar brought her a warm dish of spiced fish. The fish were small, but nonetheless the portion was enough to last her for three meals. On seeing the dish, she gazed at it fondly, and she began to anticipate eating it. At once she grew angry at herself for looking too long and too fondly at such a delicacy. Much later that night she was still fretting, and she feared that the Lord would chastize her for her offense. She wept and perspired greatly, and sat immobile with fear of divine reprehension. Nor were her fears groundless: in a vision, God forced her to behold the fish, and told her, "If you delight in seeing and contemplating these, may you be contented and satisfied in contemplation of them." Sobbing, she cast herself down on the floor and begged the Lord to send her confessor so she could relieve herself of the misdeed. For two hours she wept, unable to release herself from the reproachful vision. Even after she had confessed and received communion the next morning she still felt great sorrow for her failing.[12]

Apart from the evidence already cited, there is further testimony in the saints' lives regarding frequent sacramental confession. Flora of Beaulieu confessed daily, and examined her conscience so minutely that she presented with sighs and sorrow, as grave misdeeds, items which the most experienced priests commonly viewed as singular virtues. She cherished her confessors as ministers of Christ, dispensers of God's mysteries, and fathers whom she followed with filial love, despite their apparent laxity. The moral sensitivity of Catherine of Siena brought her also to daily confession. Elizabeth of Portugal went to confession frequently, and had priests accompany her on her travels for this and other holy purposes. Elzear of Sabran made confession part of his regular preparation for communion, and required the members of his household to confess weekly. Urban V confessed often; before celebrating mass he would first confess, then recite certain psalms, presumably the traditional penitential psalms. Catherine of Sweden confessed daily, sometimes two or three times a day, knowing "that confession is the salvation of souls, the dissipator of vices, the restorer of virtues, the assailant of demons, and that it stops up the mouth of hell and opens the gates of heaven."[13]

Two occasions in particular called for confession: religious conversion and death. James Oldo made a careful confession of his sins after his conversion, and when Henry Suso won over a man who had not confessed in eighteen years, the man confessed with such remorse that both of them wept. One may assume that all of the saints confessed as death approached, and in some cases that fact is specified in their vitae. The biographer of Urban V mentions that he did so. Elzear of Sabran made a general confession, with devotion and tears, as he saw death coming, and afterward he made frequent further confessions. And Catherine of Siena made two general confessions of all her sins, passing into the afterlife with tears of contrition, thus following the examples of St. Martin, St. Jerome, and St. Augustine.[14]

An associate who was present at Catherine of Siena's death, and who narrated the details of the scene to another friend, gives some sense of how deep the penitential fervor ran. As she lay dying, having received extreme unction, she suffered through an hour and a half of agonizing demonic temptations. For part of this time she cried out, "I have sinned! Oh Lord, have mercy on me!" More than sixty times she repeated this formula, each time raising her right arm and then letting it fall on the bed. Then she repeated, "Holy God, have mercy on me!" and other formulas. Suddenly her mood changed to one of radiant consolation. But when she saw a cross she began beating her breast and lamenting her sin:

> It is my fault, oh eternal Trinity, that I have offended Thee so miserably with my negligence, ignorance, ingratitude, and disobedience, and many other defects. Wretch that I am! for I have not observed thy commandments, either those which are given in general to all, or those which Thy goodness laid upon me in particular! Oh mean creature that I am! . . . Didst Thou not command me, oh, my God! to abandon all thought of myself and to consider solely the praise and glory of Thy Name in the salvation of souls, and with this food alone, taken from the table of the most holy Cross, to comfort myself? But I have sought my own consolation. . . . Thou hast placed me in charge of souls . . . but I have been to them nothing but a mirror of human weakness; I have had no care of them; I have not helped them with continuous and humble prayer in Thy presence, nor have I given them sufficient examples of the good life or the warnings of salutary doctrine. Oh, mean creature that I am! with how little reverence have I received Thy innumerable gifts, the graces of such sweet torments and labours which it pleased Thee to accumulate on this fragile body, nor have I endured them with that burning desire and ardent love with which Thou didst send them to me. . . .

The narrator concludes that Catherine accused herself of these offenses "rather, as I think, for our example than for her own need." The logic here is what we have seen elsewhere: if so great a saint felt the burden of guilt to be so heavy, ordinary Christians should a fortiori acknowledge their guilt and repent.[15]

Well might even a saint approach death with trepidation. As Johan Huizinga points out, there was a widespread belief in the late fourteenth century that since the beginning of the Great Schism no one had gone to heaven.[16] Yet what is perhaps remarkable about the moral sensitivity of the saints is that it is free of obsession with the afterlife and its torments. Umberto Eco has characterized this age as one which "replaced the penitence of the soul with a penitence of the imagination, a summons to supernatural visions of suffering and blood," inducing fear not so much of sin but of punishment in hell.[17]

This is not, however, the tendency of the vitae. If the saints were absorbed in their sinfulness, their penitence brought them to an intense introspective concern with their souls rather than to an imaginative preoccupation with the afterlife.

Whatever the motives for this moral sensitivity, the saints' own contemporaries and biographers did not always view it as a desirable trait. On occasion they were at least ambivalent, seeing the habit of self-accusation as an unfortunate condition that the religious person must overcome, even if it signaled a holy intent. Thus, when Henry Suso learned that his early admission to the Dominican order had been secured by simony, he feared that his soul was doomed, no matter what he did. This apprehension lasted about ten years, and then Meister Eckhart, evidently seeing it as unrealistic, relieved him of it. Elzear of Sabran underwent a phase of extreme and more generalized penitence just after his religious conversion. He thought himself worthy of hell, indeed of a punishment a thousand times worse, rather than of God's mercy. It seemed to him that he was capable of committing all the evils in the world, and that he would in fact have committed them if God had not prevented him. In the midst of such meditations, though, he heard a voice say, "Do not afflict yourself so in considering your defects and sins, for my mercy is greater than your sins. But live with confidence, and trust firmly that I will not let you lose my grace at any time." Then he laughed, and desired that all could feel what he felt then. Gertrude of Delft, likewise, spent two weeks after her conversion crying incessantly for her sins; because of her tears, she merited remission of her sins, and when God revealed to her that they were forgiven she was able to live with confidence. Later, when certain beguines were in a church bewailing their sins, Gertrude told them that they had indeed offended the Lord greatly and should wipe out their sins with tears now, but that she knew they would not ultimately be damned. Such revelations were comforting, and bespoke a more positive mentality than frequently appears in the texts. In the case of Gertrude, though, the penitential stage is still presented as useful and even necessary, if temporary. And Elzear maintained his keen moral sensitivity, if not his brooding melancholy, throughout his life.[18]

At times obsession with sin was ascribed to the devil, who presumably was trying to induce despair. Thus, when Rulman Merswin gave up his mercantile career in 1347 it was to expiate his sins; but it was the devil who reminded him of all his past sins, he said, including those he had meanwhile forgotten. Eventually he overcame his brooding sense of guilt, and the one dark spot that still needed to be removed from his soul was his tendency to criticize others.[19]

If visions and revelations were at times consoling, they could also be incriminating. After Catherine of Siena had been distracted from one of her visions, both Mary and St. Paul appeared to her and scolded her for this offense. It was in a vision that Jane Mary of Maillé heard the Lord scold her harshly for her guilt, and in a vision that she then beheld the gravity and the general consequences of original sin. When Henry Suso declined an invitation to preach on the feast of the Assumption, and suggested a more eloquent preacher in his place, an angel came and berated him for refusing to fulfill the Virgin's desire. He wept and asked for reconciliation, and the angel replied that Mary seemed already to have gotten over her anger. Elzear of Sabran, having taken part in combat, fell sick with a high fever, and began to repent of his military engagement. He heard Christ say, "Elzear, you must know that in the war in which you fought you put yourself in danger of losing my grace. After you have repented, I want to inflict discipline on you for the offense." Then Elzear bent down and recited a psalm, while Christ beat him hard on the back at each verse—an incident commemorated in a statuary group still on display at Avignon. He fell asleep, and when he awoke he was cured and consoled. When Catherine of Sweden was in Rome with her mother Bridget, she became homesick and wanted to return to Sweden. She consented to being beaten until she recovered from this temptation; it was not wholly uprooted, though, until Mary appeared to her and upbraided her, whereupon she apologized to her mother for having offended God, the Virgin, and her so grievously.[20]

Even demonic apparitions sometimes served to bring a saint to consciousness of sin, and thus from the late medieval perspective they could have salutary effect. When Catherine of Sweden was a small girl, her companions induced her one day to indulge in the vain practice of playing with dolls. The next night she saw numerous unclean spirits in the form of dolls enter her room and flog her with whips. She was left black and blue all over her body but cured of her dissolution. Villana de' Botti, too, underwent a diabolically inspired conversion. Having fallen away from a life of piety when she became married, and having repudiated ashes and hairshirt in favor of gold and jewels, she was dressing herself one day in a fine robe, with gems and other ornaments. Looking into a mirror, she saw how much her soul was deformed: checking again and again, she saw in the mirror the image of a demon rather than her expected reflection. Crying, she cast off her fancy dress, went to a Dominican church, accepted penance for her sins, and began a new life.[21]

Some individuals entered religious life specifically to atone for their sins. Andrew Corsini had been dedicated to Mary even before his birth. While pregnant, his mother had a dream in which she gave birth to a wolf, which entered a church and was transformed into a white lamb. As he grew into adolescence, he became disobedient and quarrelsome, and took far greater delight in games, arms, and hunting than in religion. Once, when he said something unseemly to his mother, she said he was indeed a wolf, and then she explained his prenatal religious history. He repented, asked Mary to beg Christ's forgiveness, and ended up in the Carmelite order as a devotee of the Virgin to whom he had long since been dedicated. Gonsalvo Sancii, a Spaniard whose life in some ways resembles that of Ignatius Loyola, was given over to the wantonness of a military life until he became ill, and then he recognized the perversity of his ways. He repented, and in a revelation he learned that he could avoid damnation by renouncing the world and entering the Franciscans. His penitence lasted throughout his life: keenly aware of his own sins, he did not dare to judge anyone else; he thought of everyone else as good and holy, and only of himself as the worst of sinners; if he saw children beaten or friars punished for their faults, he sympathized with them, and said, "Alas for me, who should be hit and punished as a miserable sinner—but what have these innocent ones done?"[22]

There was a long tradition in Christian hagiography of the penitent saint, or rather there were two traditions. On the one hand there were the saints whom legend represented as perpetrators of some particular sin, such as theft in the case of Dismas or lust in that of Mary the Egyptian. These saints were commonly seen as driven by providence toward their conversions, whereupon they abruptly turned in horror from that overwhelming sin with which they were beset. One of the best examples is Julian the Hospitaller, whose blood lust was destined (so a deer prophesied) to lead him to parricide; he fled from his home to avoid that sin, yet in the end killed his parents one day when he failed to recognize them sleeping together in his bed, and assumed that his wife was in bed with a lover. Recognizing his sin, he converted and spent the remainder of his life running a hospice and ferryboat for travelers.[23] Quite distinct from these saints are those others whose sinfulness is vaguer, amounting essentially to a general worldliness, and whose conversion is more gradual and subtle. The classic case is Augustine, whose devotion to the world was manifested in but not exhausted by his lust and ambition, and who recognized even at the time he wrote his *Confessions* that his life was still one of proclivity toward sin.[24] Other examples include Francis of Assisi, Ignatius Loyola, and Teresa of Avila. By and large, the saints of the fourteenth century who underwent conversions fall into the latter category: they began immersed in a secular way of life, their conversions were by their own admission painfully incomplete, and they continued to view themselves as sinners.

A saint often chosen as a special model and patroness during this

century was Mary Magdalene, the traditional patroness of penitent
sinners and of weepers. James Oldo, on being converted to a religious
life, took her as his model. Dalmatius Moner did the same. Likewise,
Catherine of Siena, to whom Christ gave the Magdalene as a mother
after her own mother died, identified with her as a fellow penitent,
lover of Christ, and contemplative. Along with Mary Magdalene,
Catherine lay prostrate at Christ's feet, in tears, begging for mercy,
deploring her sin, and hoping to hear the words, "Your sins are forgiven you." She developed a special devotion for Mary Magdalene,
and imitated her as much as she could, in hopes of forgiveness for her
sins. Echoes of the same devotion occur in the life of Dorothy of
Montau.[25]

But if the saints themselves looked backward to Mary Magdalene as
a model, the prophets among them might have looked forward to a
parallel that is perhaps more illuminating: the case of Martin Luther.
While the reformer was a theologian and churchman rather than
popular cult figure, his life does illustrate broad trends in the religious culture of late medieval Europe. Tortured with feelings of
guilt in his early years (if we may trust his own later accounts), the
reformer-to-be tried to soothe his conscience by following the regimen of his convent, by availing himself of penance and the other
sacraments, and by drawing upon the saints' treasury of superabundant merits, but to no avail.[26] During these early years he would
gladly have received Gertrude of Delft's sense of assurance that she
had merited forgiveness by virtue of her penitence. Ultimately his
solution was closer to that of Elzear of Sabran, or rather that given to
Elzear by a divine voice: "Do not afflict yourself so in considering
your defects and sins, for my mercy is greater than your sins. But live
with confidence, and trust firmly that I will not let you lose my grace
at any time."

It is relatively easy to comprehend Luther's scruples, in part because his life is preserved for us in far richer detail than that of any
fourteenth-century saint, and largely because the details that we have
for Luther are stripped of obviously legendary elements (though the
demons encountered by Catherine of Sweden and Villana de' Botti
did have their rough analogue at the Wartburg and elsewhere). No
doubt many modern readers find it easier to sympathize with Luther
because he *overcame* his brooding preoccupation with sin, as few of the
late medieval saints appear to have done or tried to do. For them, or
at least for many of them, a life of continual affliction with guilt was a
given: from their viewpoint they were in fact guilty, and they deserved the torment of recognizing that guilt. Yet if Luther's response
to this situation was ultimately different from that of Catherine of

Siena, Peter of Luxembourg, or Dorothy of Montau, the situation itself was similar, and arose from the same broad historical background.

Penitential Practice and Literature

The penitence seen in the saints' lives did not arise in a vacuum. For
more than a century, the Church had endeavored to cultivate penitence by means of required sacramental penance. The classic document in this context is the canon *Omnis utriusque sexus* issued in 1215
by the Fourth Lateran Council. This decree required everyone who
had reached the age of discretion to confess his or her sins once a
year, at Easter time, to his own parish priest.[27] The text has been
called "the most important legislative act in the history of the
Church," because for the first time the universal Church required
that each individual bare his conscience before a representative of the
ecclesiastical institution; the Church was exerting its authority as never before.[28] Even before 1215, though, there had been efforts in this
direction. Around 1200, Alan of Lille mentioned a local expectation
that clerics would confess weekly, if they had committed serious sin,
and that laypeople would confess every year at Christmas, Easter, and
Pentecost. This and other such stipulations arose from the Church's
growing perception that the religious needs of its people required
systematic attention.[29]

   If the priests of Western Christendom were to have large numbers
of penitents coming to them, they needed instruction on how to deal
with these waves of penitents. They needed to cultivate the skill of
listening carefully and sympathetically to those who confessed to
them. They had to be able to aid in examination of conscience; this
meant helping the penitents recall their sins, weigh their gravity, and
comprehend the attenuating or aggravating circumstances surrounding them. The Lateran Council had explicitly called for priests who
would "diligently inquire into the circumstances of both the sinner
and the sin." They had to know, furthermore, what penances they
should impose. And to help the penitents avoid future sins they had
to give sound moral counsel. All these matters were discussed in the
theological and canonical summas of the age, but these were too long,
too technical, and too expensive for the ordinary parish priest. What
most confessors needed was a simple and practical manual that would
cover such matters, and that is what began to emerge. Numerous
specimens of this genre are extant; they allow us to survey the literature more accurately than we can the actual penitential practice, for
which records are lacking.[30]

One early manual of this sort was Robert of Flamborough's *Penitential Book* from around the time of the Fourth Lateran Council. It was an exceptionally influential work for generations to come, and survives in forty-three manuscripts, which attest to its popularity. Its first four books constitute a running dialogue between a fictitious priest and an equally fictitious penitent. The method employed is illustrated by a passage from the fourth book, concerning virtues and vices. The confessor is instructing the penitent on the sin of pride:

> Priest: Are you suffering from pride?
> Penitent: What is pride?
> Priest: To be proud is to go above others [*Superbire est super alios ire*]: when, therefore, you extol yourself above all others, then you are proud.
> Penitent: I do this frequently and from habit.
> Priest: Beg forgiveness and leave off this thing.
> Penitent: I am sorry father, and by the grace of God I will leave off this thing.[31]

In the process of learning about humility, the penitent learns a lesson in application of this virtue: it is by submitting humbly to the priest's instruction that he begins to overcome his vice and to undergo the process of conversion.[32]

Several other such manuals were composed in the fourteenth century, many of them more elaborate in their scholarly apparatus than Robert of Flamborough's work had been. Thus, when Astesanus of Asti wrote his *Summa on Cases* around 1317, he gave a wealth of patristic citations, appealed in learned fashion to rational demonstrations of his arguments, and quoted judgments that had been passed in canon (and sometimes also civil) law. Other manuals of the century went in a different direction: they endeavored to provide for the laity what had already been made accessible to the clergy. Between 1309 and 1312, the Franciscan John Rigaud wrote a *Formula of Confession* for laymen, at the request of a layman. Its six sections dealt with that which precedes confession, that which accompanies it (its qualities), that which constitutes it (the examination of conscience), that which follows it (restitution and satisfaction), the necessity of repeating it, and a "general confession summarizing all that has been said." The examination of conscience is organized with reference first to the five senses, then to the capital sins, then to the ten commandments, the works of mercy, the sacraments, the virtues, and finally the possible aggravating circumstances. Likewise intended mainly for the lay penitent was *The Mirror of True Penitence*, composed in Italian by the Dominican James Passavanti of Florence. Drawing heavily from

Scripture and from edifying anecdotal literature, this work contained moral exhortations alongside practical advice for confession.[33]

The literature and practice of confession left an imprint on late medieval culture. As W. A. Pantin has said in his survey of the late medieval English church, "The correct use of the sacrament of penance is a theme which dominates or underlies most of the religious literature of the thirteenth and fourteenth centuries, from the constitutions of the bishops down to such unexpected places as certain passages in Langland, Chaucer, and Gower."[34] In *Piers Ploughman,* Langland gives a series of confession scenes which draw heavily upon the confessional manuals. Chaucer represents the characters in many of his *Canterbury Tales* as representatives of one or another sin, or of various combinations of sins, and in his prologues in particular he draws upon the confessional literature in describing these sins and their consequences.[35]

One clear example of the literary impact of confessional theory and practice is John Gower's *Confession of the Lover,* in which a figure who has sinned against the rules of courtly love so confesses to a priest referred to as Genius. Most of the work is devoted to the deadly sins; while the Lover's sin is construed as sin against courtly love, it is clearly patterned after the standard Christian notions of sin against God. This is evident from the outset, when Genius questions the Lover about the first deadly sin:

> Confessor: The first of them thou shalt believe
> Is Pride, which is principal,
> And hath with him in special
> Ministers five full diverse,
> Of which, as I shall rehearse,
> The first is said Hypocrisy.
> If thou art of his company,
> Tell forth, my Son, and shrive thee clean.
> Lover: I know not, father, what you mean:
> But this I would you beseech,
> That you to me in some way teach
> What is to be a hypocrite. . . .[36]

The confessor explains this sin, and the Lover resolves henceforth to avoid it. To an extent, the Lover's penitence seems weak and even insincere: he admits to disobedience, for example, but protests that he only disobeys when his lady wants him to love someone other than her. Likewise, he accuses himself of melancholy specifically when she turns a deaf ear to him. As the confession proceeds, however, he becomes more and more aware of his failings, and more effusive in his self-accusation. At the end, Venus forces him to recognize his amato-

ry inadequacy by handing him a mirror and making him see that he
is, alas, old—the ultimate sin against courtly love. More or less in the
same way that sacramental penance brought the sinner ideally to ab-
ject awareness of his sinfulness, and thus made him submissive to
God, so here the Lover is made to feel thoroughly inadequate.[37]

What if the Church's efforts to cultivate penitence succeeded too
effectively, and left a person cringing in fear and scrupulosity? This
was a problem that theologians and moralists began to take seriously
especially in the early fifteenth century. John Gerson dealt with this
question in various contexts, and tended to emphasize the need for
consoling such a person. In one of his works he dealt with various
types of individuals who need reassurance, including those who can
never persuade themselves that they have been sufficiently contrite in
going to confession:

> They always have a scruple that they have not yet properly
> confessed. They exhaust themselves and their confessors
> with repeated confessions, especially of light and unimpor-
> tant sins. . . . To all of these alike should be given the coun-
> sel to trust not in their own justice but in the pure mercy of
> God; and as they overestimate their own negligence, so let
> them also exaggerate the infinite mercy of God.[38]

But in the fourteenth century there seems to have been relatively little
of such comfort.[39]

The penitential fervor of the era manifested itself in numerous
ways. Indeed, much of the age's piety was designed to counteract the
effects of one's sins, and the system of indulgences, which came to be
extended and rationalized in the fourteenth century well beyond previous bounds, was yet another way of dealing with the burden of one's
guilt.[40] More accurately, one might say that indulgences forestalled
the punishment of purgatory—a theme seldom raised in saints' lives
of the era—yet fear of punishment in any case entailed recognition of
guilt. The most poignant form of this penitence, however, came in the
practice of flagellation. There were flagellant confraternities in Italy,
whose members regularly whipped themselves to atone for their sins.
In the mid-fourteenth century a movement of flagellation spread
across northern Europe in an effort to ward off the wrath of God and
check the course of the Black Death. In some places the flagellants
read a heaven-sent letter in which God informed them that the plague
and other recent calamities—earthquakes, famine, "wild beasts to de-
vour your children," and so forth—were scourges to punish human
iniquity. If people did not repent, God would send bloody rain, mon-
strous birds and beasts, and other afflictions. To ward off all this, the

flagellants took to scourging themselves. One chronicler told how at a particular stage in their rituals they would lie on the ground in postures that signaled the sins they had committed: a raised hand stood for swearing, lying on one's back or stomach or side represented other sins. At another juncture they would fall flat on their faces, regardless of mud, thistles, and stones, in recollection of Christ's passion. Through these and other means the flagellants endeavored to atone for their own sins and those of their fellow Christians.[41]

Analysis of additional texts (sermons, treatises, and other forms of literature) and practices would show in still further ways the efforts of fourteenth-century Christian society to heighten its awareness of sin so as ultimately to rid itself of guilt and its consequences. The materials already cited, though, may convey some notion of how penitence, like patience and devotion to Christ's passion, was firmly established in the religious culture of fourteenth-century Europe.

Asceticism as Penance

Both the awareness of sin and the means to escape it betray an implicit or explicit dualism: the world and the flesh were seriously liable to corruption, and if not kept under constant guard could be sources of the gravest temptations. Sin arose in large part from failure to subjugate one's flesh properly and keep oneself detached from the world. Efforts to rid oneself of sin could succeed only if one undertook such subjugation and detachment. This conviction, alongside the desire to imitate Christ, motivated the asceticism of the age. Commonly the term "penitence" was used as a synonym for "asceticism," and the penitential life was that in which one abstained from worldly pleasures and imposed rigors upon oneself in an effort to subdue the urges of the world and the flesh.

Dualism of spirit and matter (or soul and body) appears routinely in the saints' lives. When Francis Patrizzi "desired with all his heart to leave the tabernacle of the flesh," and prayed for liberation from his bodily prison, he was speaking not only for himself but for his era. Catherine of Siena implored Christ to take her from her "contemptible" and "worthless" body, and from that wretched life in which nothing attracted her; she too represented her body as a prison from which to be freed, as did Urban V. Rulman Merswin "hated his body and turned against it"; out of hatred for the world and his body, he tortured his flesh so much that he became sick and approached death. Recognizing that worldly things are marked by "shortness, burdensomeness, thorniness, laboriousness, contrariness, and deceptiveness," Cicco of Pesaro turned away from them and toward things of the spirit. And Catherine of Sweden, knowing that the desires of the world and the flesh are the greatest impediments to devotion, strove to remove them from her mind as if they were a lethal poison.[42]

The other side of the picture emerges less frequently but shows in Francis Patrizzi's counsel that, while being sparing in one's refreshment, one should not deny necessary foods to one's "ass and servant," to wit, one's body. If not cared for, the body will be recalcitrant, whereas it should be ready and able to perform any good deed: "we know that to them that love God, all things work together unto good" (Rom. 8:28).[43] This text bespeaks a sacramental conception of nature rarely emphasized in this era. On balance the negative emphasis was stronger and more persistent. Even if they were from a certain perspective holy, the world and the flesh were clearly not in themselves sources of value: they were good only when they served spiritual ends, and throughout life their base impulses needed to be held in check.

While this dualism itself was entirely traditional, the recurrent emphasis on it served as an inducement to the penitence that characterized the era. The deeds of which the saints repented were accommodations to the world and the flesh: Catherine of Siena's willingness to have herself adorned, Dorothy of Montau's eagerness to eat fine food, or Peter of Luxembourg's taking bodily refreshment between meals. It was the person who felt ill at ease with the world who was most likely to be seen as saintly. This ascetic outlook also goes hand in hand with the emphasis on patience: one might keep aloof from the world as a source of temptation, or one might submit to its adversities as a means for one's perfection—indeed, the temptations themselves could be adversities that led to spiritual betterment—but in any event one viewed it as an alien and potentially hostile environment.

In an effort to subjugate their bodies, the saints exercised fasting and abstinence, kept close guard over their chastity, and learned to do without that bodily comfort afforded by sleep. To wean themselves from attachment to the world, they cultivated humility and shunned worldly honors, they reduced themselves to poverty, they refused to wear sumptuous clothing, and they fled at times from human company, preferring solitude and silence. In all of these respects they deprived themselves of normal human comforts and pleasures. Going beyond all this, they mortified their bodies with physical abuse: flagellation, hairshirts, and other such devices. All of this constituted the penitential life which helped to overcome and atone for sin.

In an early formulation of Christian ascetic theory, John Cassian represented gluttony as the root from which all other vices spring.[44]

In fourteenth-century hagiography, the battle against gluttony by means of fasting and abstinence arises more frequently and more insistently than any other ascetic concern. Andrew Corsini made a point of always rising from the table hungry. Clare Gambacorta imposed such strict rules of fasting and abstinence on herself that even if she wanted an apple and they were in abundant supply she would still refuse herself the pleasure. Catherine of Sweden acknowledged abstinence as a practice which "prolongs life, preserves chastity, pleases God, repulses demons, illumines the intellect, strengthens the mind, overcomes vices, overpowers the flesh, and stirs and inflames the heart with love of God."[45]

The specific patterns of voluntary fasting and abstinence varied, but certain practices—dietary restrictions and times for fasting and abstinence—were routine. The saints often abstained from meat, either altogether or on specific days. Some of them abstained from wine, or watered it down. More extreme, yet more frequently cited, was routine or frequent fasting on bread and water. More than any other form of asceticism, fasting and abstinence became interwoven with the Church's liturgical calendar, both through ecclesiastical prescription and by choice of the individual. Thus, Advent and Lent were normal times for fasting. Frequently the saints fasted on specific days of the week: Monday, Wednesday, Friday, and (in honor of the Virgin) Saturday. In addition, it was common to fast on the vigils of the feasts of those saints to whom one was particularly devoted. The result for Elizabeth of Portugal was that she ended up fasting on the greater number of days in the week; doubtless the same was the case for many others.[46]

Even on days when they did eat, some of the saints made it their practice to have only one meal a day. And the quality of their food was poor: Gertrude of Delft ate whatever she happened upon, such as moldy or hard bread, and she drank coagulated milk or other such liquids; Clare Gambacorta gathered scraps of food left by others, and in effect ate their garbage, or if eating a kind of simple sandwich she might sprinkle ashes on it to spoil whatever taste it might have; Francis of Fabriano, too, mixed his food with ashes, in imitation of Francis of Assisi.[47]

Catherine of Siena gradually reduced her consumption of food, and eventually underwent a miraculous transformation of her digestive process which made it both impossible and unnecessary to eat. Toward the end of her life she supported herself with nothing but communion. James Oldo too proposed to sustain himself through one Lent by taking nothing but the eucharist, but after eight days he was ordered to moderate his rigor—though he had tried to conceal his fast by sitting at table and pretending to eat.[48]

When the saints violated their own standards of fasting and abstinence, their gluttony could be the occasion for grievous compunction.
Cicco of Pesaro smelled a roast pig one day as he was out begging. A
demon took advantage of him and aroused his gluttony, so that he
had a companion go and buy part of the pig and take it back home.
Several days later he found it spoiled, noisome, and crawling with
worms. Nonetheless, he deliberately exposed himself to its stench,
and smeared its grease over his naked body, thus conquering this vice
for good. Worse still was the punishment meted out to Henry Suso,
who after several years of abstinence ate some meat. He had barely
swallowed his unaccustomed fare when an "immense infernal being"
threatened to kill him, because, having violated his abstinence, Suso
deserved death. The beast drove a gimlet into Suso's mouth, and
wounded him so badly that for days thereafter he could eat only by
sucking through his teeth.[49]

Almost as much a matter of concern as gluttony in the fourteenth
century was the vice to which, according to John Cassian, gluttony
leads: lust. Saints who were not married commonly went out of their
way to avoid being placed in marital bonds by their parents; those
who were married sought to avoid sexual contact with their partners
and usually succeeded in this effort.

The flight from marriage, and more generally the flight from the
opposite sex, usually began in childhood. Clare Gambacorta was
twelve when she wished to have no other spouse but Christ, and wore
an engagement ring on her finger as if to forestall any earthly betrothal. Catherine of Siena took a vow of virginity when she was seven
years old, though her biographer affirms that she had the maturity of
a seventy-year-old. Andrew Corsini fled the company of women, and
in youth was ashamed to speak even with his mother and sisters; if he
had to talk with a woman, he kept his eyes on the ground. When he
was in Paris as a student, his fellow-students referred to him as "Andrew the blind, deaf, and dumb," because he so systematically kept all
his senses from lewdness.[50]

Those who did enter marriage usually did so with little enthusiasm,
and strove to maintain their virginity in marriage. On her wedding
night, Jane Mary of Maillé regaled her husband with examples of the
saints, and thus persuaded him to accept a virginal marriage; after his
death she made a vow of chastity before the archbishop of Toulouse.
James Oldo and Gonsalvo Sancii were already married when they underwent religious conversions; they managed to free themselves from
marital bonds and enter the Franciscan order, despite loud protest
especially from their wives' families.[51]

When Elzear of Sabran was married, his wife induced him to accept
a virginal marriage; she informed him on their wedding night that

her parents had forced her into the ceremony and that she had resolved to retain her treasure of virginity. He was evidently surprised,
and did not yet share her resolve, but "seized with divine fear" he
heard her kindly and refrained from touching her or saying anything
unseemly to her, as she spent the night praying with tears and sighs
and commending her virginity to the Lord's care. On subsequent
nights, as soon as they went to bed she forestalled any alternative developments by addressing him with "chaste, upright, and devout
words," and thus they remained virgins. He concealed their arrangement from others; once, when he was away from home and his companions tried to induce him to extramarital relations, he replied, "I
have a lovely and beautiful wife, as you all know, and that is enough
for me." It was only after he had had an ecstatic conversion, though,
that he shared his wife's religious fervor, and recognized how all
along God had preserved him in his virginity. Thus he resolved never
to worry about heirs or his inheritance, but to keep his virginity per-
petually, as his wife had encouraged him to do. They still slept together, but neither felt any inclination toward sexual relations.
Eventually they confirmed their mutual resolve with a formal vow of
virginity. Before a small group of friends, kneeling and with his
hands on a missal, Elzear took his vow:

> Lord Jesus Christ, from whom every good thing and every
> gift comes, I, a frail and infirm sinner, cannot remain con-
> tinent or chaste without your special gift. But confident of
> your singular help, I vow and promise to you and to the
> glorious Virgin and to all the saints that I will live chastely
> and maintain my virginity throughout my life, which your
> clemency has guarded in me up to now. And to keep this
> promise I am prepared to suffer whatever tribulations and
> pains are necessary, even bodily death.

Then his wife made a similar vow or, rather, repeated in this gather-
ing what she had already vowed before God. Elzear strictly ordered
that the vow be kept secret, though toward the end of his life it became widely known.[52]

If even marital relations were problematic, illicit sex was unthinka-
ble. Someone once joked with Urban V that it would be good for him
to have a son, because he would learn from experience what the love
of children is like. Not amused, he replied in a rebuking tone that he
would rather be dead and buried than stained with that sin. And
Elzear of Sabran ordered that all those in his service should live chaste-
ly or be expelled from his household. Servants who committed for-
nication were in fact dismissed. He did not want anyone in mortal sin

to eat his bread, lest such a person infect others, and lest he himself appear to be nourishing the sin. It is not surprising, then, to read that Henry Suso was so scrupulous in this regard that for a long time he avoided touching himself on any part of his body except his hands and feet.[53]

In combat against the vice of sloth, the saints stayed awake much or all of the night, usually immersed in prayer. The biographies are frequently vague, and merely mention these vigils without further information, but in some cases the accounts are fuller. Urban V stayed awake praying almost all night every night. Catherine of Siena began by staying awake until matins, but gradually overcame her need for even that much sleep; eventually she slept no more than half an hour every other day, though she acknowledged that this was the most difficult thing she ever learned to do. And Jane Mary of Maillé on solemn feasts held vigil in church before the consecrated host as she prayed assiduously. When her body was worn out she would sleep a bit on the stone steps of the altar. While praying, she would lie prostrate, holding her mouth to the dust on the floor. There was even a period when she spent her nights routinely in a certain chapel at Tours, until the chaplains ousted her in preparation for an expected onslaught of pilgrims.[54]

When the saints did sleep, it was commonly in the most uncomfortable of accommodations. John of Caramola, during his later years in a monastery, had a small and crooked bed on which he had to lie in a contorted position, so that he appeared to be laboring rather than resting. When his fellow monks bore posthumous testimony to his holiness, not a single one had ever seen him sleeping. Andrew Corsini is described as having slept on straw, or as having used a bed of twigs with a mat on top and a bundle of twigs for a pillow, which he concealed with a painted cloth as if for decoration. Though Nicholas Hermansson's bed would be carefully prepared, he was often found lying on the floor on a bearskin, with a brick or something equally uncomfortable for a pillow. Urban V, as a child, lay on the ground with a rock under his head, and when his parents forbade this austerity he would secretly render his bed uncomfortable by strewing sand over it.[55]

The sins of worldliness, such as pride and avarice, seem to have occupied the attention of fourteenth-century saints less than those of the flesh, yet they did exert themselves to practice the virtues of detachment from the world.

To distance themselves from worldly honors, they deliberately humbled themselves, performing menial tasks and refusing honors and pomp. When Andrew Corsini was ordained, his relatives wanted him to sing a mass with great ceremony, but he went to a remote convent and sang mass instead with great devotion. He washed the feet of his brethren, performed other humble tasks, and fled the praise of men. Elzear of Sabran had such deep humility that he totally undermined his own self-esteem. Worldly honors were displeasing and onerous to him, and although he went along with them outwardly, he bore them with inner discomfort. He was relieved when others failed to pay him the honor due his rank.[56]

Poverty, which in the twelfth and thirteenth centuries had been the key virtue of those seeking to imitate the apostles, receded somewhat into the background in the fourteenth century, as patience came to the fore. The Franciscan Spirituals had carried the demand for poverty to extremes that provoked papal condemnation, and even the traditional Franciscan motif of poverty was under a cloud. To be sure, the saints' lives still acknowledged poverty as holy and as an integral part of the holy life, and there are many passing references to it. Only occasionally, though, does poverty assume a major role in the vitae.[57]

In both the biography and the canonization proceedings for Jane Mary of Maillé, the poverty she adopted in widowhood was a recurrent and dominant motif. Even as a girl, she would sometimes exchange her fine garments for the ragged clothes of her poor playmates; her governess would chide her for such behavior, saying it was not befitting a "future queen," but her biographer hails this and other such deeds as signs of her future poverty. Later in life she made herself a beggar for Christ's sake, especially when she was ejected from her estate on her husband's death. Even what she had in her own right, her dowry and inheritance, she gave away with no hope of future compensation. When she went traveling she did not ride a carriage or a horse, as her nobility prescribed, but went with the staff of poverty, carrying her sack on her shoulder, like a poor woman. At one point she fell so seriously ill that she was expected to die. Her one concern was that she should die completely impoverished, because Christ had been born poor, had taught poverty by his word and example, and had died poor and naked on the cross.[58]

Even where poverty was exalted, its exercise was sometimes qualified out of recognition for the conventual principle, the notion that ownership is required for the good of an institution. Clare Gambacorta was puzzled in her early life by Proverbs 30:8, in which God is asked to send neither beggary nor riches, but only the food one needs; she thought that poverty was not real unless there was a lack even of necessities. Later, though, when she was charged with care for a convent, including an infirmary, she said she understood the sense of the passage. Urban V often said he wished he could be poor, but out of reverence for his ecclesiastical office and for the good of his subordinates he could not be penurious. Perhaps the most poignant

case of adaptation to this conventual principle comes in the life of
Flora of Beaulieu, who at first was scandalized at her convent's
richness in temporal goods, and wondered how she could please
Christ amid such luxury. When a priest known for his holiness came
to the convent, she went to him for confession, and told him she feared damnation because of this affluence. He told her not to fear, since
if she used such goods soberly when necessity urged she would obtain
great merit. She should thank God for giving temporal goods to the
convent in such abundance that the cares of the sick might be more
effectively satisfied. Furthermore, he said, there were many who
would quickly lose heart if subjected to stark deprivation, but who
amid such abundance could learn to reject superfluities and grow in
love for God. Flora accepted this consolation, and while she herself
attended only to God and became oblivious to earthly concerns, she
no longer protested the lavishness of her surroundings.[59]

In their style of clothing, the saints took care to preserve various
virtues: humility, poverty, and modesty. The Blessed Virgin appeared once to Jane Mary of Maillé and instructed her to wear more
humble clothing; indeed, she gave her precise instructions as to what
she should wear. Jane Mary followed these directives, and in consequence was mocked by many, who taunted her as a hermit. Nicholas
Hermansson wore coarse rather than fine clothes, and asked what
point there was in decorating the flesh which would soon be given
over to worms. Urban V abhorred all irregularity of dress, and used
his powers as pope to inflict both spiritual and temporal punishments
on those who violated his standards. He had many laymen stop wearing long hair, womanly styles, shoes with pointed toes, and unduly
short garments. Whenever he issued a plenary indulgence, he enjoined its recipients to observe propriety in clothing.[60]

While it would scarcely be accurate to label the saints of this era as
antisocial, and while they generally lived in the cities and mingled
with the urban population, still there was some tendency among them
to flee from human company. This was particularly the case for wom-
en, who even in the mendicant orders were more secluded than their
male counterparts. Thus, Clare Gambacorta went into seclusion even
from her family when she entered the cloister. Other saints yearned
in a romantic fashion for the life of the desert fathers: Villana de'
Botti, for example, on reading the lives of these hermits, conjured up
dreams of fleeing to the desert.[61]

More important and widespread was an aversion not to society itself but rather to frivolous, vain, and worldly companionship. Henry
Suso avoided many unwholesome impulses in his youth by shunning
frivolous company. When he associated with friends they poked fun
at him, and he had no kindred spirits to whom he could pour out his

tribulations. Thus he went about as "a stranger and unloved, shunning all society with great self-control," but later he reaped the rewards of this aversion to baneful influence. Flora of Beaulieu, too, disdained the childish speech and manner of her youthful contemporaries, and fled from their puerile diversions. Even churchmen, who mingled routinely, could shun the vanity of secular society. Urban V took consolation only from conversation with God, and associated with fellow human beings only as a means for pleasing God. And Nicholas Hermansson remained serious even when he entertained others; when he was kept at table longer than usual, he would obviate scandal by saying, "My friends, do not take example from my staying so long at table."[62]

Elzear of Sabran unwillingly spent five days once at a wedding celebration for a member of his mother's family. He found himself in the midst of ribald courtly society, where those about him spent their time in singing, dancing, and other merriments, with immodest banter that discomforted him greatly. All of this kept him from praying and contemplating as he was accustomed. Because he was in the habit of "tasting divine things," his spirit languished out of desire for things eternal. The one consolation that the Lord sent him during those days was that if he awoke during the night he would find his eyes, face, and clothes drenched with tears: for "what he could not do while awake, his inflamed heart and mind made up for in his sleep." Thanking God for this gift of tears, he was in some measure consoled.[63]

Pious conversation seems to have been highly valued among the saints of this century, but the monastic virtue of silence did not go wholly unobserved. John of Caramola, who had been a hermit before joining a monastery, was so silent that he could be characterized more as speechless than as taciturn. Even outside the monasteries, meals in particular were occasions for silence. Nicholas Hermansson observed such strict silence during his meals that he scarcely allowed anyone dining with him even to clear his throat, much less indulge in idle chatter. Talkativeness was associated with childishness: Andrew Corsini, for example, indulged in great silence rather than silly or "childish" talk.[64]

Self-mortification is a practice already discussed in connection with the passion; it was essentially a way of identifying oneself with Christ. Because it could also serve as a way of disciplining the body, keeping it from sin, and atoning for past misdeeds, it arises in this context as well. There were essentially two methods: beating oneself, usually with a scourge but at times with an iron chain; and wearing hairshirts and other devices that caused grave discomfort. The first procedure was for specific moments, while the second was a constant feature of many saints' lives.[65]

Self-flagellation was common. Andrew Corsini beat himself daily to the point of drawing blood. Francis of Fabriano beat himself for what seemed interminable periods, and when he died the skin on his shoulders was so worn and calloused from this exercise that it could scarcely be pierced. Francis Patrizzi disciplined himself for the sake of the living and the dead every morning; he beat himself so hard that anyone hearing it would assume he was striking wood or stone. Catherine of Siena beat herself with a rope when she was a child, and encouraged her playmates to do the same. Her parents gave her a room of her own, in which she could pray and scourge herself as much as she wanted. At one stage in her life she disciplined herself with iron chains three times a day—for herself, for the living, and for the dead. In some instances the motive may have been imitation of Christ, but we are told that Francis of Fabriano disciplined himself vigorously to subject his flesh to the spirit.[66]

Even more common than flagellation was wearing of hairshirts and other devices, though there is seldom much information, and routinely the fact itself was at least theoretically kept secret. When Clare Gambacorta had to wear elaborate attire on account of her station, she wore her hairshirt beneath the elegant clothes. Sometimes one of her brothers would see her in a new and expensive gown, and would say, "Oh what a lovely gown! How well a hairshirt would suit you underneath it!" She would respond with a gentle smile, concealing the hairshirt she was in fact wearing. Other devices to cause discomfort included iron chains, iron girdles, knotted cords that dug into one's flesh, and nettles underneath one's clothing. The figure most ingenious at inflicting such suffering upon himself was Henro Suso. For some time he wore a hairshirt and an iron chain, causing his blood to flow out "like a river." Then he had a tight-fitting hair undergarment made for the upper part of his body, with a hundred fifty nails embedded in straps in this garment, with the points directed inward, and he slept in this device.[67]

In the fourteenth century, as at other times, asceticism was seen as a vocation. Some were called to lives of extraordinary rigor, while others were expected merely to obey the commandments and practice abstinence in moderation. Thus, while Gerard Cagnoli was himself a rigorous ascetic, he did not pass judgment on those who were living otherwise. And when a disciple of Henry Suso began to mortify herself with hairshirts, chains, iron nails, and other such implements, he told her to modify these austerities. He was in part concerned with her "feminine weakness" and health, but the principle went beyond such concerns. His essential point was that "we are of different natures: what is suitable for one is not fitting for another." In general, he said, it is better to practice only moderate austerities. And if it is difficult to determine what constitutes moderation, it is preferable to stop short than to venture too far in the direction of rigor.[68]

The saints of the era seem to have been willing to view all such questions as strategic. Rather than opting a priori for one or another form of asceticism, or "penitence," they were evidently willing to employ whatever was suited for the discipline and sanctification of a given individual. The factor that all individuals had in common was the need to use whatever means were most effective for them in reforming their lives by turning them away from creature comforts and orienting them increasingly toward the divine.

The ultimate reward for asceticism, in the fourteenth century as at other times, was eternal bliss. Short of that there was the consolation of mystical experience: if one could wrench oneself effectively from all that was of the world, one might become intimate even during this life with that which was not of the world.

6
Rapture and Revelation

Penitential fervor was arguably the saints' most ordinary and accessible way of cultivating their inward spirituality, with its consciousness of the gulf between human weakness and divine perfection, and its reliance upon God's work in the soul. The mystical experiences of the saints, their ecstasies and visions, were the most extraordinary and inaccessible manifestations of precisely the same spirituality.

One might suppose that these experiences stood as a counterbalance to the darker and more obviously disquieting elements in the saints' lives, and in some ways they did: visions often served as God's means for comforting his saints when the tribulations of life would otherwise have grown too severe. As we shall see, though, mystical experiences themselves could become disquieting. In any case, they involved surrender to the deity, they required spiritual passivity, they came unbidden and beyond the saints' control, and just as effectively as adversity and compunction they could arouse a sense of being overwhelmed. They were forceful signs of God's work on behalf of the saint, who commonly emerged from the experience with ever keener yearning for release from this life and attainment of celestial reward.

The fourteenth century is commonly seen as a high point in the history of Christian mysticism. The Dominican mystics of Germany, the relatively reclusive figures of England, and spiritual virtuosi in other parts of Europe established the era as one of mystical fervor. Many of the saints of the century were mystics, including several of the most prominent: Catherine of Siena, Bridget of Sweden, Julian of Norwich, Richard Rolle, Henry Suso, and John Ruysbroeck. Less widely known figures such as Dorothy of Montau, Margaret Ebner, Christina Ebner, Adelheid Langmann, Flora of Beaulieu, Jane Mary of Maillé, and others swell the list. German convents often boasted of numerous such women, whose mystical experiences filled the convent chronicles (or *Nonnenviten*) of the era.[1] This dimension of Christian spirituality was by no means new, yet the increasing literacy and consequent development of lay piety in late medieval Europe brought about a democratization of mysticism, with broader audiences to read about and emulate the mystics. The development was complex and in a way paradoxical: while the heights of mystical experience were accessible only to the virtuosi or saints, mystical literature adapted for the needs of the laity could draw upon a long tradition of mystical themes to persuade the laity that their normal Christian lives were somehow on a continuum with those of the great mystics. Meister Eckhart went so far as to glorify the ordinary life of active service, infused with consciousness of God's presence, as the highest ideal, and applied to this life the mystical terminology earlier reserved for distinctive forms of experience. Thus, while the saints remained important for their exceptional mystical fervor, the spirituality that they exemplified could arouse mixed sentiments of wonderment and identification in the readers of the *vitae*.

In hagiographic manifestations of mysticism, the fourteenth century has little new to offer. It was specifically in this area that the tendencies of fourteenth-century spirituality had most clearly been anticipated in earlier saints' lives: the vitae of Hildegard of Bingen and Elizabeth of Schönau, just as clearly as those of their late medieval counterparts, recount intense mystical experiences in which the saints became passive before a God who worked on their behalf within their souls.[2] While the unfolding of this motif in fourteenth-century hagiography is thus not particularly original, the theme occupies such a prominent place in this century that one cannot neglect it in an examination of the era's saints.

The Varieties of Mystical Experience

The term "mysticism," more familiar in modern scholarly parlance than it would have been to the mystics themselves, can mean various things. For present purposes it may be taken as covering two closely linked phenomena: ecstatic experiences (raptures), in which a person's consciousness of the spatio-temporal order is temporarily lost or diminished; and extraordinary glimpses of spiritual or otherwise hidden realities (revelations), whether communicable or ineffable.

Both raptures and revelations occur in the vitae of fourteenth-century saints, and at times they are so prominent that they virtually displace other extraordinary signs of holiness, such as miracles. To be sure, we are told that some of the saints were shy about relating these phenomena. Peter of Luxembourg confided one vision of his in secrecy to an associate; judging from the ecstatic quality of his prayer and from the flooding of his oratory with a supernatural light, people concluded that it was only from humility that he kept other such experiences secret, and his canonization proceedings mention the apparently widespread belief that he "had many and great visitations and consolations from God, though this was unknown to human persons."[3] Because other saints were less reticent, though, the records are plentiful.

Turning to rapture, one finds that it typically left the saint oblivious to surrounding realities, or at most vaguely conscious of them. John Ruysbroeck would become quite unconscious of those around him, even important personages, and would remain utterly silent, with his face in his hands. Richard Rolle was sometimes so absorbed in his raptures that his cloak could be removed, mended, and replaced without his taking notice. Flora of Beaulieu, who commonly feigned sleep when she sensed these experiences coming on, would remain unmoved for an extended time, as if she were no longer among the living. If anyone approached Villana de' Botti while she was in prayer or at mass, even though her eyes were open she would not perceive the person. Clare Gambacorta was once called by another nun, but did not respond; her companion went to her cell and found her rapt in prayer and immobile as a column. At length the other nun touched her, and Clare came to herself, as if awakening from a deep sleep. Elzear of Sabran found that he "tasted divine things" quite unexpectedly, even when he was eating with other people or at a dance with singing and playing of instruments, and when this happened he would become oblivious even to such surroundings, so that his wife was afraid he might trip and fall. When he was knighted at Naples, he followed the traditional custom of spending the night before the ceremony in vigil in a church. When a great multitude of knights and other nobles entered in with lights, and passed before him with the sound of trumpets and other instruments, he remained virtually oblivious to it all. The need for such abstraction is clear from the life of Robert of Salentino, who found that the throngs of people flocking to him distracted him in prayer, until God gave him the blessing of deafness while he prayed.[4]

Henry Suso was standing by himself in the choir of a church one day, rather dejected, when he entered into rapture:

It was without form or shape, and yet it bore within itself

all forms and shapes of joyous delight. His heart was hungry and yet satisfied, his mind joyful and happy, his wishes were calmed and his desires had died out. He did nothing but gaze into the brilliant light, in which he had forgotten himself and all things. He did not know whether it was day or night.

He was uncertain how long the experience lasted—perhaps half an hour, perhaps an hour. Likewise, he did not know whether his soul remained in his body or not. When he came back to his senses, he had a feeling that he had returned from a different world, and the return itself made him feel for a moment the kind of pain that one suffers in death. He cried out in his heart, "Alas, God, where was I, where am I now?" No one else noticed that he had changed, but he himself felt as though he were floating in the air, and for some time he could smell a celestial odor like the aroma of balsam.[5]

The life of Catherine of Siena was filled with such incidents. Whatever she was doing, even as she attended to household chores, she would be carried away suddenly in rapture.

No sooner did the thought of her Heavenly Bridegroom come into her holy mind than she lost the use of her bodily senses, and her extremities, that is to say her hands and feet, became quite paralyzed. Her clenched fingers would press so tightly into the palms of her hands that it was as though they were nailed there, and it would have been easier to break them than force them open. Her eyes, too, shut tight, and her neck became so stiff that any attempt to move it would have been really dangerous.

In such states she "became rapt like another Mary Magdalene," and her body sometimes lifted off the ground as a sign that a higher power was drawing her upward. Once she fell into such a state as she was turning a spit over an open fire; her sister-in-law hastened to take over turning the spit. After everyone else had eaten Catherine was still sitting there in rapture. When she had finished cleaning up, her sister-in-law went back "to see the end of the ecstasy" some hours afterward, and discovered that Catherine had fallen into the smoldering embers—yet, like the young men in the book of Daniel, she remained unharmed. On other occasions those about her tested her mystical states by kicking her or lifting her up and throwing her out of church. Once a person pricked her with a needle all over her body, and she remained in rapture, though on regarding consciousness she was aware of having been hurt. The perpetrators of these forms of abuse were duly punished; one died without benefit of the sacraments, while another went mad and began raving, "For the love of God help me! The executioner is coming to cut my head off!" Such were the dangers of tampering with so holy a phenomenon as rapture.[6]

Richard Rolle, who often experienced the delights of rapture, cited its effects as "sweetness, warmth, and melody"; his writings often make reference to these phenomena. In the saints' lives, the sensation of music is not commonly used as a way of conveying the experience of rapture, but three images that do recur are those of sweetness, heat, and light—sweetness and heat as expressions of the saint's inner experience, and light as a manifestation to others of the ecstatic state. Elzear of Sabran was overcome with "great sweetness of divine love" and an "inner ardor and flame" that made him warm all over and even caused him to flush as if he were feverish. (The warmth was in this case apparent even to his companions, who led him to his room for rest.) On another occasion he savored spiritual and eternal things "with great sweetness of mind." Flora of Beaulieu was repeatedly refreshed with "fervor of spirit, or an inner sweetness of mind," among other such experiences. While Gertrude of Delft was still in the world, before adopting a distinctively religious career, she was so prone to inward devotion that she often felt as much "sweetness of divine bounty" in the midst of a crowd as she later would in her beguinage. Clare Gambacorta had such experiences even when she was held captive by her own family in an effort to keep her from joining a convent: Christ comforted and strengthened her with "such sweetness of spirit that it overflowed to her bodily senses, and all things in her prison seemed sweet to her." Later she often felt "wondrous sweetness" when she withdrew to her cell for prayer. Jane Mary of Maillé found herself infused with heat from a fiery globe that descended upon her and extended its effects throughout her body.[7]

Those who were privileged to witness the saints in ecstasy frequently reported that they were enveloped in light. When Elzear of Sabran was in rapture, his wife found him with light emanating from his face brighter and more lovely than that of a candle; his face itself was illumined, and he had a lovely aura around himself. An associate of Flora of Beaulieu peeked into her room once and found that the entire chamber was glowing with light, as if it were ablaze. Much the same happened when a companion caught Peter of Luxembourg in ecstasy. When John Ruysbroeck went off into a forest by himself and did not return, his brethren began to look for him; not finding him in the monastery, they eventually sought him out in the forest. One of them happened upon him, spying him from afar as he sat under a tree. The entire tree was surrounded as if a fiery beam were descending upon it from above, and the "man of God" was sitting entranced (*semiraptus*), in "great fervor of divine sweetness." The outward light was a sign of that splendid fervor which he maintained in his soul.[8]

Another, rarer way in which rapture found outward manifestation was in levitation. Jane Mary of Maillé was often raised two cubits off the ground by angels, and once by St. Ives of Brittany. Flora of Beaulieu was once singing *Veni creator Spiritus* when all of a sudden, in the presence of all the sisters in her congregation, she was carried into rapture and raised up more than two cubits from the ground, where she remained hanging for some time. Gerard Cagnoli enjoyed a similar experience, as did Catherine of Siena.[9]

The occasions on which rapture ensued were various. Most commonly, it occurred as the saints were praying: it was when she withdrew to her cell for prayer, for example, that Clare Gambacorta felt "wondrous sweetness." Flora of Beaulieu sometimes went into ecstasy during recitation of the canonical hours; verses such as "I saw the Lord face to face" (*Vidi Dominum facie ad faciem*) or "I saw a great throng" (*Vidi turbam magnam*) especially induced such experiences. In the last analysis, however, any reference to heaven or divine things could bring her to ecstasy, even the priest's words of absolution in confession.[10]

When the saints entered rapture they did not merely swoon or fall asleep. While it might seem to those around them that they were totally dazed, they themselves beheld wondrous things, whether by way of visions or in direct and ineffable union with God. Catherine of Siena once had such an experience which others, who thought she was dead, clocked at four hours, though she herself lost all sense of time. She reported that she had seen "divine mysteries that no living soul can utter because memory has no hold over them and there are no words capable of describing things so sublime: any words that were used would be like mud compared with gold." She beheld the glory of the saints, the agonies of sinners, and the essence of God himself.[11] For Dorothy of Montau and her confessor, the inner experience was associated with rapture by definition, rapture being "an elevation of the mind by the divine Spirit from that which is according to nature to that which is above nature—that is, to supernatural things—with abstraction from the senses, which is to say alienation of the senses."[12] In short, rapture was integrally linked with revelation.

In the context of hagiography, supernatural revelations usually came in the form of visions. Often these were quite simple: Christ, a saint, an angel, or an unsainted deceased person would come to the living saint to impart information or instruction. In these simple visions the spirits who appear are typically not described in detail, since their manner of appearing is less important than the message they impart. In other cases the visions are more complex: they involve sequences of events, and are often set in heaven or other spiritual environments which may be described in at least some detail. The simpler visions could serve various purposes, including chastisement or warning; the more complex, narrative visions were usually signs of special favor or sources of consolation.

The hagiography abounds with visions in their simpler form, but a few representative examples may suffice. Christ appeared frequently to Bridget of Sweden to instruct her regarding her personal life: he advised her to move to Rome, for example, and instructed her how to deal with her daughter Catherine. The Virgin, similarly, appeared to Bridget's daughter and exhorted her to set aside her own will and submit to Bridget. When Jane Mary of Maillé received a vision of the Virgin, it was to instruct her that she should wear humble clothes in imitation of Christ, who humbled himself in taking the form of a servant (cf. Phil. 2:7). Saints and angels at times brought similar messages. Souls in purgatory would appear to request prayers for their deliverance. Henry Suso had made a pact with a friend that whichever survived the other would say masses for the soul of the deceased; but when the friend died he had to come and remind Suso of this arrangement, and begged him to say the promised masses so that Christ's blood might "flow down upon me, and so that this fierce fire may be extinguished." Souls of the blessed might appear to console those they had left behind, or to thank them for securing their release from purgatory.[13]

At times the visual element in such experiences was lost altogether, and what the saint had was not a vision but a mere locution. Thus, Jane Mary of Maillé heard a voice instruct her to have an altar built in honor of St. Stephen. And when a woman prayed for Elzear of Sabran in his youth, she heard Christ "with her bodily ears" assure her that his own mother would guard over the young saint; the woman was unsure whether this voice was an illusion, until the next day at mass she heard a voice from the consecrated host saying, "What I told you last night about young Elzear is true and certain, and you should not doubt it."[14]

Far more elaborate than these simple visions and locutions were those narrative visions in which the saints witnessed sequences of events. Often these have a dreamlike quality to them, and at times they in fact occurred while the saints were sleeping. Christina Ebner dreamt that she was pregnant with the Lord, and was so charged with grace that it extended to every member of her body. She then dreamt that she gave birth to him without any pain, and was so filled with joy that she could not conceal it, but took the child in her arms and went into the refectory, where she told the rest of the nuns they should all rejoice, and showed them the child she had borne. At this point, overwhelmed with joy, she awoke. Another of her dreams was more fore-boding, but ended on just as positive a note. This time the Lord came as he was when he was thirty years old, to see how the nuns in the convent were living. She loved him greatly, but was afraid that he would perceive her offenses, of which she was ashamed. He entered a garden; seeing him from afar through a window, she went out and hid behind a tree so he would not find her. In an instant, though, he was standing before her and chastizing her. She admitted to him that she was but "dust and earth," overcome as she was with shame. Her inner senses were opened, and she became aware of all her defects, as if they were written in a book. She lowered her eyes in shame, and was speechless. Then the Lord spoke gently to her, saying all her sins were forgiven; he drew her to himself, pressing her so close that she was like wax being pressed by a seal, and transforming her soul into the likeness of the Trinity. She could not express how wondrous and sweet this experience was.[15]

A few of the saints had the privilege of being transported to para-dise in their visions—or to the "divine consistory," as it is called in the proceedings for Bridget of Sweden. On one occasion two angels came to Flora of Beaulieu as she prayed, and clothed her in precious gar-ments, the color of fire. She wondered at this honor, and the angels said she would be thus clad in heaven if she persevered in virtue, though in the meantime they wanted the garments back for safekeep-ing. As Flora pondered these matters, humbly thinking herself un-worthy of such splendor, an angel led her to the eternal heavenly seats reserved for the blessed, and showed her secret things which are beyond human thought and speech. She saw gems, thrones, and or-naments of unspeakable splendor, and good things of every kind. Among them was a particularly marvelous and sweetly smelling throne. The angel said, "This is to be your eternal seat; sit here for a little while, where, with God's consent, you are to sit after this life." When she expressed her unworthiness, the throne was raised up higher—and when she later submitted the validity of the vision to the judgment of a pious theologian, a further vision revealed that her throne had been raised higher still as a reward for her humility. An-other time she had a vision of the angels and saints in heaven, who were celebrating a great feast that was not on the liturgical calendar of the Church militant below. There was much singing and other solem-nity. She asked her angelic escort what the feast was, and he an-swered, "Have you not heard that there will be great joy in heaven whenever a sinner repents of his past life?" (Lk. 15:7). He then ex-plained that a notorious sinner had just repented; when she returned from her ecstatic state, Flora was pleased to confirm this revelation.[16]

Several times Christina Ebner, too, had celestial visions. Once the

Lord took her about heaven announcing that she was his bride. He told the angels, "This is your sister by virtue of her purity." To the martyrs he said, "This is your sister; what you suffered in your bodies, she has suffered in her heart." So likewise, he represented her to the confessors, virgins, and monks as their sister. On another occasion, one Friday, she entered into rapture on receiving communion, and saw the luminous streets of heaven, strewn with pure gold, lilies, and roses. She also saw that Christ was preparing a special celebration, and was inviting all his saints to it. She beheld a dance in heaven, in which God and Mary took part along with the saints. Their proximity to God reflected their level of spiritual attainment, with Mary as the closest of all. Whenever the Lord raised his foot, he emitted a great flame, which flared out like wildfire upon the lilies and roses; the Holy Spirit flowed out of God like flashes of lightning upon these flowers. King David proclaimed that when he was on earth he had foreseen this event, but could only express it in the words, "Sing to the Lord in his saints" (cf. Ps. 150:1). The entire heavenly host came before the Lord and asked why this great feast was occurring that day; the Lord answered that this was a great day, on which he suffered bitterly, and on which his people on earth honored him, and for that reason there was much joy in heaven.[17]

In other visions the location is paradisal, but is not identified specifically as heaven; the aura of bliss is reminiscent of paradise, but the full context of God surrounded by both angels and saints is missing. Henry Suso once saw angels ascending and descending in the sky and singing a song to the Virgin, in which he joined. On another occasion he found himself led in a vision to a beautiful field, and there an angel host came to comfort him in his distress. One may assume that paradise was the location for the "mystical marriage" which Catherine of Siena (like Catherine of Alexandria) was privileged to undergo: the Lord came to her and proposed to celebrate a wedding feast with her soul; Mary, John, Paul, and Dominic appeared on the scene, David came to play his harp, and the Virgin presented Catherine's hand to her son, who placed on her finger a golden ring studded with a diamond and four pearls.[18]

The peak of mystical experience, as viewed by most of the mystics, was neither the subjective experience of rapture nor the ostensibly objective experience of visions, but that fleeting experience of total union with God in which one loses all sense of the distinction between oneself and the divine. When this occurs, one no longer clings to the pleasantries of sweetness and warmth that characterize rapture, and there are neither visual nor auditory symbols that can capture what one encounters. Not surprisingly, an experience of this sort, which does not lend itself readily to any form of description, particularly transcends the powers of narrative authors. Thus, there are relatively few references to it in the saints' lives. At times the saints are represented as emerging from such union with breathless exclamations of its ineffability—but such is not the stuff of a good story.

Occasionally, however, one finds a bold spirit among hagiographers who attempts to convey some sense of the *unio mystica*. Such a spirit was the biographer of Flora of Beaulieu. Once, he says, Flora saw the creator of the world while she was in rapture, and she recognized that he is so great as to exceed all height. As she contemplated what lay before her, she realized that in that abyss there was neither quantity nor quality, nor pain, nor end, nor beginning, nor any species, nor any dimension. Struck with wonder and fear, she asked her angel escort what this was that could not be shown to her without any representation, yet worked such exultation within her. The angel replied, "This is a holy and terrible place. Divinity itself, never known on earth to any mortal, is presented to your mind. It is given to you to behold it in similitude and species, as once to Moses in the form of a bramble-bush and fire." A celestial torrent then flowed upon her, to her delight, and in that excess of exultation and jubilation she sang in a loud voice the antiphon for the feast of martyrs: *Gaudent in coelis animae sanctorum* ("The souls of the saints rejoice in heaven").[19] Even this experience, one might contest, does not qualify as full mystical union, since "similitude and species" were not done away with. Yet the insistence on the *via negativa,* the purely negative manner of referring to God as transcending all human terms, does suggest that what Flora beheld was that abyss of divinity which is the object of mystical union, even if the narrator was forced to convey it in figurative language.

The saints who were schooled in mystical theology could, of course, speak of mystical union in the same terms that might be used in treatises on the subject, or in sermons. Thus, Henry Suso could refer to individuals who "are so completely lost in soul and mind in God that, so to speak, they know nothing else of themselves save that they apprehend themselves and all things in their prime origin," which is to say in God, as archetypes in the divine mind. He continues, "All this takes place when thy own will is abandoned; for such persons are driven out of themselves by the thirst of longing to the will of God and to His righteousness." Catherine of Siena, too, could speak in the sophisticated language of mystical theology, and her confessor related words of hers to this effect:

> The soul that sees its own nothingness and knows that its whole good is to be found in the Creator forsakes itself and all its powers and all other creatures and immerses itself

wholly in Him, directing all its operations towards Him and never alienating itself from Him, for it realizes that in Him it can find all goodness and perfect happiness. Through this vision of love, increasing from day to day, the soul is so transformed into God that it cannot think or understand or love or remember anything but God and the things of God. Itself and other creatures it sees only in God, itself and others it remembers only in God. Thus it is like a man who dives into the sea and swims under water: all he can see and touch is water and the things in the water, while, as for anything outside the water, he can neither see it nor touch it nor feel it. If the things outside the water are reflected in it, then he can see them, but only in the water and as they look in the water, and not in any other way.

What this passage is referring to is a sense of mystical union that is not necessarily ecstatic, but rather ongoing and habitual, the sense of being so closely joined with God throughout one's experience that everything else becomes conditioned by that focusing of one's attention, and one perceives other things only as creatures of God. In any case, this text demonstrates that, if the biographer abandons the narrative approach, the range of mystical states that can be described becomes greatly expanded. Because most biographers were reluctant to shift to a different mode of discourse, passages of this kind are rare in the hagiography.[20]

In one curious episode involving Elzear of Sabran, the content of the revelation was doctrinal but nonetheless ineffable. As he spent the entire night in prayer, he received supernatural instruction on how the persons of the Trinity are generated, why the world was created, what effects the fall brought about, how even damnation can be a fitting punishment for sin, how the love of Christ manifested itself in his becoming human, what inexplicable works God worked in the Virgin, and so forth; virtually the entire creed was laid open for him. Yet he found the next day that he could scarcely speak of what he had learned. He could only say, "Oh, how badly and imperfectly I speak! I do not know and cannot formulate what I saw, or express in speech what I learned by experience." Another time he enjoyed such revelation of divine mysteries, and told his wife that the experience confirmed him powerfully in his faith. He could never be won over to infidelity, even by Antichrist. Indeed, even if he learned on trustworthy report that the pope and cardinals wished to change the faith, and if the whole world were crying out for the revision, he would not be able to deviate in a single point from that true Catholic faith which God had shown him, and would even be prepared to die for its sake. Again, the revelation remained essentially personal. One might expect such mystical experiences to hold dangerous potential: they might lead a person to doctrinal conclusions that did in fact vary from those of the Church. For obvious reasons, cases of doctrinal deviance do not arise among the saints, or else they would never have been recognized as such. Elzear's preference for private revelation over public authority is tempered by the consonance between his revelation and long-standing tradition. Yet in entertaining the possibility of papal error, perhaps even papal heresy, he was raising by implication the same potentially revolutionary questions that thirteenth-century canonists had raised in their discussions of papal fallibility.[21]

A further variety of revelation, sometimes linked with rapture and sometimes not, is what the late medieval sources refer to as prophecy: preternatural knowledge of future, distant, or secret affairs. Because prophetic revelation did not always come in rapture, one might be reluctant to characterize it as mystical. Like other forms of revelation, though, it was an extraordinary sign of divine favor, indicating privileged contact with its divine source.

The subject matter of prophecy was diverse: John of Caramola prophesied that a countess who had long been sterile would bear many children; Gerard Cagnoli foretold that the queen of Sicily, who had given birth to seven daughters, would at last have a son; on other occasions the same saint predicted that a disease would be cured, that lost cattle would be regained after seven months, and that a difficult pregnancy would end in successful delivery; Bridget of Sweden knew in advance that Nicholas Hermansson would become bishop of Linköping. Gertrude of Delft brought pleasant tidings about such diverse subjects as eternal salvation and real estate: on one occasion she assured penitent women that they would not be damned; on another she predicted that good houses would be put up for sale at Delft. Perhaps just as often, however, the predictions were of misfortune: Andrew Corsini had a premonition that a nobleman's infant would become either a religious or a source of great trouble to his family; Villana de' Botti revealed to her father that bad luck would befall him (soon afterward he suffered shipwreck), and that their family would soon become extinct; Francis Patrizzi, having been denied liquid refreshment on a hot day, told his companion that the locality where they were would suffer God's wrath, and the next night an unaccustomed tempest destroyed vineyards and orchards; Peter Olafsson prophesied that a great prince would not fulfill his vow to visit the Holy Sepulcher because he would be "ensnared by the devil"; Gertrude of Delft predicted to her confessor that one Master Theodore of Renen would be killed by his enemies, and when the master was killed and mutilated, so that the pieces of his body had to be picked up and collected in baskets, her confessor became increasingly respectful of Gertrude's prophetic gifts. Not infrequently the subject of prophecy was death, either the saint's own or someone else's. John of Caramola, for example, foreseeing the death of a certain lord who owed a debt to the monastery, advised his abbot to warn the man, so that he could pay off that debt before he paid the debt of all flesh. When a companion was sad at James Oldo's impending demise, the saint reassured him, "I beg of you not to mourn, brother, for the Lord is inviting you as well as me," and it was only a matter of days before the man became sick and died.[22]

Although in all these cases the prophecies were independent of visions, there were other instances in which visions served as the vehicles for prophecy. James Oldo had a dream vision about a great treasure to be found beneath the floor of his house. But the next morning, when he got up and dug, he found "neither gold nor silver, nor anything else of value." Regretting that he had trusted his dream, he did penance for his foolishness. Later on, however, he turned his room into a chapel, and it was precisely on that spot that the altar was erected, where "the most precious of all treasures," the sacrifice of Christ's body, was available every day. When Clare Gambacorta was near death, her fate was revealed to one of her nuns in a dream. She saw a group of nuns wearing black veils over their faces, but despite the veils their faces shone with greater or lesser splendor. One of them was especially beautiful; her face was whiter than snow. A voice said, "This is our prioress," meaning Clare. The dreaming nun said to herself that this could not be so, since Clare was swarthy, while the nun in her dream was sheer white—but the same voice insisted, "Still, it is she." On awaking, the nun knew that the dream was a sign of Clare's approaching demise. In the case of Bridget of Sweden, Christ himself told her, presumably in a vision, that she was to die on a certain day and at a certain hour, and instructed her to inform her confessors and daughter so they would be prepared to make the proper arrangements.[23]

The prophetic charism did not necessarily refer to future events, but could apply to events occurring at a distance. Thus, Gertrude of Delft had knowledge of a battle being fought some distance away. Gerard Cagnoli was praying for a sick man, and received a revelation that the man had been cured; he sent a messenger in the depth of the night, who confirmed that the prophecy was true. Such clairvoyance could prove useful for practical purposes. When Catherine of Sweden arrived in Rome, her mother Bridget was out of town, and Catherine sought her anxiously for eight days. Meanwhile, Peter Olafsson, who was traveling with Bridget, felt "wondrous movements and instincts in his soul," and was aroused to go back to Rome; the impulse was so strong that he could neither eat nor sleep until he undertook the journey. When he arrived, he found Catherine and her companions in St. Peter's.[24]

The saints' lives refer to yet another kind of special knowledge: insight into the secret lives of those around them. The saints were privy to their companions' thoughts, and knew both their sins and their graces. Thus, Peter Olafsson was sitting one evening in the refectory of his house, reading the canonical hours with one of his brethren, when someone entered the room, heard them reading, and quickly departed. Not knowing who had come in, Peter asked his companion to go after him and find out the man's identity. Having ascertained who it was, Peter said that the man "has the spirit of God, and will be great in the spiritual life," since, when he entered the refectory, he emitted "an odor of wondrous sweetness, at which my heart and soul exulted wondrously." Jane Mary of Maillé frequently knew the thoughts of a certain companion who later testified at her canonization proceedings. Once this person was reflecting how silly it would be for her to bewail her sins: "If I should weep for my sins as other persons do, I would have red and unsightly eyes, and would be despised by others as hideous, and they would poke fun at me." As she was thinking these things, Jane Mary said to her, "It seems to some persons that if they wept for their sins they would have red eyes and appear hideous to others, and by fleeing from such contempt they lose out on much goodness." Her companion, feeling herself confounded, recognized that Jane Mary had perceived her thoughts clearly.[25]

Prophecy could entail divinely revealed criticism of the political or ecclesiastical leaders of Christendom. Thus, God charged Ursulina of Parma to visit both the Roman and the Avignonese popes in an effort to induce agreement between them and bring an end to the schism—a mission which almost ended in her being tried for sorcery.[26]

One saint with a particularly strong claim to the title of prophet was Catherine of Siena, who, called by God to serve both private individuals and Christendom as a whole, did so in large measure through use of her prophetic gifts. At the papal court in Avignon, she impressed the pope with her knowledge of the moral status of those present. Catherine claimed that even when she was far off in Siena she could smell the sins of the Avignonese more keenly than could their perpetrators. Once she had to speak with the mistress of a highly placed prelate; she afterward told her confessor, "If you had smelt the stink that I could smell while I was talking to her you would have been sick." Yet she was also capable of making subtler judgments about the spiritual lives of others. When she visited the Carthusian monks at Corgona she preached to them, addressing each one individually. The prior, who served as their confessor, marveled that what she said to each monk was appropriate for his spiritual and moral circumstances, even though Catherine had not had the opportunity to get to know them. In 1375, while cities and city-states in Italy were rebelling against the pope, Catherine prophesied that there would be a schism, but that in the end God would purify his Church:

> After all these tribulations and miseries, in a way beyond all human understanding, God will purify Holy Church by awakening the spirit of the elect. This will lead to such an improvement in the Church of God and such a renewal in the lives of her holy pastors that at the mere thought of it my spirit exults in the Lord.

She also prophesied that a new crusade would soon take place. Later, when critics pointed to the failure of this prophecy, her confessor and biographer defended her by saying that she had never set a date, that some prophecies came true only after a long time, and that, as Augustine says, what is slow for human beings is quick for God. In some instances, he said, prophecies serve merely to emphasize how critical a situation is, as in the case of Jonas's prophecy that God would destroy Nineveh for its sins after forty days.[27]

If even a figure such as Catherine was open to criticism, lesser prophets must have been also. Contemporaries had good reason to question a prophet's utterances, since they so often made claims upon others, and were all too often proven false.[28] The opinions of the humanist Petrarch concerning an unknown prophet are instructive. In the spring of 1362, Petrarch received a letter from Boccaccio, who was deeply disturbed by a report he had heard. A holy man of Siena named Peter, renowned for his piety and miracles, had had a vision of Petrarch, Boccaccio, and various others, and was inspired to deliver secret messages to all these personages. Unable to do so before his death, the holy man prayed for a messenger who could complete the mission, and his wish was fulfilled. The messenger had already spoken with Boccaccio, and would eventually reach Petrarch. Whatever the content of his other messages, the announcements which had so badly shaken Boccaccio were two: that he would soon die (in fact he lived thirteen more years), and that he should give up the study of poetry. Petrarch's reaction was highly guarded. He did not disdain legitimate prophecy, but doubted seriously that this particular revelation was legitimate, and insisted that "it is an old and much-used device, to drape one's own lying inventions with the veil of religion and sanctity, in order to give the appearance of divine sanction to human fraud." When the messenger reached him, he would judge from his entire manner of behavior—his facial expressions, his dress and bearing, his gestures and manner of speech, and especially his apparent intentions in delivering the message—whether to believe him. In the meantime, he advised his friend not to abandon those literary studies which could in fact accomplish much good. What Petrarch could articulate with some eloquence, his contemporaries might readily intuit without being able to express.[29]

The Devotional Context

As we have seen in previous chapters, the relationship between the sanctity of the fourteenth century and the normal Christian piety of the era was complex. The saints embodied and reinforced the spirituality of their contemporaries, while at the same time arousing suspicion by the extremes to which they went. Their mystical experiences were dramatic manifestations of a devotional trend which, translated into a vernacular idiom and transformed for a secular milieu by writers such as Meister Eckhart, was increasingly popular in the later Middle Ages. If Catherine of Siena's associates were skeptical about her raptures, and if Petrarch was doubtful about specific prophecies, this did not mean that the public at large was unwilling to recognize mystical spirituality as a sign of sanctity; when John Marienwerder promulgated the cult of Dorothy of Montau, he could be confident that accounts of her mystical experiences would evoke reverence from the masses and might arouse sympathy from those literate townspeople who had exposed themselves to the popular devotional literature of the age.

One of the clearest ways in which the mystics lent their authority to ordinary Christian piety was through visions that drew upon current devotional trends. We have already seen how visions of the passion related to the century's widespread devotion to the passion. Other devotions as well—to the Virgin, the saints and angels, and the eucharist—received confirmation from the saints' visions. Furthermore, the liturgical setting in which visions frequently occurred lent support to broader currents in late medieval piety.

Marian piety was one of the strongest of devotional trends in the late Middle Ages.[30] Devotion to the Virgin was one of the most common sources of inspiration for art: alongside the crucifixion, the madonna and child was by far the most common single subject for artistic representation; specific events such as the annunciation and the coronation as queen of heaven were less often depicted but in the fourteenth century were coming into their own as topics for art, and polyptychs showing scenes from the life of the Virgin were certainly well known. The proliferation of Marian feast days inspired a dispro-

portionate number of Marian hymns and motets, which formed a
substantial portion of composers' output in the fourteenth century.
Popular literature reinforced these trends, with intense devotion to
Mary reflected, for example, in poetic compilations of the Virgin's
miracles. The century was rich in Marian imagery, and provided ample resources which would be further elaborated in the following
century.

When the Virgin appeared to saints, it was often to comfort and
strengthen them. She came to Andrew Corsini as he said his first
mass, and told him, "You are my servant, for I have chosen you, and
in you I shall be proud." She visited Gerard Cagnoli just before his
death, comforted him, and invited him to join her soon in the glory of
paradise. When Bridget of Sweden lay in childbirth there were doubts
about whether she would live, but a woman garbed in white silk appeared, soothed her body with her touch, and brought her relief.
After experiencing that vision, Bridget gave birth easily. In a later
revelation, the Virgin informed the saint that she herself had been
that woman. Soon after James of Porta joined the Franciscans, he
went to an image of the Virgin and with tears asked for the grace of
perseverance in the religious life. Then he lay down on a bed, and she
appeared to him, putting her finger into his mouth; he held on to it
firmly with his teeth, and she pulled him up to a sitting position. He
was filled then with a sensation of great sweetness, and after this God
did great things with him.[31]

At times she appeared to give instruction, reprimand, or warning.
Thus, she appeared to Catherine of Sweden and instructed her that
she should set aside her own will and remain in Rome with her mother, in obedience to both her mother and her spiritual director. When
Catherine had difficulty persuading another woman to abandon her
fine attire and to dress more simply, the Virgin lent support: the two
women were together before an image of Mary, and Catherine's companion dozed off and had a vision in which Mary herself appeared,
looking pleasantly at Catherine but angrily at the companion. Greatly
disturbed, the sleeping woman asked, "My Lady, why are you looking
at me so fiercely?" The Virgin replied, "Why do you not obey the
counsels of my beloved Catherine? If you correct your habits and
manners according to her counsel and example, I will look at you, too,
fondly." The woman quickly complied.[32]

Another important motif in Marian visions was that of intercession.
Francis Patrizzi in a dream saw Mary speak with her son, whom she
held in her lap: "Oh my beloved, the beloved of my womb, what shall
I repay my beloved [Francis] for the reverence he has shown me?"
Christ said Francis should be honored on earth, "to your glory." Then
he reached out to Francis and invited him to enjoy eternal glory

among the blessed. Just then, the saint was abruptly awakened and summoned to lauds.[33]

The Virgin appeared frequently to Jane Mary of Maillé. Even when the saint was a young child, the Virgin came to her in a dream, holding Jesus in her arms, and censed her with a thurible which held drops of Christ's blood. In a later experience she gave the saint instruction on what kind of clothes to wear—humble ones, for the sake of Christ, who humbled himself in taking the form of a servant (cf. Phil. 2:7)—and cleansed her in ritual fashion by touching her face. When Jane Mary took part barefoot in a procession on the feast of the Purification, she saw the Blessed Virgin joining in the procession with her child in her arms; afterward, during mass, she had a vision of the Presentation itself, and then she had the privilege of holding Jesus in her own arms. One witness described how the saint lay ill in a forest chapel near Tours for three weeks; she lay on a pile of hay and straw, and was in such bad health that her death seemed near. Yet one night when the witness awoke after a brief sleep, it seemed to her that there was such brightness in the chapel that it was like noon, and the Blessed Virgin was standing in front of the saint. The next morning, it became clear that this apparition had effected a cure. Another witness told that when the saint lay sick the Virgin appeared and said, "Make haste to pray"; the saint replied, "Oh glorious Lady, Virgin Mary, do not wait for us to request it, but anticipate us in prayer." The saint's husband, too, enjoyed the Virgin's patronage: when he was taken prisoner in war, she visited and consoled him, eventually obtaining his release.[34]

One of the most interesting specimens of Marian literature from the fourteenth century, Bridget of Sweden's *Angelic Sermon*, was represented as the product of a vision.[35] The work is a rich mine of Marian theology. In the prologue, the saint tells how, while she was residing at Rome, she pondered what lessons she should prescribe as common reading in the convent of Vadstena which she had founded back in Sweden. She was praying about this when Christ appeared to her and said he would send an angel to dictate a series of lessons to her; she was to copy them down faithfully, and send them to her nuns so they could read them at matins. As it happened, Bridget had use of a room with a window overlooking an altar, so that she could look out upon the eucharist (an arrangement typically provided for anchorites' cells). Every day, sitting by this window, she prepared herself to write at the angel's dictation. When he arrived, he stood by her side, facing the altar, and would give her a portion of the series. She would then show the writing to her spiritual director. Sometimes the angel would fail to arrive, and when her director asked for that day's dictation she would have to say, "Father, today I have not written anything, for I waited long for the angel of the Lord, that he might dictate and I might write, but he did not come." At length, however, she copied down a series of three lessons for each day of the week.

The lessons for Sunday described how God loved Mary above all creatures from all eternity, in her archetypal pre-existence, before he created anything. The allegorical character of these reflections can be seen in Bridget's extended comparison between Mary and Noah's ark. She was in God's mind before he created her, as the ark was in Noah's mind when God had prescribed its plan but before Noah had carried out God's command. Noah rejoiced that his ark was impervious to storms; God rejoiced because the Virgin's body would be impervious to sin. And so forth. All this is followed in the *Sermon* by lessons on how the angels and patriarchs rejoiced in Mary's future creation, how she was conceived and born and matured, how she kept faith in her son when others despaired, and further topics. It is appropriate, Bridget says, that she should be called a blossoming rose, for just as a rose grows among thorns, so this venerable virgin grew in this world among tribulations; and just as a rose opens up more as its thorns become stronger and sharper, so also as she grew in age she was stung more sharply by the thorns of tribulation. Just as God and the angels took pleasure in her constancy, so likewise human beings took delight in how patiently she encountered tribulations, and how prudently she met with consolations. All this and more Bridget copied down faithfully from the angel.

While the Virgin occupied a special place in late medieval devotion, there were many saints to whom Christians were devoted as well.[36] Indeed, the fourteenth century was an age of particularly fervent veneration of the saints. It was during this period especially that the custom of naming children after saints became widespread in European society. Relics of the saints, while long popular, captured the imagination of lay as well as clerical society in the later Middle Ages as never before: they were more commonly owned by laypeople, and even when owned by ecclesiastical institutions they were more often put on public display in monstrance reliquaries. The shrines and feast days of the saints grew in popularity. Representation of the saints proliferated—alongside Marian art and art of the passion—in panel painting and in statuary. Legends of the saints, which underlay the other manifestations of devotion, had been catalogued in the thirteenth century in James of Voragine's classic *Golden Legend* and other such compendia, and further elaboration occurred as Latin and vernacular authors spun out ever new variations on traditional stories.

Numerous saints appeared to fourteenth-century visionaries. Commonly the saints in question were the ones whose pictures were widely displayed in churches: the New Testament saints, the early martyrs,

and the founders Francis and Dominic. When these founders appeared, it was often for partisan purposes. Before Catherine of Siena
became a Dominican, for example, she had a dream-vision in which
Dominic appeared to her; she recognized him because he was holding
a lily in his hand, as he typically did in art. (This flower, like the burning bush of Moses, was aflame without being consumed.) Founders of
other orders were likewise present, and they competed with Dominic
by inviting her to join their orders; yet she favored Dominic, who held
out the habit of his order and promised that some day she would wear
it. Somewhat less bold was a vision in which Francis of Assisi appeared
to Bridget of Sweden and invited her to see his house at Assisi, thus
inspiring a pilgrimage to that holy city.[37]

The canonization proceedings for Jane Mary of Maillé tell of several incidents in which the saints appeared to her. Mary Magdalene,
Stephen, and John the Baptist (in addition to Christ himself) often
came to her and accompanied her. Once Saints Gatianus and Martin
appeared to her with episcopal vestments, mitres, other insignia, and
a wealth of gems, showing the splendor of their merits. Another time,
on Pentecost of 1387, Francis of Assisi appeared along with the
Blessed Virgin; both of them were hovering in the air, praying for the
salvation of humankind. The vision of Francis lasted forty days, during which time Jane Mary saw him unceasingly. On two occasions
these apparitions were linked with the saints' relics. John the Baptist
and Stephen appeared to her one night, lying on the ground; she
invited them to stand up, whereupon they rose up into the air, and
John the Baptist proceeded to preach a sermon on contempt of the
world. After this, they vanished. A few days later, when she was in the
Franciscan church at Tours, she asked if there were any relics there,
and was shown relics of precisely these saints, unworthily hidden away
in the sacristy beneath a wooden altar. Evidently the vision was a sign
that the relics deserved to be brought out of this obscure repository
and placed on prominent display. On another occasion, Mary was
spending the night in a castle chapel where the head of one of St.
Ursula's 11,000 virgin companions was temporarily being kept on the
altar. While she prayed, the head was somehow brought to her from
the altar; she kissed it "in the usual manner," and then a youth appeared to her, and on bended knee he kissed her. She was given to
understand that the head belonged not to a female virgin but to a
man, though she did not ask his name, and it was not revealed to
her.[38]

While angels played a lesser role in the general culture and in the
saints' lives, they did make occasional appearances. One saint who
often beheld them was Flora of Beaulieu. She had great veneration
for the angels, and was able to perceive when they were present. At

times she asked her confessor whether he was able to see angels standing about, and she would point out to him in what direction he should
look, but he seemed to lack her sensitivity to them. One day while she
was praying an angel came and stood beside her, carrying a two-
pointed sword, marvelously wrought, which she took as a weapon
against the assaults of the enemy; it was, her biographer says, an apt
symbol of that word which the Apostle speaks of as more piercing
than any two-edged sword (Heb. 4:12). Another time an angel in the
form of an elegant youth came to her and handed her a gold cup with
divine nectar, saying, "Drink, and take in hand this chalice of salvation." She had scarcely tasted the heavenly liquor when she perceived
its ineffable sweetness, and at once she attended in contemplation to
the angel who ministered the cup. As if in play, he splashed on her
face what was left in the chalice, and then he suddenly departed. With
wet mouth, she returned to herself, and found that she was able to go
days without terrestrial food.[39]

Henry Suso was another recipient of frequent angelic visitations.
Spirits appeared to him most commonly in groups. On the feast of all
the angels a band of them appeared to him in the form of youths; one
of them, who seemed to have the dignity of an archangel and who
appeared as a heavenly minstrel, was apparently the leader of the
group. Encouraging Suso to be joyful, he took his hand and danced to
In dulci jubilo. They "made the highest, wildest leaps and bounds";
their dance was "like a heavenly flowing forth and back again into the
lonely abyss of the divine mystery." On this and on other occasions
they did much to cheer him up. Once, when he was afflicted with
illness and other problems, angels came to him, sang sweetly, and
encouraged him to sing. One of them assured him that he would not
die but would "live to sing such a song that God in His eternity will be
praised, and many a suffering soul will be comforted thereby."[40]

The connection between visions and general religious culture in all
these cases was fairly straightforward: it was perfectly natural that the
saints should share in the devotional life of their era, and that in their
visions they should behold those figures to whom they were most devoted; stories of these visions would in turn reinforce the popular
veneration of these celestial visitors. In the case of eucharistic devotion, the connection was more complex. In popular piety, the eucharist was increasingly conceived in magical terms: publicly
displayed not only at the elevation of the mass but also in elaborately
encrusted monstrances, it was an object capable of working miracles
of all sorts. The fourteenth century was the age in which miraculous
bleeding hosts became popular centers for pilgrimages. At the same
time, the mystics of the century continued the tendency of earlier
female mystics to perceive the eucharist as a catalyst for inward, mys-

tical transports. Some of the mystics, such as Meister Eckhart, tended to conflate the experience of mystical union with that of communion: partaking of the eucharist was a way of joining one's soul with God in a way analogous to that of mystical absorption, and Eckhart was willing to use standard mystical language in referring to the eucharist. In various ways, for certain of the fourteenth-century saints mystical experiences were linked with intense devotion to this sacrament. The most straightforward connection was one of cause and effect: the reception of communion, or even exposure to the consecrated host, was the stimulus that aroused the saint to ecstasy, or the occasion for a vision in some way related to the eucharist. Another possibility was for the saint to be carried away in a kind of mystical swoon out of desire to receive the host, as often happened to Dorothy of Montau. Yet the possibilities extended further, to experiences in which mystery and miracle became intermingled.[41]

Raptures occasioned by the eucharist were not rare. Flora of Beaulieu underwent them regularly during mass, at the moment the priest took the eucharist in his mouth; she would not return to herself until vespers. When she herself was fed with this heavenly food, every Sunday and feast day, she would suddenly be "rapt to the higher table of the Lord, where she received heavenly sweetnesses and delights of heavenly charisms." Standing in the halls of the Lord's own house, she learned the most hidden of mysteries. As she approached for communion, she burned so vehemently within herself, as if boiling over from excess of love, that two sisters had to help her going and coming. Afterward she was unable to take wine or even water. She would be taken back to her room, where the sheer intensity of the experience left her for a long time unable to depart. She assumed that other people, especially priests, were likewise affected by the sacrament, and she marveled that any priest could handle the sacred elements without entering ecstasy.[42]

Eucharistic apparitions were also known. Christina Ebner sometimes saw Christ in human form in the hands of the celebrant. Jane Mary of Maillé, too, had a vision when a priest elevated the host at one mass: she saw a small child with wounds in his side, hands, and feet, with blood gushing out of various parts of his body. Clearly such visions were related to the spread in veneration of miraculous bleeding hosts; both the visions and the miracles were signs of a popular liturgical realism.[43]

Perhaps the most revealing incidents are those in which the saints obtained the eucharist in miraculous ways. When Jane Mary of Maillé was lying ill, she prayed that she might take a drink from the priest's chalice, and suddenly she found her mouth filled with blood. Flora of Beaulieu likewise benefited from such a miracle. In a church three leagues distant from her convent, a priest she knew was saying mass and broke the host into customary three parts, and put two of them on the paten, but then could not find the third one anywhere. He was much distraught, and after mass went to consult with Flora. He had not yet entered the convent when she came up to him, smiling, and said, "Do not be troubled, Father, for the third part of the host, which departed from you, has not been lost; rather, an angel of the Lord took it and brought it to refresh me."[44]

Perhaps the most important feature of this eucharistic mysticism is that it was the specialty of women. Raptures and visions generally were more important to the female than to the male saints, with few exceptions: when men did have visions, they were seldom integral to their lives as for the women. (The one most important exception is Henry Suso.) Eucharistic mysticism, all the more clearly, was a phenomenon associated with the women. Indeed, this was the case even earlier, as the female mysticism of the twelfth and thirteenth centuries attests. It has been suggested that the reason for this is that women, being unable to consecrate and administer the eucharist, felt a particularly keen need to associate themselves with this sacrament—the most important sacramental means for joining oneself on a regular basis with God—through extraordinary experiences.[45] Flora of Beaulieu need not have been surprised, then, that priests could handle the sacred elements without ecstasy. For the males who were ordained to consecrate the eucharist, it was a manifestation of that divine order by which the process of sanctification was routinely carried out, and though it was miraculous it did not require a sense of intense mystical identification on their part. There were practical reasons as well for the absence of eucharistic mysticism among the priests. Apart from the fact that for them it was a routine, they were faced with the demand to get on with the mass, without its being interrupted with mystical intrusions. Surely the more significant factor, though, was that if they wanted intimate contact with the eucharist they could easily attain it simply by carrying out their sacerdotal role. One might ask why married laymen, excluded from the priest's privileges as much as were women, did not share their eucharistic mysticism. Perhaps they represent too small a class on which to pass judgment. If there had been more individuals such as Elzear of Sabran (who was indeed devoted to the eucharist, though without the mystical involvement of the women) there might have been a male counterpart to this female phenomenon. But the most pertinent consideration here, no doubt, is that laymen, not being biologically precluded from priesthood, had no sense of radical distance from the eucharist to be overcome through mystical means. They were de facto excluded, but must always have been aware that it was in principle possible for them to have become priests, and even to exchange their marital status for priesthood (if circumstances and uxorial tolerance allowed).[46]

Apart from the specifically eucharistic mysticism that flourished among the saints, there were mystical experiences associated with the broader liturgical context of the mass. Christina Ebner's visions, for example, frequently took place during mass, and commonly she was assured that those attending mass with her would receive various favors: contrition for their sins, the grace to live better lives, special forgiveness, release from punishment in purgatory, or other such favors. Once she was "rapt into heaven" while she was at mass, and saw the Lord with a wondrous crown. He spoke to her, saying that none of those who were at that mass would ever be separated from him. When the people at mass sang, the Son remarked to the Father, "How beautifully they are serving me!" The Father blessed all who were present. Then the Son stood before the Father with arms out-stretched, and said, "Father, I stood thus on the holy cross until my soul went out from me. Thus, I wish to receive all of them in the arms of my mercy, and give them the kiss of my love." All the angels and saints then came and fell on their faces before him, kissing his feet. He allowed Christina to suck from the wounds in his divine heart, as the bees do from flowers. Throughout, she seems to have remained vaguely conscious of the mass that was being celebrated on earth. While in this case the mystical experience was a full-fledged narrative vision, there are other saints for whom the mass occasioned simpler visions: Christ appeared to John Ruysbroeck during mass, for instance, and said, "You are mine and I am yours."[47]

It was not only the celebration of the mass that could inspire such experiences, but the liturgical calendar as well. It was on the feast of All Saints that Flora of Beaulieu found her mind raised up to heaven, where she conversed with the blessed, witnessing how they enjoy a "torrent of delights." She could not yet see the source of their bliss— that is, she herself did not share in the beatific vision of God—but she had a passionate yearning to do so. On November 22, the feast of St. Cecilia, Flora meditated on that blessed martyr's marriage with her "heavenly bridegroom." She beheld a virgin, wondrously attired, standing forth among the other virgins. Stunned by the elegance of their form, by the sweetness of their songs, by the splendor of their ornament, and by the brightness and pleasantness of the place where they stood, she asked her angel escort who the central figure was, and the angel identified her as St. Cecilia.[48]

Visions focusing on scenes from the life of Christ could readily be inspired by the liturgical cycle. Thus, Jane Mary of Maillé witnessed the events of the Annunciation on the feast of the Annunciation, and on the feast of Mary Magdalene she joined with that saint in holding the feet of Jesus as he reclined in the house of the Pharisee. Flora of Beaulieu followed the liturgical cycle, attending with special fervor to the mysteries celebrated at each juncture, and she received visions and manifestations of these mysteries from heaven. At Christmastime she envisaged the "infant God" as if on that very day he were wrapped in swaddling clothes and ensconced in a manger. On the feast of the Purification she saw how the "boy God" was offered in the Temple. On Easter she saw with her own eyes how the Lord spoke with the women at the tomb, and she listened carefully to his words. On the Ascension she contemplated the Lord as he ascended on high and blessed her along with his disciples. The Holy Spirit bestowed spiritual joy and consolation on her for the feast of Pentecost. In all of this she "followed the mind of the Catholic Church" in its liturgical celebration, and thus manifested that liturgical realism—the sense that the liturgy represents a higher level of reality than daily life, in that it makes the events of Christian history actually present—that we have seen elsewhere.[49]

The Agony of Ecstasy

The aspects of mystical experience thus far covered were essentially unproblematic for the saints who enjoyed such favors. Often they took consolation from them; commonly the experiences were marks of special privilege. This was clear from the visions of Christina Ebner, to whom Christ declared, "What more shall I do for you? I have worked such great wonders with you that one's heart can scarcely believe it. I have poured out the treasury of my sweetness into you. You are one of those persons to whom I have given my gifts most lavishly." This exaltation of the mystics was further enhanced by the intercessory role they sometimes played. It was for Christina's sake that God lavished favors on her companions, and just as he honored Israel for the sake of his mother, so also Christ gave special treatment to Nuremberg because of Christina.[50] While the saints' narrative visions and their experience of mystical union served essentially to enrich their own spiritual lives, there were other forms of experience in which God worked through the saints, for the benefit of society: in simpler visions the saints often received messages that could be communicated to others, and their prophecies were almost always transmitted as a service to those about them. To this extent, the raptures and revelations we have discussed present a counterthrust to that tendency seen elsewhere in the saints' lives, the focus on their disquietude and on God's work specifically for them. Looking more closely, however, one finds a darker side even to such mystical experiences.

Shortly after Bridget of Sweden's husband died, the saint was praying in her chapel for help in adjusting herself to the state of widowhood, when suddenly she entered a state of rapture. She beheld a shining cloud, and from the cloud she heard a voice proclaim, "Woman, hear me." Terrified that it might be a delusion, she fled to her bedchamber, then went to confess and to fortify herself with communion. A few days later the shining cloud again appeared to her in the same chapel, and again the voice demanded, "Woman, hear me." As before, she fled in terror to her chamber, confessed, and received communion. In a few more days the experience occurred once more. This time the voice said, "Woman, hear me—I am your God, who wishes to speak with you." She was again terror-struck, and feared that it was a delusion, but the voice continued: "Do not be afraid, for I am the creator of all, and not a deceiver, for I do not speak with you for your sake alone, but for the salvation of others. Hear what I speak, and go to Master Matthias, your confessor, who is expert at discernment of spirits, and tell him for me what I am saying to you—for you will be my bride and my channel, and you will hear and see spiritual things, and my spirit will remain with you even to death." This was the first of many revelations that she received, awake and in prayer, over several years, which went into the making of her *magnum opus*, the *Revelations*. While she eventually became accustomed to these incursions of divine majesty, their initial impact on her was discomforting in the extreme.[51]

Bridget's fear of demonic delusion was not unique. Another saint who had such fears was Catherine of Siena. When she went off to a cave outside of town and began the life of a hermit, she found herself levitating uncontrollably to the top of the cave, and she attributed this occurrence to the devil's intervention. In adulthood, too, Catherine was wary of the devil's touch when she had mystical experiences. More often, when the devil attacked his presence was unmistakable. He appeared to Peter Olafsson as a horrible monster, whose head towered over the rooftops, and who hurled a large stone against the door of the saint's house with such force that it left a mark there "as a sign of the cunning of that ancient serpent, who leaves his deadly venom on the paths of the innocent." He afflicted Catherine of Siena as she lay in bed by causing her to bang her head against an earthenware jar, so that she broke it and the burning coals inside it spilled over her. To John Ruysbroeck he appeared as a toad or some other "terrible creature." Once, when this saint was an old man and was sleeping in the same cell as the provost of the monastery so that the latter could take care of him, he perceived that the Evil One was about to appear, and he cried out, "Father, he is coming! Father, he is coming!"—no doubt to the provost's great consternation.[52]

The saints who suffered these assaults from the netherworld were often the same ones who enjoyed consolations from celestial spirits. It is as if they possessed a sensitivity toward spiritual realities that opened for them experiences of all sorts, both positive and negative, that were closed to ordinary mortals. More broadly speaking, the saints were uniquely conscious of both benevolent and malevolent forces about them, and this consciousness often manifested itself in the form of visions. It is no wonder that such sensitivity aroused an ambivalent response to that numinous realm where they did not know what they might encounter.

The most dramatic instance of demonic assault in the saints' lives may be found in the life of Catherine of Siena, in a passage clearly modeled after the classic temptation of St. Anthony.[53] Seeing her rise to great spiritual perfection, the fiend feared that she would bring salvation to many others as well, and would be of service to the Church. He adopted "a thousand cunning and malicious ruses to lead her astray." The Lord allowed her to be assaulted, so that in fighting she would make more spiritual progress than if left alone. He had "armed His tower with the defence of sound doctrines," then "opened its gates to its enemies to see whether they could take it by storm." The besieging hordes first tried carnal temptations, provoking Catherine with unclean thoughts and visions, which she overcame with sleeplessness and by beating herself with an iron chain. They took on the form of sympathetic counsellors, who advised that she do some good for the world by taking a husband and having children, but she endured these temptations too, trusting not in herself but in the Lord, and refusing to engage the enemy in debate. The devil then "brought vile pictures of men and women behaving loosely before her mind, and foul figures before her eyes, and obscene words to her ears, shameless crowds dancing around her, howling and sniggling and inviting her to join them." In addition, she was apparently abandoned by her heavenly bridegroom. She began spending more time in church, where she was less troubled by such temptations. Ultimately she overcame them with prayer. Suddenly illuminated by the Holy Spirit, she understood that the temptations were given to enhance her fortitude, whereon she resolved cheerfully to bear them as long as the Lord required. One bold demon threatened to persecute her to the very death, but Catherine replied, "With joy I have chosen the way of suffering and shall endure these and any other persecutions in the name of the Saviour for as long as it shall please Him to send them, in fact I shall enjoy them." The evil spirits then withdrew in shame, and suddenly, as in the temptation of Anthony, the experience ended in a glorious vision:

> there came from on high a great light that lit up the whole room, and in the light was the Lord Jesus Christ, nailed to the cross and bleeding as when he entered the holy of holies through the shedding of His own blood. From the cross He called down to the holy virgin, "Catherine, my daughter, you see how much I suffered for you? Do not be sad, then, that you must suffer for me." Then His appearance changed and He came closer to her, and to comfort her He spoke sweetly of the victory she had gained. But like Anthony she said, "My Lord, where were you when my heart was disturbed by all those temptations?" "I was in your heart," said the Lord. "May your truth always be preserved, Lord, and all reverence to Your Majesty," said Catherine, "But how can I possibly believe that you were in my heart when it was full of ugly, filthy thoughts?" "Did those thoughts and temptations bring content or sorrow, delight or displeasure to your heart?" asked the Lord. "The greatest sorrow and displeasure," answered Catherine. "Well, then," said the Lord, "who was hidden at the centre of your heart?"

Christ then assured her, "since you fought the good fight not by yourself but with me, you deserve greater grace from me, and from now on I shall appear to you oftener and closer."

This scene differs from the patristic model on which it is based mainly in the intrusion of motifs that were fundamental to fourteenth-century piety as they had not been in the fourth century: the patience manifested in Catherine's willing acceptance of suffering as a means for greater virtue; the penitence shown in her reluctance to imagine that the Lord could have been present within her mind when it was filled with unclean thoughts; the devotion to the passion revealed in the final vision of Christ crucified; and the promise of mystical consolations as a reward for what she had endured. To be sure, there were fourth-century analogues to all these phenomena, yet the phrasing and emphases are distinctive to Catherine's era.

Yet it was not only demons and fear of demons that created problems; the difficulties lay deeper. Even divinely bestowed experiences were so intense as to leave the saints exhausted both spiritually and physically. Second, the fleeting taste of ecstasy was often enough to make all earthly joys insipid, so that the saints were left yearning and languishing for the final release of death, which would bring perpetual bliss. And third, the intermittent moments of rapture that God afforded his saints might be interspersed with long periods of spiritual dryness and a sense of abandonment. The mystical life was by no means necessarily one of uninterrupted bliss. Indeed, many of the saints in this period appear feverish in their piety largely because their privileged experiences left them anxious and enervated.

That the positive and negative features of these experiences were integrally intertwined is suggested by those passages in which the intense bliss itself appears as excruciating. When Jane Mary of Maillé had a vision of the Annunciation, she rejoiced greatly at it, yet her heartfelt piety moved her to much weeping, and she could not restrain the tears that flowed from her eyes. The abbess of the convent where she was staying heard her crying out bitterly, and fetched a cloth so she could wipe off her face and eyes. Rulman Merswin, too, wept uncontrollably when he had his first experience of ecstasy, and even noted that his heart was beating irregularly. In one of her experiences Flora of Beaulieu found that she "could scarcely bear the torrent of inner sweetness" that gushed upon her; in another, she was moved to wonderment and even terror at beholding the abyss of divinity. And Dorothy of Montau's biographer says expressly that the joys and anguish of her spiritual life occurred not in alteration but simultaneously and indistinguishably.[54]

Frequently the saints are spoken of, in terms borrowed from the Song of Songs, as "languishing" in reaction to their mystical experiences. Flora of Beaulieu was stunned (*stupefacta*), seemed to burn and boil over with the heat of divine love, and languished (*diffluebat*) in sweet tears. John of Alverna "almost fainted" for the magnitude of what he felt in his soul. And as we have already seen, "languishing" love was one of the mainstays of Dorothy of Montau's spirituality.[55]

Having tasted the sweetness of ecstasy, the saints could scarcely content themselves with normal human pleasures and involvements. Elzear of Sabran, having enjoyed a revelation of all the mysteries of the Christian faith, was greatly transformed; he could not eat the next day, and found it painful to converse, so that those around him thought he was ill. He kept silent, ruminating the wonders God had shown him. God had commanded that he return to the humdrum world of secular affairs, but to occupy himself with such distractions was acutely painful and laborious for him; his biographer comments that the patience with which he endured this pain must have been highly meritorious.[56]

The ultimate release for which the saints longed was that of death. Flora of Beaulieu had a keen desire for eternal glory, and had more appetite for the angelic than for human life. Having enjoyed the contemplation of spiritual matters, she desired to be "dissolved," and to depart from this life as quickly as possible, to be with Christ. That death which is terrible to all normal mortals was pleasant and lovable for her. Often her desire for it seemed to exhaust all the powers of her heart.[57] It may have been for similar reasons that Peter of Luxembourg faced death with grand enthusiasm.

The saints were, in short, keenly aware of their alien status in this life, and the postponement of their entry into their homeland, with all the burdens that they had to endure as they waited, was a source of excruciating anguish for them.

7
Unquiet Souls

O n one occasion when the Holy Spirit came to Dorothy of Montau, he infused in her a wide variety of loves, including "impa-
tient" and "inquietative" love; her soul became eager for the Lord and
unquiet (*inquieta*), and in her desire for God she raved (*insaniebat*) a
great deal, finding it impossible to obtain rest in this life. Again, the
Lord once sent his Spirit with great "desiderative, satiative, boiling,
maddening, and inquietative love," causing her to grow delirious and
unquiet (*insana et inquieta*) in her yearning for eternal life. Her heart
burned fervently, as if it were on fire, and began to bubble up as if it
were a heated pot. Ardent tears flowed from her eyes. She perspired
as if she were sitting in a hot bath. The more she burned, and the
more she cried, the more she grew unquiet and desirous of fulfillment. Such experiences were not manifestations of grief, but of exquisite delight. In particular, after the extraction of her heart she
often enjoyed such ineffable delights that she could neither stand nor
walk even sit down to rest, because she trembled all over. Laboring to find rest (*quietis impatiens*), she would first stand and then sit,
and then lie down, folding and wringing her hands, thus demonstrating that alongside the passive component of suffering there could be
an intensely active involvement in one's anguish. Though she be-
haved like a person in great sorrow and misery, in her case these
actions were expressions of intense joy and love. Likewise, when she
received the eucharist on one occasion the Lord came to her in a disquieting (*inquietativus*) manner, causing her great unrest (*inquietem*),
and hunger and thirst of both body and soul. And when she was enclosed in her cell, the Lord sent the Holy Spirit with insatiable and

indefatigable love which caused her to have no rest (*quietem*) what-soever. While in many such passages her biographer underscores the bliss that accompanied such experiences, elsewhere he remarks that her consolation and her afflictions were inextricably intertwined. Clearly there was reason for ambivalence about these states of soul.[1]

Such passages would surely have reminded an educated four-teenth-century reader of the classic lines in Augustine's *Confessions* in which that father of Western spirituality proclaimed that we are made to be with God, and the human heart is restless (*inquietum*) until it finds its rest (*requiescat*) in him.[2] To be sure, Augustine is not known to have shown this mentality as dramatically as the fourteenth-century German mystic and many of her contemporaries. He was inwardly intense, perhaps, but not excitable, nor prone to feverish displays of spiritual disquietude. He was never bedridden for several days with Dorothy's "languishing love." Nonetheless, what Dorothy's biog-rapher recounts is a late medieval rendition of Augustine's yearning. In each case, the prevailing sense is one of a soul tormented—subtly in Augustine's case and quite unsubtly in Dorothy's—by the sug-gestion of a spiritual fulfillment not yet attained, or an ideal as yet unrealized. In Dorothy's case as in Augustine's, the theme of dis-quietude underscores the position of the human being on earth as a *viator,* a wayfarer, destined ultimately for a paradisal repose and capa-ble of only temporary refreshment until that final rest is attained.[3]

To what extent was Dorothy typical of her era? There were several other saints during the fourteenth century who showed a similar ex-citability; Flora of Beaulieu comes readily to mind. More important, the intense consciousness of a gap between ideal and reality is some-thing that arises frequently enough in fourteenth-century hagiogra-phy to form a characteristic motif. The raptures of fourteenth-century saints are often disquieting experiences, which leave a burn-ing desire to transcend this earthly life and enter into eternal bliss. The penitential fervor of the age rendered this sense all the more poignant: not only was the world in general imperfect and distracting, but one's own soul fell all too far short of the ideal. Devotion to Christ's passion was disquieting not only because it induced a keen sense of compassion with the excruciating pain of the Savior, and a craving to share in that suffering, but because it heightened one's feelings of guilt for having occasioned Christ's burden. Similar expe-riences can be found in the saints' lives of any era, but they are seldom so intense as in the fourteenth century. While the pious Christians of that century labored to maintain patience in the face of external ad-versity, their accommodation to outward affliction did not leave them serene, confident, and composed. Rather, they remained acutely vulnerable to inward torment. Such, in any case, is the view of saintliness found in many of the hagiographic texts.

One senses at times that the saints took a certain delight in this affliction, or perhaps rather in their ability to withstand it. If that was indeed the case, then the eagerness to undergo outward suffering and the tendency toward inner anguish may have stemmed from a common urge to test and prove themselves. Protesting their own frailty, they demonstrated to themselves and their contemporaries that they were in fact able to live in the midst of afflictions from both within and without. If the sources permitted, it would be fascinating to satisfy one's curiosity about these matters.

The intensity of religious fervor during this era can be gauged to an extent by the frequency with which the saints were moved to tears of devotion. The phenomenon was certainly ancient, and gospel precedent could always be cited,[4] but again it was fourteenth-century saints who developed the art to perfection. Francis Patrizzi, for example, wept bitterly as he prayed to the Virgin, and was accustomed to say that one should never request a grace of God or his mother without shedding tears. Clare Gambacorta was endowed with the wonderful gift of "prayer and tears," and even at age twelve would weep in a "marvelous" way while praying. Gonsalvo Sancii "prayed and wept" constantly, and Catherine of Sweden shared this inclination. When Ademar of Felsinio entered the Franciscan order, he went so far as to set aside a part of each day for prayer, meditation, and "profuse tears," so firmly established were his emotional inclinations. Dorothy of Montau, similarly, was blessed with a rich flow of pious tears, as her biographer mentions on numerous occasions. Dalmatius Moner "prayed ceaselessly with abundant tears, and afflicted himself with frequent sighs and beatings of his breast."[5] Such profusion of tears must, of course, be understood against the background of a culture that was generally not shy about displaying emotion. Even within such a milieu, however, the saints distinguished themselves by the depth of their fervor. Their tears were by no means a sign of weakness but rather of their sensitivity toward the divine and toward the gulf which unfortunately separated themselves from God. In their raptures and in their identification with the crucified Savior they sought to close this gap, but their penitential exercises reminded them that it still remained.

Margery Kempe: The Harvest of Fourteenth-Century Spirituality

While the fourteenth century brought an exceptionally steady stream of saintly disquietude, one should not imagine any artificial boundaries between the fourteenth-century saints and their predecessors or successors. Earlier saints such as Mary of Oignies shared many of their traits, though such spirituality was less widely venerated in the earlier period; and Rose of Lima imitated Catherine of Siena as nearly as one could do in seventeenth-century Peru.[6] While the intensity of saintly fervor became more intermittent as time went on, it was not altogether lost. One figure who serves as a reminder of this continuity in religious ideals, and who thus provides a convenient capstone for this study, was Margery Kempe, an Englishwoman of the late fourteenth and early fifteenth century who sums up conveniently the spirituality of the era.

Margery was born in about 1373, the year Bridget of Sweden died, and the year in which Julian of Norwich received her revelations.[7] Hailing from a patrician family of King's Lynn, she married a man from a lower social class in 1393, and bore him fourteen children. After one childbirth she was seriously ill, feared she would die, and sent for her confessor. When he arrived, she came close to telling him a sin that she had (at the devil's suggestion) long left unconfessed; but he treated her too harshly, and even now she could not bring herself to tell that one unspecified offense. Over the next eight months she was greatly vexed with fear of damnation, and saw visions of demons opening their mouths to pull her down into "burning waves of fire." The demons encouraged her to abandon all effort at virtue; as she tells us, she followed their counsel and led a wicked and slanderous life. Utterly disconsolate, she bit her hand and left a permanent scar, and scratched the skin over her heart. She had to be constrained forcibly, at last, day and night, until Christ appeared to her and she was cured.

Even then she was held back from a life of religious fervor by her love of ostentatious apparel, which she wore (she said) to maintain her family's reputation. To further their financial condition, she went briefly into the brewing trade, but failed; the same fate befell her when she tried milling. Recognizing these business disasters as God's scourge, she imposed great bodily penances upon herself, especially fasts and long periods of prayer in church. For two years she performed these austerities easily, with no sense that her body was resisting them. She continued having sexual relations with her husband only out of obedience, though she found her marital debt so "abominable" that she would rather have "eaten or drunk the ooze and the muck in the gutter." To counter her sense of pride in her religious accomplishments, God then sent her three years of temptations. Lust in particular assailed her, though she craved relations only with men other than her husband. At one point she went so far as to consent to a certain man's proposition, but it turned out that he was not serious, and he said he would rather have himself chopped into mincemeat than sleep with her. Uncomfortable with these inclinations within herself, for some time she went through an agonizing cycle of penitence and despair.

At last she had a decisive conversion experience as she knelt one day in a chapel, weeping and begging God's forgiveness. Christ again came to her, "ravished her spirit," assured her that she would attain salvation without even passing through purgatory, promised his succor in times of hardship, and instructed her how she should live from then on. He told her to go to a certain anchorite for guidance; when she did so, the anchorite advised that she relate to him all the thoughts she felt were from God, so that he could discern whether they were in fact from God or from the devil. She went through one further period of temptation, as punishment for doubting that a certain revelation was from God. Apart from that, the rest of her life was one of devotion. She went on pilgrimage to Canterbury, to the Holy Land, and to Santiago de Compostela. In 1415 she celebrated in Rome the confirmation of Bridget of Sweden's canonization. Later she went to Norway and Danzig; it has been conjectured by more than one author that in Danzig she may have learned of Dorothy of Montau.[8] On a trip to Rome she made a reverential visit to the house where Bridget of Sweden had lived, and despite the language barrier she spoke with that saint's former maid. She traveled also to Norwich, where she spoke with Julian of Norwich and obtained reassurance that her spiritual experiences were divine rather than diabolical. Indeed, for the remainder of her life she enjoyed a steady stream of revelations, to which we will return shortly. Furthermore, she finally obtained release from her marital obligations. One sultry day, when she and her husband had gone several weeks without intercourse, they were walking down a road with some sort of cake and a bottle of beer, and he asked her whether she would prefer resuming sexual relations or having her head lopped off. When she opted for the latter choice, he concluded that she was "no good wife." Ultimately, in 1413, they took formal vows of chastity before the local bishop, and began to live separately.

While Margery herself could not read, she knew a priest who read the Bible and biblical commentaries to her, as well as the works of Bonaventure, Bridget of Sweden, Richard Rolle, Walter Hilton, and others.[9] A more significant result of such literacy-by-extension came in response to one of her revelations: Christ commanded her, so that his beneficence might become known to many, to have an account written of her own life. She dictated an account to a man who had spent part of his life in England but most of it in Germany. After he died, she showed his manuscript to a priest, who discovered that it was virtually incomprehensible because of the man's scrawl and his poor command of both English and German. After much procrastination, and an abortive attempt to decipher the script with the aid of a pair of spectacles, the priest kept on trying, and with divine aid he found at last that he could make out the text and recopy it. What was thus produced was the earliest autobiography in English. Kept for centuries in the holdings of a private family, and assumed by the scholarly community to have been lost, the book reached the Victoria and Albert Museum in 1934 when its binding needed repair. Because an expert on fourteenth-century piety happened to be on hand to inspect the contents, the work was at long last identified and made public.

What Magery's autobiography makes clear is that she shared in all the tendencies of fourteenth-century saints: she cultivated fervently the virtue of patience, she was keenly devoted to the passion, penitence was a major theme in her life, she enjoyed raptures and revelations in great abundance, and in every aspect of her piety there was a spirit of intensity that made her stand out as a noteworthy character.

She had ample occasion to exercise the virtue of patience. While some of her contemporaries thought it possible that she might be a saint, others reviled her. In her own words: "Some said it was an evil spirit which afflicted her, some said it was a sickness, some said she had drunk too much wine; some cursed her, some wished her in the harbour, some would have liked her out at sea in a bottomless boat." Many saw her as an hysterical woman or an exhibitionist, particularly because of her long hours of weeping and sobbing in church. Largely for that reason she had trouble keeping traveling companions. At one point a man dumped a bowl of water on her head as she was walking down the street. In a more serious episode, after a day spent weeping and praying in the cathedral at Canterbury, she found herself confronted by a throng of monks and laypeople, who came close to burning her as a heretic; as she stood outside the town gates at sunset, members of the gaping crowd called out for her to be burned. Her husband, in the meantime, walked off and pretended not to know her.[10]

As she sat one day in a church at York, Christ remarked to her that she seemed overcome with tribulation. Gloomy and ashamed, she did not answer. Christ suggested that if his love was ill compensation for her sufferings he would withdraw it—to which she asked him rather to give her strength to suffer as he willed, and meekness and patience to endure this suffering. From then on, knowing that it was God's will that she suffer, she accepted it gladly and gratefully; eventually she reached a point at which she was disconsolate if she did not suffer tribulation of some kind. Christ had already promised that she would be crucified only by the suffering of "cruel words." Happy to imitate

him at least to that extent, she recognized her own affliction as mini-
mal: "I have cause to be right merry and glad in my soul that I may
suffer anything for His love, for He suffered much more for me."
Expanding on this point, she said she did not suffer as much as she
would like to for the sake of the Lord's love, since she suffered only
verbal abuse, while he underwent blows, scourging, and shameful
death. Yet Christ assured her that it was more pleasing for him that
she should suffer "despites and scorns, shames and reproofs, wrongs
and discomforts" than if her "head were smitten off three times a day
every day for seven years." Furthermore, he promised that on her
death all her suffering would be turned to joy.[11]

Like some of her predecessors in the fourteenth century, Margery
dreamed of undergoing the ultimate suffering of martyrdom, though
she immediately added that she preferred beheading, as the easiest
form of martyrdom she could imagine. Christ appeared to her and
thanked her for this sentiment, assuring her that because of it she
would enjoy a martyr's reward in heaven, yet frustrating her hopes by
telling her she was not called to actual martyrdom.[12]

As has perhaps already become clear, penitence formed another
dominant motif in her autobiography, particularly during those years
when she verged on despair over the fate of her soul. On the first
page of her book, she refers to herself as a "sinful caitiff"; if the reference is in some measure conventional, the sentiment is nonetheless
heartfelt. After her first conversion experience, when she had two
years of easy sanctity, she confessed her sins as often as two or three
times a day, dwelling in particular on that sin which she had previously concealed. It was to undo the effects of her sin that she imposed ascetic penances upon herself: she wore a hair-cloth under her
clothing, in addition to other forms of penitence. During one of her
revelations she begged Christ to forgive the sins of others, just as he
had forgiven hers: "I wish I had a well of tears to constrain You with,
so that You would not take complete vengeance upon man's soul by
separating him from You for ever." Not surprisingly, she had a special devotion to Mary Magdalene.[13]

Yet another keynote in her piety was her abiding preoccupation
with the passion. In the revelations, Christ encouraged her to keep it
in mind: "When you weep and mourn for my pain and my passion,
then you are a very mother having compassion on her child." After
her initial conversion experience she found herself wishing often that
the Crucified would release his hands from the cross and embrace
her; later, Christ told her in a revelation that he would offer her soul
to the Father with those very hands. She meditated intently on the
passion, and beheld the scene as vividly as if she were there, with
Christ hanging on the cross before her, "his precious, tender body all

ragged and torn by scourges, more full of wounds than ever was a dovecote full of holes, hanging upon the cross with the crown of thorns upon his head, his blessed hands, his feet nailed to the hard tree." At Leicester she entered a church and saw a crucifix "piteously painted and lamentable to behold, through the sight of which the passion of our Lord entered her mind." When she saw a pietà at Norwich, she felt such compassion for Christ and his mother that she wept aloud. A priest upbraided her for this, saying that Christ had been dead for a long time, but she insisted, "Sir, his death is as fresh to me as if he had died today, and it seems to me that it should be so to you and to all Christian people." At one point she had a long and particularly detailed vision of the passion. Being as sensitive as she was, when she went to Jerusalem and stood on the spot where Christ was supposed to have been crucified, she underwent more than her usual spasms of tears. Indeed, she fell to the ground and cried aloud in unquiet rapture. Even when she was at home, however, she could obtain the benefits of a pilgrim: in one revelation Christ assured her that she needed only to say or think the words, "Honored be all those holy places in Jerusalem in which Christ suffered bitter pain and passion," and she would obtain the same indulgence as a pilgrim to these sites.[14]

The centrality of revelations and other mystical experiences in Margery's life is likewise evident. Her revelations were of two main sorts: in some Christ himself spoke to her, giving her instruction and consolation; in others she beheld various scenes from the life of Christ, especially his infancy and passion. In the latter revelations or visions she was apparently influenced by the details given in art and literature, even though the gospel text was usually the main basis for her accounts. It has been suggested that some of the detail came from liturgy. Her rendition of the events of Palm Sunday, for example, seems to be derived from her experience of liturgical processions.[15]

Apart from these revelations, there were further mystical experiences. At times she sensed "a flame of fire about her breast, full hot and delectable," or heard "the voice of a sweet bird singing in her ear." At other times she detected odors sweeter than anything she had ever smelled on earth. Both day and night she beheld "with her bodily eyes" (as opposed to the purely spiritual visions of her "ghostly" sense) an array of bright objects flying about her like "specks in a sunbeam." A modern reader might be inclined to suggest an ophthalmological condition, but Christ told her these objects were signs of the numerous angels hovering about.[16]

Her experiences could in more than one way be disconcerting. It was not only that they aroused such intense devotion and left her with a sense of the inadequacy of terrestrial life. The further fact that impressed itself on her conscience was that these phenomena could be dangerous. "Sometimes," the autobiography tells us, "she was in great gloom for her feelings, when she knew not how they should be understood, for many days together, for dread that she had of deceits and illusions," until God gave her proper understanding of what she had experienced. Sometimes she had interpreted in a bodily way what was intended as only "ghostly," or spiritual. Thus, especially when such experiences were new to her, she agonized over these questions, and "the dread that she had of her feelings was the greatest scourge that she had on earth."[17]

The extent of Margery's sensitivity can be seen in the prominence in her book of the gift of tears. It occurred repeatedly—often in association with her meditations on the passion, sometimes in her reflections on sin, and occasionally in connection with the eucharistic devotion in which she shared. When the experience came, it did so involuntarily; she would gladly have had it stop while she was in public. In some contexts her weeping aroused others to cry. She insisted that tears had salvific effect, and appealed to precedent in Christian tradition, such as the life of Mary of Oignies, for the gift of tears. Repeatedly, however, it was her weeping that was responsible for the opposition she aroused; the cynical might characterize it as blubbering, and that term perhaps suggests the attitude with which many of her contemporaries viewed the phenomenon.[18]

In outline and in detail, then, Margery's piety resembles that of Dorothy of Montau, Catherine of Siena, and several other figures slightly earlier than she. Yet there is one major difference: when Margery died there was no hint of a cult forming around her. Why this was so is possibly the most significant question to be answered about her. Surely it is not the case that forms of holiness so dominant in the recent past, at least to some extent in England as well as on the Continent, had gone suddenly out of vogue, leaving her the hapless victim of changes in spiritual fashion. Her passage into obscurity may have been largely a matter of personality. She tells us that there were some during her lifetime who venerated her, and who wanted her to be present at their deathbeds.[19] Nonetheless, she may have lacked that charismatic spark that would give sympathetic contemporaries the impression of being in the presence of an exceptionally holy individual. She would strike them as a good woman, and possessed of unusual inclinations and powers (some viewed her as something of a clairvoyant), but not necessarily a saint.

At least as important as this was another factor: she had no clerical associate who felt strongly enough attached to her to promote her cult. She had no John Marienwerder or Raymund of Capua to suggest to the populace that posthumous veneration might be appropriate and efficacious. Indeed, during her life she found herself on shaky terms with the clergy. Quite apart from the charge of heresy, which no one seems to have taken seriously for long, she had a quick tongue which she was able to use against churchmen as well as laity. When the archbishop of York told her he had heard she was quite wicked, she returned the compliment and warned him of his fate in the afterlife.[20] Some might call this prophetic criticism, yet it leads to recognition as a saint only if uttered from a safe and well-defined position within the Church. Margery belonged to no religious order or movement, and was not officially enclosed in a cell. She was, in short, a maverick. She prevailed upon one priest, with difficulty, to transcribe her book for her, but he procrastinated for some time and never seems to have shown interest in disseminating the text. To be sure, some figures, such as Peter of Luxembourg, were recognized as saints by the populace and then accepted as such by the clergy. But Peter was himself a member of the hierarchy, whose close ties to the ecclesiastical establishment were significant in the perpetuation of his cult. Normally the process of fostering a cult required collaboration of hierarchy and people. In Margery's case, neither the people nor the churchmen seem to have been interested in promoting her cult.

One further factor must be borne in mind: we know a fair amount about Margery because of her autobiography, but for the last years of her life we are quite uninformed. We do not know, therefore, whether she found herself in increasingly hostile or friendly environs when she died, or even whether she was able to maintain her earlier level of religious commitment. Therein may lie important grounds for the lack of a posthumous cult.

Margery's autobiographical reflections lead to two questions that are of central relevance for this book: the historical question of how to explain the trends seen in her spirituality and that of many of her older contemporaries; and the theological question of how to assess these trends. In other words, one may ask from a historical viewpoint why it was that many of the era's saints found themselves in Margery's position, and why society reacted to them as it did; and one may inquire from the vantage point of theology as to the significance of such lives. While these questions require different methods of approach, both are vital for a full understanding of the subject.

Fourteenth-Century Saints in Their Historical Context

Recent work on Margery has emphasized those respects in which she typifies lay religious life of her era, or perhaps epitomizes it.[21] One article takes her as an example of what happens to "sincere persons left to their own devices," emulating monastic ideals without actually entering a convent. The author continues:

> Popular religious culture in the late 14th century did equate spirituality with asceticism and withdrawal from the world. Ordinarily the contemplative life could only be satisfied by a recluse, blind to the secular, in perpetual communion with God. But these are conditions to which no secular woman could aspire. Such circumstances readily explain the evident psychological tension that Margery Kempe suffered: Being spiritually gifted, Margery would naturally feel simultaneous attraction to the only form of religious life for which models existed and racking guilt for her inability to achieve it, a textbook prescription for her strained personality.[22]

The tension arose not because she desired to enter a cloister; even after she and her husband vowed themselves to continence, she did not take this step. Rather, she, like many other saintly figures of the era, was striving for a transplanted monastic life within secular society, where she had none of the institutional and psychological support that the cloister would have provided. Such, at any rate, is the image of herself that she portrays in her autobiography. Rather than successfully depicting an ideal religious life as an example for others, she makes an effective case for the difficulty of living an unworldly existence in a worldly society.

Margery poses for us the problem of the outsider. Whereas she evidently remained an outsider to her society throughout life and in death, however, there were other such figures whose relationship with society became more complex, and who combined the roles of outsider and insider. Having explored some of the reasons for Margery's isolation, we must turn to the thornier question of the circumstances in which an outsider to society might be recognized by that society as playing a valuable social function.

One must remember at the outset that there is always some measure of ambivalence about saints: they may be venerated, but with reservations. Integral to the notion of sainthood in Christianity (and to analogous concepts in other religions) is a tension between the imitability and the "otherness" of the holy personage.[23] The saint is someone who lives an exemplary life, carrying out in full the religious and moral values of the culture; for that reason, he or she is set up as a model for imitation. Yet the saint is also exalted and put on a pedestal, in such a way that he or she can no longer serve effectively as a model. The otherness of the saint arises partly from the sheer fact of glorification: those who venerate the saint portray his or her virtues in such idealized terms that the individual no longer serves as a realistic and effective model for others. Further, the saint is expected to play roles in and for society that differ from that of model, and may conflict with that role. The saint is expected to be a wonder-worker or intercessor, a prophet and social critic, and perhaps a visionary. The superhuman powers and experiences of the saint are not commonly available for imitation, and when they are included in the saint's vita it becomes to that extent less useful as a guide to imitation. When the saint's devotees venerated him for his excesses, that does not mean that they thought others should imitate those excesses. Rather, what it means is that once the saint is dead the excesses become signs that the saint was an exceptional individual with an extraordinary vocation, and that having passed into the afterlife he can serve Christian society all the more effectively as an intercessor. When people prayed to saints, they wanted a feeling that they were praying to individuals who were different from themselves; the rigors to which the saints had exposed themselves rendered them spiritual virtuosi and heroes, who could be recognized as effective intercessors before the throne of God.

Even the pious among the saints' associates seem to have had difficulty understanding the extremities to which the saints were driven. The family of Catherine of Siena, the close associates of Peter of Luxembourg, Dorothy of Montau's mother and to an extent also her husband—all these appear in the sources as conventionally pious individuals, who fasted and went on pilgrimages as any decent Christian did. Even these people, however, sought constantly to hold the saints within the limits of normal religious observance—to keep them, in other words, from being saints. Even though these people's actions may be as stereotypical as the saints' reactions, the recurrence of these motifs is an admission on the part of the hagiographers that sanctity was open to a challenge that would seem reasonable.

If society was ambivalent about its saints, this is not to say that it was ambivalent about any type of saintly excess whatsoever, but that it tolerated and in some ways encouraged certain kinds of excess. In these matters, as in other affairs of cultural history, there were specific and variable tastes that reveal the preoccupations of the society.

In the fourteenth century, the saint was someone who bore overwhelming affliction with heroic patience, took upon himself excruciating pains in imitation of Christ, accused himself of the foulest transgression, and distanced himself (or more often herself) from the world through mystical experiences, or desired to do so. To an extent, all of these forms of piety were widespread in the population; at the very least, there were popular versions of all these aspects of saintliness. Patience was extolled not only in devotional but in secular

and chivalric literature. (One thinks perhaps of Petrarch's defense of
the story of patient Griselda, portrayed almost as St. Griselda: true,
her patience was extreme, but one should not judge other people's
capacities by one's own.) For ordinary Christian as well as saint, devotion to Christ entailed ritual identification with him, and fascination
with his representations in art and literature. For every saint who confessed daily, there were numerous ordinary Christians who confessed
at least yearly and cultivated their own examination of conscience.
And while few could claim to have enjoyed visions, the literature of
visions included far more than just saints' *vitae:* the vision story had
become an important form in secular literature (such as the Middle
English *Pearl*) as well.[24] Thus, one can partially explain what was
going on as a kind of escalation: the more widespread lay piety became, and the more effectively the Church disseminated its devotions
among the laity, the more it took for the saint to single himself out as
distinctively and heroically holy.

What was it in the era that encouraged these particular tendencies?
The calamities of the century come naturally to mind. As already
mentioned, misfortunes such as the famines and the plague may indeed have had an important role in shaping Christian attitudes toward the world and toward suffering, though it is difficult to establish
the precise development of such amorphous cultural phenomena, let
alone their correlation with the facts of nature and of social history. It
has been suggested that "The very misfortunes of the age seem to
have stimulated spiritual activity." Heretical as well as orthodox fervor has been attributed to the difficulty of living comfortably in the
world of the fourteenth century.[25] Indeed, the precariousness of life
may well have sharpened people's sense that the world was transitory,
and that lasting comfort was to be found only in the spiritual order.
One might not abandon one's worldly belongings, but one might de-
velop a keener sense of detachment from those goods. As the mystics
conceded, if one had the proper attitude of detachment one could
own an entire kingdom without being seduced by it.[26] Likewise, if one
began with the postulate that suffering could be meritorious, the sufferings of the fourteenth century might serve as constant reminders
of this principle. In these and perhaps other ways, the material suffering of the era surely did have an impact on the mentality of many late
medieval Christians, though the precise degree and nature of that
impact might vary.

One might consider an opposite approach to the problem. It was
the centers of material prosperity, places where urban life was
blossoming and the middle classes were rising, that gave birth to the
noteworthy spiritual movements of the fourteenth century. Though
the century was one of general malaise, there were places such as

northern Italy, the Rhineland, and eastern England which, though hit harder in mid-century largely in consequence of earlier development, enjoyed a higher level of prosperity than other regions, and it was in these places in particular that spirituality blossomed, just as in the sixteenth century it was Spain that distinguished itself for its richness in both material and mystical resources. Furthermore, the classes which benefited from this prosperity are disproportionately represented among the saints of the century: Catherine of Siena came from a leading family; Henry Suso and Bridget of Sweden came from the aristocracy, as did most of the French saints; Dorothy of Montau's parents were wealthy enough to have servants, and her husband was apparently successful enough as a craftsman to support a lengthy stay in Switzerland. One could cite several further instances. Most of these saints had circles of close associates or broader clienteles, which likewise came from classes that enjoyed urban prosperity. The romantic image of the hungry mystic, like that of the starving artist, is seriously misleading if one does not bear in mind that spiritual and artistic *movements* require such clienteles to purchase and appreciate the literary or artistic works that are produced. And what this means is an aristocracy or upper middle class with sufficient wealth to buy books and leisure to read them.

What may have made the fourteenth century particularly rife in spiritual literature may have been a combination of circumstances: the rise of such an urban upper middle class, together with a strong enough measure of adversity to make the advantages of secular life conspicuously precarious, and to impress upon people the need for detachment from whatever prosperity they did enjoy. From this viewpoint, the cult of suffering found in the saints' lives becomes the expression of insight attained by people whose expectations had been raised and then shattered: individuals such as Jane Mary of Maillé, who suffered with her husband through the Hundred Years' War and then suffered further when on his death she was dispossessed and had to live without the privileges of nobility; or Margery Kempe, who had married beneath her social class and was unable to improve her lot through her own business ventures; or Clare Gambacorta, whose family was ousted from power in one of the political upheavals that were so characteristic for fourteenth-century Italian towns; or those many further saints whose families were *not* brought to ruin, but who faced greater risks than people living in more stable times.

Another factor is also relevant. Far more than in any previous era, the saints of the fourteenth century were from a sort of border zone that emerged in the later medieval Church: they stood on the boundary between the laity and the clergy. Some, such as Catherine of Siena, belonged to the third orders affiliated with the mendicants. A

few, such as Julian of Norwich or Dorothy of Montau, became officially recognized anchorites. Richard Rolle was a hermit. Gertrude of
Delft was a beguine, living a pious life in association with others of her
status. Individuals in these categories did not have the stabilizing and
moderating influence of the monastery, in which most of the earlier
medieval saints had been trained. They might have spiritual directors
who would try to exert such moderating influence; Raymund of Capua evidently tried to do so with Catherine of Siena. Without the set-
tled environment of the monastery, however, it was easy for these
saints to imbibe the fundamental notion of how one becomes saintly
and carry it to extremes. (One of the few important saints who *had*
been trained in a monastery, Elzear of Sabran, had been corrected by
the abbot for one fault: his excessive rigor.)[27] Many of these figures
had no regular responsibilities—parish work, teaching, and so forth—
which means that they had time on their hands to brood over the state
of their souls, as well as ample time for contemplation and devotional
reading. They tended to come from the aristocracy or urban upper
middle class; they were leisured, and their religion was the fruit of
their leisure. Whatever connections they had with the clergy, they
represented an essentially lay version of saintliness, and often it was a
less nuanced, more fervent, at times even more fanatical interpretation of Christian ideals than one might find elsewhere. Even Peter of
Luxembourg, who became a cardinal-deacon, wore his cardinal's hat
uncomfortably and lived in a mental world not unlike that of
Catherine of Siena; like her, he resisted all efforts to temper his enormous devotional zeal.

A parallel consideration is that most of these saints were literate—
or, like Margery Kempe, had access to others who were literate and
kept them abreast of the devotional literature—but not genuinely educated. They had, as it were, a little learning. They benefited from
the rise of general literacy that came in the later Middle Ages, and
there is much evidence from the saints' lives that they themselves in
many cases could read. In some instances they even went to great
effort late in life to learn how to do so.[28] But the materials they read
were, so far as the sources indicate, either prayerbooks and liturgical
manuals or works of popular devotional literature, which would only
have stoked the fires of their zeal. Even when they did not acquire
notions of holiness directly from reading, they lived in a literate society in which unsophisticated notions of saintliness abounded.
Catherine of Siena insisted that when she strove to imitate the rigors
of the desert fathers in her early youth she was imitating them on the
basis of infused knowledge; she had not read about them herself, and
had not been told about them.[29] One may pardonably question her
recollection, and speculate that she had picked up these ideas because

they were in the air. With the growth of lay literacy and lay piety, townspeople had ready access to popular notions of how one became distinctively holy.

At this point the analysis could go either of two ways. One might argue that because the saints came from this border zone they were prone to the extravagance attributed to them in the texts. However plausible this suggestion may seem, it remains speculative. We cannot determine the extent to which the saints actually did what their biographers said they did. (The problem is no less great when the works are autobiographical: Henry Suso, for example, may not have been beyond distortion in his account of his own life.) Indeed, even the sources' reports about social status, ecclesiastical position, and literacy are open to challenge, though information of this kind seems less often stereotyped than accounts of pious deeds, temptations, visions, and the like. The second line of analysis essentially brackets out such questions about what the saints did and what their status in society was, and proceeds to a different area of inquiry altogether: whatever the saints were like, their representation in the texts is a mirror of that society which read the hagiographic literature and venerated the saints. If the saints came often from a border zone between clergy and laity, so in a weaker sense did most of their devotees. The more religious the urban laity became, and the more it imitated monastic piety, the more difficult it would be to distinguish lay from clerical or religious mentality. Those who venerated Dorothy of Montau or Catherine of Siena for anything more than their intercessory power must have seen in her a focused version of the dilemma that they themselves faced in reconciling monastic ideals with lay existence. If most of these devotees found the problem less acute than did several of the saints, that was perhaps they were less strongly enthralled by monastic ideals. Yet the difference was one of degree, and need not have prevented the readers of the texts from feeling a bond of sympathy with the saints in all their agonies.

To go much further than this in showing the link between sanctity and historical context would perhaps require a different kind of analysis from that done in this book. It would be useful to examine the distinctive features of saints from particular regions, social classes, and so forth, in an effort to link their spirituality with their specific historical settings. To some extent the work of Vauchez and that of Weinstein and Bell has already done this, though in broad outline. What is perhaps most needed now, along these lines, is a series of detailed studies of individual saints and small groups of saints, viewed in their particular contexts. The thrust of the present book has been the opposite: having attended to broad motifs widespread throughout late medieval culture, we are in a position here to relate those themes to very broad trends in late medieval society, but not to the specific concerns of southern French aristocracy or northern German artisans and merchants. Clearly much remains to be done before we have a rounded understanding of the historical background to late medieval sainthood. Work has been done and is being done on a few individuals, such as Margery Kempe and Bridget of Sweden, but it will be long before the areas for research are exhausted.

Fourteenth-Century Saints and the Theology of Sainthood

Margery Kempe not only incorporates all the central features of four-teenth-century sanctity, but presents in concentrated form all the difficulties we considered at the outset of this study. She seems to have impressed most of her contemporaries as something of a mad-woman; since the rediscovery of her book, this opinion has gained many further adherents. In recent years, to be sure, there have been efforts to rehabilitate her. E. I. Watkin, for example, suggests that her theological naiveté cloaked a deep and genuine spiritual life.[30] Other scholars have suggested that she was the victim of an antifeminist soci-ety, which could accept a cloistered woman or a fully secular one, but not a woman who emulated the rigors of the cloister while going about in the world. Watkin honors what he finds in Margery's person-al life; her other defenders sympathize with her because of the diffi-culties she encountered in society. After reviewing these arguments in a recent article, though, Drew E. Hinderer dismisses them forcefully:

> even when the institutional and anti-feminist biases of tra-ditional criteria for evaluation are taken into account, what remains of Margery's spirituality is characterized by a con-sciousness of guilt and a persistent anxiety that did not pro-duce any of the most positive values of Christianity. Regardless of how one might disagree over particular de-tails of Margery's career, there emerges from her *Book* a woman whose preoccupation with herself and pervasive hysterical fear come close to insanity. A sympathetic reader must be moved by the depth of Margery's struggles. But an honest one must, I think, conclude that she was not entirely successful in overcoming them.[34]

Hinderer goes on to compare Margery with Julian of Norwich, who was not only more sophisticated theologically but also more balanced in her assurance of divine love, and thus represented those positive values that he finds lacking in Margery.[32]

Surely Hinderer is right in his factual description of Margery;

there is indeed a strong tone of self-centered hysteria in her writing. Most readers will agree not only with his factual account but with his assessment, or will have difficulty rejecting it, just as many readers will no doubt share William James's reservations about Henry Suso, Huizinga's aversion to Peter of Luxembourg, and other such views of fourteenth-century saints. However committed one may be to historical objectivity, few readers can refrain from judgment in the face of what appears to be obsessive guilt, effusive emotional devotion, and masochistic asceticism. Yet judgment of any sort presupposes norms by which to judge, and responsible assessment requires reflection on those standards. One cannot simply hold the saints up to unconsidered notions of "the more positive values of Christianity" and test whether they conform.

As suggested at the outset of this study, one cannot ultimately pass judgment on the saints themselves unless one is a member of the Congregation for the Causes of Saints, and is supplementing vitae and testimony of the saints' associates with evidence of cult and miracles to determine the role of a saint within the Church. Ordinary scholars must content themselves with the textual evidence at hand, and must recognize that this material, even when it is autobiographical or quasi-autobiographical, is intended more to express a vision of sanctity than to convey accurate historical data about individuals. If one wishes to venture an assessment, then, it is this vision one must assess.

The most obvious difficulty in the theology of sainthood conveyed by these texts is that pervasive imbalance discussed in Chapter 1 and encountered again in each subsequent chapter. One might argue that a balanced presentation of spirituality would too readily have led to that sort of moderation in which the extremes cancel each other out: reminded prematurely of divine graciousness, the reader might never attain a keen sensitivity to his own sinfulness; mindful all along of the resurrection, the reader might not take the passion seriously enough to feel the full weight of Christ's anguish and abandonment; in general, presented with reasonable and balanced accounts of saintliness, the reader might lose the force of a more emphatically unbalanced approach. Yet the alternative to such a bland compromise of extremes is not necessarily imbalance, but rather a Chestertonian sense of the paradoxical nature of Christian spirituality—a view of Christianity as involving at every turn a "collision of two passions apparently opposite."[33] This ideal combines passionate conviction of sin with equally passionate gratitude for forgiveness, deep absorption in mystical experience with keen appreciation for quotidian life. Such paradoxical sanctity may be difficult to cultivate and nearly as difficult to describe. The problem with fourteenth-century saints and their biographers is that they do not seem even to have striven toward this ideal. Their otherworldly orientation did not dispose them to view the present life as sacramental—as one in which evils are to be reformed and not merely borne, passion leads to resurrection, sin is met with forgiveness, and rapture enhances the value of earthly life.

One may disparage the texts because of these deficiencies, or one may proceed to recognize and appreciate that depth of insight that they nonetheless contain. One-sided as they may be, they are singularly effective at conveying what they set out to convey. One cannot expect to find sophisticated expressions of ascetic and mystical theology in hagiography, but with all their imbalance the hagiographic sources of the fourteenth century present in striking fashion a vision of saintly life which carries an implicit theology. The vitae of Dorothy of Montau clearly portray her as overwhelmed with both grace and guilt, and as a woman upon whom God was constantly at work. The canonization proceedings for Peter of Luxembourg hold him up not as a model for imitation but as an extreme example of purity admist corruption, an object for wonderment that should shame others into reform, a figure whose passionate aversion to vice brought light to those about him, *lucem in burgo*. Whatever its eccentricities, the autobiography of Margery Kempe is eloquent in its emphasis on the sheer strenuousness of the religious life and the extraordinary difficulty of living an ideal existence in a setting that is far from ideal. Remote as these figures may seem from biblical notions of Christ-like holiness, they reflect clearly the attitudes of late medieval Christians toward the demands of religious life.

Virtually all these saints were marked by depth of sensitivity. Their contemporaries, as well as modern readers, might prefer to speak of hypersensitivity; yet from the hagiographers' viewpoint it was noble to have the capacity for deeply felt submission, contrition, compassion, and ecstasy. Keenly aware of God's aid in coping with afflictions, the saints become more sensitive than they would otherwise be to matters spiritual, and they tend to engender such sensitivity in receptive individuals around them. In that way they carry out the Pauline theme of strength perfected in weakness: were it not for their vulnerability, they would be less effective signs of divine aid.

In a few cases, this sensitivity to spiritual matters is linked with reformist zeal: Bridget of Sweden's efforts at reform, for example, grew out of her childhood obsession with the sufferings that sinners inflicted on Christ, and were closely linked with her own conviction of sin. At other times this sensitivity blossomed in a depth of religious insight, and found expression in literary works. Simone Weil provides a twentieth-century example of a woman afflicted with many of the tendencies seen in fourteenth-century saints, yet capable of a depth of insight which has gained wide admiration.[34] The parallel with artistic creativity comes to mind. With the saint as with the artist, there is a constellation of factors that can be closely linked: emotional intensity, feverish quest of fulfillment through aesthetic or spiritual experience, craving for intuitive comprehension of that experience, and a need to express one's sensitivities to others. While a more normal individual might be content with that modicum of insight needed to live a comfortable life of basic Christian commitment, the tortured soul is driven by constant malaise to a never-ending quest of ever deeper understanding. Henry Suso's religious and poetic sensitivity inspired writings which are profoundly moving even when they are most alien; his patient endurance of affliction is particularly touching when it leaves him all the more deeply absorbed in his love affair with Eternal Wisdom. Julian of Norwich had a type of religious sensitivity which led her in youth to penitential self-affliction, though as she matured this gave way to a brighter outlook. One might represent Richard Rolle, too, as an individual for whom depth of sensitivity brought depth of insight. What the hagiography extols, though, is not so much the insight as the sensitivity; whether or not it is accompanied by intellectual gifts and learning, openness to spiritual realities is in itself seen as a valuable gift and a mark of saintliness.

Some would go so far as to suggest that intense commitment to the pursuit of virtue suffices in itself for saintliness, even if the saint conceives virtue in a seriously distorted way. This is the argument that Lawrence S. Cunningham pursues: "If the saints cannot be fully emulated, their witness cannot be ignored. It is the intensity and seriousness of their lives that compels attention." From Cunningham's perspective the value of the saints for Christian society remains undiminished by their defects and aberrations. "The value of the saintly personality, eccentricities and all, is that it provides a norm or standard by which we may measure our religious seriousness."[35] Yet Cunningham does not spell out what sorts of aberration he would be willing to tolerate. Sinners as well as saints can be intensely dedicated to their ways of life, and while the saints may commit themselves to principles they see as religious, their perception of those principles remains always open to theological criticism. It is not self-evident, for example, that zeal in the pursuit of suffering necessarily contributes to sanctity.

The hagiographers of the late Middle Ages would surely not have argued that their subjects were worthy of veneration simply because they were intense in their commitment; the object of that commitment was vital. Whether they represented their saints as exemplars of patience, as penitents, as devotees of *Christus patiens,* or as ecstatics, they sought to reinforce norms which applied also to ordinary Christians. And affirmation of these norms required overstatement. If moralists were to heighten the moral consciousness of fourteenth-century society, and if devotional writers were to foster ever more fervent devotion, they could do so more effectively through the dramatic example of outlandish sanctity than by pointing to specimens of normal good conduct. The saints' excesses called secular modes of life into question more strikingly than moderate virtue ever could. This was the point of the argument *a fortiori* which underlay the emphasis on wonderment rather than imitation.

For those who had already accepted the values affirmed by these texts, the saints served as heroes whose extremism afforded dramatic affirmation of shared values. There is nothing distinctively medieval (or late medieval) in this phenomenon: other times and other societies furnish examples of the hero whose apparently irrational extremes become symbols for values widely recognized as rational.[36] If an outsider to late medieval culture cannot make sense of Dorothy of Montau's commitment to suffering or Peter of Luxembourg's admissions of guilt, that is not so much because these figures are extreme, but because they are extreme manifestations of a spirituality that is no longer in favor. A viewer sharing the ascetic outlook of late medieval Christianity could more readily see these saints' exasperating behavior as a divinely sanctioned (indeed, divinely instigated) affirmation of ascetic principles.

It would do the sources an injustice, though, to represent them as having practical value but as utterly lacking theologically fruitful perception of the human situation. Their focus on the constant need for divine aid—for God's efficacious work within the saint—is from one perspective the essence of their theological contribution. From a broader viewpoint, what they have to offer are signs of concern about the disparity between ideals and realities. The fourteenth century has often been characterized as an era captivated by ideals but markedly unable to bring ideals and realities into alignment.[37] Chivalric literature portrayed a genteel society that did not exist, a dream society in which the beleaguered Europeans of the fourteenth century liked to imagine themselves as living. The art of the period often conveys the same sense of dreamlike unreality and mystery: it has been suggested that one characteristic of late medieval art is its "strange tension between the realistic image and its supra-real sense."[38] One reason the lives of the saints hold great fascination is that they show intersections between ideals and realities. The subjects of these vitae were individuals who made it their life's task to translate ideal into reality, and it was their success in this task, however full or partial, that aroused others to venerate them. The saints were recognized as such because they lived out ideals which their contemporaries recognized but left unfulfilled, either because ordinary Christians felt themselves too weak to strive for sanctity (a difference in degree) or because they viewed sanctity as a calling for the exceptional few (a difference in kind). At the same time, while the saints labored to implement the ideals, their biographers engaged in their own idealization. There are some vitae which have greater verisimilitude than others, and without making any extravagant claims one may suppose that some of them are substantially faithful and sober accounts of historical fact. In general, though, the biographers were less concerned with the canons of historical accuracy than with stirring their readers to veneration. Thus, if the saints appear in their biographies as figures who brought ideal and reality into harmonious accord, that is partly because they realized the ideals, and partly because their biographers idealized the realities. Even so, the portrayal of spiritual ideals that one reads in the saints' lives is more graphic, more vivid than what one would encounter in a purely abstract treatise on the spiritual life, and in that sense the vitae give a uniquely "realistic" representation of contemporary religious ideals even when they improve upon historical fact.

Unquestionably, however, the most important point about ideals and realities in fourteenth-century hagiography is its demonstration of the gap: the saints' lives make abundantly clear that the saints themselves yearned for a better life in heaven, and while on earth they were painfully ill at ease with the world and with themselves. Once again, this disquietude is not a phenomenon unique to the fourteenth century, but one cannot help but be impressed by the intensity and the diffusion of such discontent which make it a central characteristic of this era.

Guide to Primary Sources

The list below is not exhaustive, but merely provides bibliographic information for primary sources cited in abbreviated form in the notes. The following abbreviations are used for collections of sources.

AF   *Analecta franciscana, sive Chronica aliaque varia documenta ad historiam Fratrum minorum spectantia* (Quaracchi: Collegium S. Bonaventurae, 1885–).

AS   *Acta sanctorum,* 3d ed. (Paris: Palmé, etc., 1863–). Not all volumes in this series are in their third edition; since earlier editions were incomplete, certain individual volumes published since 1863 represent the second or first edition of those particular volumes. The series as a whole, though, is the third undertaken with this title.

In addition, the following abbreviations are used for types of source material.

P.C.   *Processus canonizationis*
Vit.   *Vita*
V.Lat.   *Vita latina*
V.P.   *Vita prima*

Adelheid Langmann	Philipp Strauch, ed., *Die Offenbarungen der Margaretha Ebner und der Adelheid Langmann,* trans. Josef Prestel (Weimar: H. Böhlaus Nachfolger, 1939)
Ademar of Felsinio	AF, vol. 3, pp. 464–67

Andrew Corsini	AS, January, vol. 3, pp. 680–92
Bernard Tolomeo	AS, August, vol. 4, pp. 475–87
Bridget of Sweden	Isak Collijn, ed., *Acta et processus canonizacionis beatae Birgitte* (Uppsala: Almqvist & Wiksells, 1924–31)
Catherine of Siena	AS, April, vol. 3, pp. 862–967. The most recent English version is Raymond of Capua, *The Life of Catherine of Siena*, trans. Conleth Kearns (Wilmington, Dela.: Glazier, 1980). Quotations are from Raymund of Capua, *The Life of St. Catherine of Siena*, trans. George Lamb (New York: Kenedy, 1960)
Catherine of Sweden	AS, March, vol. 3, pp. 503–15
Charles of Blois	*Monuments du procès de canonisation du bienheureux Charles de Blois, duc de Bretagne, 1320–1364* (Saint-Brieuc: Prud-homme, 1921)
Christina Ebner	Georg Wolfgang Karl Lochner, *Leben und Gesichte der Christina Ebnerin, Klosterfrau zu Engelthal* (Nuremberg: Schmid, 1872)
Cicco of Pesaro	AS, August, vol. 1, pp. 656–58
Clare Gambacorta	AS, April, vol. 2, pp. 503–16
Clare of Rimini	Giuseppe Garampi, ed., *Memorie ecclesiastiche appartenenti all'istoria e al culto della B. Chiara di Rimini* (Rome: Pagliarini, 1775), pp. 1–76
Conrad of Piacenza	AS, February, vol. 3, pp. 167–70
Dalmatius Moner	"Vie inedite du B. Dalmace Moner O.P.," ed. "V.O.," *Analecta Bollandiana*, vol. 31 (1912), pp. 49–81
Delphina of Puimichel P.C.	Jacques Cambell, ed., *Enquête pour le procès de canonisation de Dauphine de puimichel, comtesse d'Ariano (+ 26-XI-1360)* (Turin: Erasmo, 1978)
V.Occ.	Jacques Cambell, ed., *Vies Occitanes de Saint Auzias et de Sainte Dauphine, avec traduction française, introduction et notes* (Rome: Pontificium Athenaeum Antonianum, 1963)

Dorothy of Montau

Dt.L. "Deutsches Leben," in Theodor Hirsch, Max Töppen, and Ernst Strehlke, eds., *Die Geschichtsquellen der preussischen Vorzeit bis zum Untergange der Ordensherrschaft* (= *Scriptores rerum Prussicarum*), vol. 2 (Leipzig, 1863; repr. Frankfurt a.M.: Minerva, 1965), pp. 197–350

P.C. Richard Stachnik, ed., *Die Akten des Kanonisationsprozesses Dorotheas von Montau von 1394 bis 1521* (Cologne & Vienna: Böhlau, 1978)

V.Lat. Hans Westpfahl, ed., *Vita Dorotheae Montoviensis Magistri Johannis Marienwerder* (Cologne & Graz: Böhlau, 1964)

V.Lin. "Vita Lindana," in AS, October, vol. 13, pp. 499–560

V.P. AS, October, vol. 13, pp. 493–99

Elizabeth Achler Karl Bihlmeyer, "Die schwäbische Mystikerin Elisabeth Achler von Reute (+1420) und die Überlieferung ihrer Vita," in Georg Baesecke and Ferdinand Joseph Schneider, eds., *Festgabe Philipp Strauch zum 80. Geburtstage am 23. September 1932* (= *Hermaea: Ausgewählte Arbeiten aus dem Deutschen Seminar zu Halle*, vol. 31) (Halle: Niemeyer, 1932), pp. 88–109

Elizabeth of Portugal AS, July, vol. 2, pp. 173–213

Elzear of Sabran

P.C. Jacques Cambell, ed., "Le sommaire de l'enquête pour la canonisation de S. Elzéar de Sabran, TOF (+1323)," *Miscellanea Franciscana*, vol. 73 (1973), pp. 438–73

V.Lat. AS, September, vol. 7, pp. 494–39

V.Occ. See under Delphina of Puimichel

Flora of Beaulieu AS, June, vol. 2, pp. 43–54 of appendix; cf. C. Brunel, ed., "Vida e miracles de Santa Flor," *Analecta Bollandiana*, vol. 64 (1946), pp. 13–49

Francis of Fabriano AS, April, vol. 3, pp. 992–99

Francis of Patrizzi Peregrinus Soulier, ed., "Legenda beati Francisci de Senis, Ordinis Servorum

	B.M.V.," *Analecta Bollandiana*, vol. 14 (1895), pp. 174–97
Gerard Cagnoli	AF, vol. 3, pp. 489–97
Gertrude of Delft	AS, January, vol. 1, pp. 349–53
Gonsalvo Sancii	AF, vol. 3, pp. 549–52
Henry Suso	Heinrich Suso, *Deutsche Schriften*, ed. Karl Bihlmeyer (Stuttgart: Kohlhammer, 1907); quotations are from Henry Suso, *The Life of the Servant*, trans. James M. Clark (London, 1952)
Imelda Lambertini	AS, May, vol. 3, pp. 181–83
James Oldo	AS, April, vol. 2, pp. 597–606
James of Porta	AF, vol. 3, pp. 617–39
Jane Mary of Maillé, P.C. Vit.	AS, March, vol. 3, pp. 744–62 AS, March, vol. 3, pp. 734–44
Joan of Castres	Chrysostomus Henriquez, *Lilia Cistercii, sive sacrarum virginum Cisterciensium origo, instituta, et res gestae*, vol. 1 (Douai: Bellerus, 1633), pp. 122–31
John of Alverna	AF, vol. 3, pp. 439–47; cf. AS, August, vol. 2, pp. 459–74
John of Caramola	AS, August, vol. 5, pp. 860–62
John Colombini	AS, July, vol. 7, pp. 365–409
John Domenici	AS, June, vol. 2, pp. 393–412
John Ruysbroeck	"De origine monasterii Viridisvallis, una cum vitis B. Joannis Rusbrochii, primi prioris hujus monasterii, et aliquot coaetaneorum ejus," *Analecta Bollandiana*, vol. 4 (1885), pp. 283–308
Julian of Norwich	Edmund Colledge and James Walsh, eds., *A Book of Showings to the Anchoress Julian of Norwich* (Toronto: Pontifical Institute, 1978)
Luitgard of Wittichen	Franz Joseph Mone, ed., *Quellensammlung der badischen Landesgeschichte* (Karlsruhe: Macklot, 1848–67), vol. 3, pp. 438–68
Margaret Ebner	See under Adelheid Langmann

Margaret of Faenza	
Rev.	"Revelationes," in AS, August, vol. 5, pp. 851–54
Vit.	AS, August, vol. 5, pp. 847–51
Margery Kempe	Sanford Brown Meech, ed., *The Book of Margery Kempe* (London: Milford, 1940); quotations are from W. Butler-Bowden's translation (London, 1936)
Nicholas Hermansson	
P.C.	Tryggve Lundén, ed., *Sankt Nikolaus av Linköping kanonisationsprocess: Processus canonizacionis beati Nicolai Lincopensis* (Stockholm: Bonniers, 1963)
Vit.	Henrik Schück, ed., "Två svenska biografier från medeltiden," *Antiqvarisk Tidskrift för Sverige,* vol. 5 (1895), pp. 313–400
Peter of Fulgineo	Joanne Gorini, "Beati Petri de Fulgineo confessoris legenda," ed. Michaele Pulignani, *Analecta Bollandiana,* vol. 8 (1889), pp. 365–69; cf. AS, July, vol. 4, pp. 665–68
Peter of Luxembourg	
P.C.	AS, July, vol. 1, pp. 462–97
V.P.	AS, July, vol. 1, pp. 448–54
Peter Olafsson	Henrik Schück (see under Nicholas Hermansson), pp. 295–312
Richard Rolle	Stephen Willoughby Lawley, ed., *Breviarium ad usum insignis ecclesie Eboracensis,* vol. 2 (Durham, etc.: Andrews, 1883), pp. 785–820; cf. Frances M. M. Comper, *The Life of Richard Rolle, together with an Edition of his English Lyrics* (London & Toronto: Dent, 1928), pp. 301–11
Robert of Salentino	AS, July, vol. 4, pp. 495–509
Rulman Merswin	*Mystical Writings,* ed. Thomas S. Kepler (Philadelphia, 1960), pp. 39–52
Sibyllina Biscossi	AS, March, vol. 3, pp. 68–71
Silvester (and Paula)	*Leggende di alcuni santi e beati venerati in S.*

	Maria degli Angeli di Firenze: Testi del buon secolo, vol. 2 (Bologna: Romagnoli, 1864)
Urban V	J.-H. Albanes, ed., *Actes anciens et documents concernant le bienheureux Urbain V Pape, sa famile, sa personne, son pontificat, ses miracles et son culte*, vol. 1 (Paris: Picard; Marseilles: Ruat, 1897), pp. 375–430
Ursulina of Parma	AS, April, vol. 1, pp. 721–35
Venturino of Bergamo	P.A. Grion, "La 'Legenda' del b. Venturino da Bergamo, secondo il testo inedito del codice di Cividale," *Bergamum*, vol. 50 (1956), no. 4, pp. 38–110
Villana de' Botti	AS, August, vol. 5, pp. 864–69; also in Stefano Orlandi, *La Beata Villana, terziaria domenicana fiorentina del sec. XIV* (Florence: "Il Rosario," 1955), pp. 55–73 (Italian), 76–90 (Latin)
William Gnoffi	AS, April, vol. 2, pp. 462–70

Notes

1. Introduction

1. William James, *The Varieties of Religious Experience: A Study in Human Nature* (London: Longmans, 1902), pp. 306–10. James does not accord Suso that respect which he elsewhere (pp. 127–65) grants to the melancholic or "sick" soul. J. Huizinga, *The Waning of the Middle Ages: A Study of the Forms of Life, Thought and Art in France and the Netherlands in the XIVth and XVth Centuries*, trans. F. Hopman (London: Arnold, 1924), pp. 167f.

2. Günter Grass, *The Flounder*, trans. Ralph Manheim (New York: Harcourt, Brace, Jovanovich, 1978), pp. 12f., 107–68 (quote is on p. 167); Barbara Tuchman, "Hazards on the Way to the Middle Ages," *Atlantic Monthly*, vol. 236, no. 6 (December 1975), p. 72; Marcel Eck, "La mortification dans la vie chrétienne," in *Saints d'hier et sainteté d'aujourd'hui* (Paris: Desclée de Brouwer, 1966), pp. 174f.

3. Millard Meiss, *Painting in Florence and Siena after the Black Death: The Arts, Religion and Society in the Mid-Fourteenth Century* (pb. ed., New York: Harper, 1964); David Knowles, "A Characteristic of the Mental Climate of the Fourteenth Century," in *Mélanges offerts à Étienne Gilson de l'Académie Française* (Toronto & Paris: Vrin, 1959), pp. 315–25.

4. For references, see the "Guide to Primary Sources" on pp. 203–8. Note the bibliographic information for *Acta sanctorum* on p. 203.

5. For the development of canonization proceedings, see André Vauchez, *La Sainteté en occident aux dernieres siècles du Moyen Âge, d'après les procès de canonisation et les documents hagiographiques* (Rome: École Française de Rome, 1981), and Eric Walram Kemp, *Canonization and Authority in the Western Church* (London: Oxford University Press, 1948).

6. Bibliographic information is in the "Guide to Primary Sources"; cf. Vauchez, pp. 655–76.

7. For the history of this theme, see especially Georg Misch, *Geschichte der Autobiographie* (Frankfurt am Main: Schulte-Bulmke, 1949–69). Cf. Karl Joachim Weintraub, *The Value of the Individual: Self and Circumstance in Autobiography* (Chicago: University of Chicago Press, 1978), esp. pp. 196–209. See also, e.g., Margaret Ebner.

8. Vauchez, *La Sainteté*, pp. 439f. See also, e.g., Elizabeth Achler.

9. Misch, *Geschichte der Autobiographie*, includes material on earlier saints (esp. vol. 2, pt. 2, pp. 310–55, and vol. 4, pt. 1, pp. 37–111), but is particularly useful for Henry Suso (vol. 4, pt. 1, pp. 113–310).

10. Melanie Starr Costello has done work, as yet unpublished, on this aspect of Catherine.

11. Biblical quotations are from the Douai-Rheims version. References to the Psalms likewise follow the Vulgate and Douai-Rheims enumeration.

12. Dorothy of Montau, V. Lin., prol. Cf. Barbara Newman's forthcoming book, *Sister of Wisdom: St. Hildegard's Theology of the Feminine*, for use of 1 Cor. 1:27.

13. Nicholas Hermansson, prol. For Gedeon see Jud. 7:20

14. For this formulation, which is of central relevance to this study, I am grateful to Barbara Newman. Vauchez, *La Sainteté*, p. 622, makes a related yet distinct point: in their passivity, the saints manifested God's power rather than collaborating with God.

15. *St. Augustine's Confessions*, tr. F. J. Sheed (New York: Sheed & Ward, 1943), x.6 (p. 216), xi.4 (p. 264); Marion A. Habig, ed., *St. Francis of Assisi: Writings and Early Biographies* (Chicago: Franciscan Herald, 1973), pp. 130f., 494–500; Herman Joseph, i.5.32 (*Acta sanctorum*, April, vol. 1, p. 695).

16. See, for example, Albert Auer, *Johannes von Dambach und die Tröstbücher vom 11. bis zum 16. Jahrhundert* (Münster i.W.: Aschendorff, 1928), p. 159. There are elements of this approach in Gordon Leff, *The Dissolution of the Medieval Outlook: An Essay on the Intellectual and Spiritual Change in the Fourteenth Century* (New York: Harper, 1976), e.g., p. 128.

17. Mary of Oignies, i.1.12 (*Acta sanctorum*, June, vol. 5, p. 550).

18. Herman Joseph, i.3.14 (*Acta sanctorum*, April, vol. 1, p. 689); Habig, *St. Francis of Assisi*, p. 672; James of Porta, p. 620 (an austere life, "magis admirandam quam imitandam"); Elzear of Sabran, V. Lat. i.11.

19. Mary of Oignies, i.1.14 (*Acta sanctorum*, June, vol. 5, p. 550).

20. Vauchez, *La Sainteté*, pp. 149–58 (esp. p. 154), 446–48; Donald Weinstein and Rudolph M. Bell, *Saints and Society: The Two Worlds of Western Christendom, 1000–1700* (Chicago: University of Chicago Press, 1982), p. 104. The classic text on the specific matter of weeping is Jerome, in J. P. Migne, ed., *Patrologiae cursus completus*, Series latina (Paris: Migne, etc., 1844–64), vol. 23, col. 351 (hereafter cited as PL).

21. Phyllis Hodgson, ed., *The Cloud of Unknowing and Related Treatises on Contemplative Prayer* (Salzburg: Institut für Anglistik und Amerikanistik, 1982); on the intended audience, see prologue (p. 2).

22. As above, n. 20. On the significance of the topic, see Bernard McGinn, "Medieval Christianity: An Introduction to the Literature, 1957–1977," *Anglican Theological Review*, vol. 60 (1978), pp. 304f.; McGinn suggests that the "changing modes of sanctity" in the fourteenth and fifteenth centuries are especially fruitful areas for future research.

2. Three Representative Saints

1. See especially Vauchez, *La Sainteté*, and Weinstein and Bell, *Saints and Society*.

2. The primary sources are listed above, in the Guide to Primary Sources. The *Vita Lindana* is good for simple narration, though the *Deutsches Leben* is fuller, and the *Vita Latina* provides useful discussion of her spirituality. In addition to these sources, see the various articles on Dorothy in the *Dorotheenbote*, a newsletter devoted specifically to her.

3. V.Lin. ii.42–44, iii.55–56, iii.76–79; V.Lat. ii.44f., iii.6–15, iii.23–26; Dt.L. ii.9–14, ii.24–26.

4. V.Lin. iii.55.

5. V.Lin. iii.55–62; V.Lat. iii.9–12.
6. Ibid.
7. V.Lin. ii.42–44; V.Lat. ii.44f.; Dt.L. ii.9–14.
8. V.Lin. ii.38, ii.40, iii.70; cf. iii.47.
9. V.Lin. i.15, ii.44; cf. i.17; Dt.L. i.6. Cf. Weinstein and Bell, *Saints and Society*, p. 244.
10. V.Lin. i.13f., i.21, i.35, ii.40, iii.69; cf. i.19; Dt.L. i.4, ii.19.
11. V.Lin. i.13f., i.35; Dt.L. i.4.
12. V.Lin. i.24f., ii.35f.; Dt.L. i.15.
13. V.Lin. ii.36.
14. This tentative diagnosis was provided for me by Ann Johnston, M.D. A chronic pemphigoid condition—a severe dermatological affliction characterized by sudden eruption of blisters along the trunk and extremities, with itching and stinging sensations—would at least be consistent with Dorothy's known symptoms. She may have had some other autoimmune disease; considering that she survived as long as she did, however, she is unlikely to have had pemphigus vulgaris (the disorder imitated by pemphigoid conditions). Infectious diseases and genetic disorders are implausible, since her condition seems to have been so rare as to strike her contemporaries as unfamiliar.
15. V.Lin. i.23, i.26f.; Dt.L. i. 14, i.17.
16. V.Lin. i.22.
17. See Newman, *Sister of Wisdom*, on Hildegard and Elizabeth of Schönau.
18. V.Lin. iii.63; cf. iii.65; Dt.L. ii.15.
19. V.Lin. iii.65.
20. Song of Songs, 2:5, 4:9, 5:8.
21. V.Lin. v.101–16.
22. V.Lin. v.101–18; cf. iii.47, iii.52, iii.76.
23. V.Lin. iii.45, iii.48, iii.51, iii.54, iv.97, v.85–94; V.Lat. vi.22, vii.15–18; Dt.L. ii.1f., iii.21–32.
24. For a broad survey of this phenomenon, see Louis Gougaud, *Ermites et reclus: Etudes sur d'anciennes formes de vie religieuse* (Vienne: Saint-Martin de Liguge, 1928). See also Vauchez, *La Sainteté*, pp. 380–88.
25. Dt.L. iii.1f., iii.4. See "Die Klause Dorotheas in ihrem jetzigen Zustand," *Der Dorotheenbote*, no. 32 (Advent 1973), p. 269 (cf. no. 30, p. 231).
26. V.Lin. iv.95f.; V.Lat. iv. 5, v.1, v.7, v.12f., v.17, v.19f., v.23f., v.38; Dt.L. iii.3, iii.6–17. See Hans Westpfahl, "Dorothea als Klausnerin," *Der Dorotheenbote*, no. 9 (summer 1956), pp. 3–14; "Zum Vollkommenheitsstreben der seligen Dorothea: Dorothea als Klausnerin," *Der Dorotheenbote*, no. 19 (spring 1964), pp. 2–10 (with photos).
27. V.Lin. v.126–28.
28. Ann Kosser Warren, "The Anchorite in Medieval England, 1100–1539" (Ph.D. diss., Case Western Reserve University, 1980), pp. 423f. Even Gougaud, *Ermites et reclus;* while giving a survey of eremitic life throughout Europe, cites only English materials for the fourteenth and fifteenth centuries.
29. This notion is a constant theme in the P.C.
30. On the general context, see James M. Clark, *The Great German Mystics: Eckhart, Tauler and Suso* (Oxford: Blackwell, 1949).
31. Grass, *The Flounder*, especially pp. 12f., 107–68. For reaction to this novel, see various materials in *Der Dorotheenbote*, no. 38 (summer 1978), pp. 407–13.
32. The P.C. is published in the *Acta sanctorum*, but the entries are arranged systematically rather than (as in the MSS) according to witness; thus, while the MSS give all the testimony for each of the witnesses together in one section, the published edition has a separate section for each of the items raised in the inquiry. For present purposes, this rearrangement is not a major drawback. Of the secondary works, Henri François's *Vie*

du Bienheureux Pierre de Luxembourg, evêque de Metz, cardinal à Avignon (1369–1387) (Ligny-en-Barrois: Gettliffe, 1927) is particularly useful.

33. Bibliothèque Calvet (Avignon), MSS 697, 698, and 3064; cf. MSS 2397 and 2477. A critical edition is needed.

34. P.C., test. 2, 10, and 11.

35. P.C. viii.27; François, *Vie*, pp. 25–27. Nicolas Jorga, *Philippe de Mézières, 1327–1405* (repr. London: Variorum, 1973), pp. 460–62, draws upon the P.C. for pertinent information. Another aspect of Philip's spirituality is conveyed in Murial Joyce Anderson Brown, "Philippe de Mézières' Order of the Passion: An Annotated Edition" (Ph.D. diss., University of Nebraska, 1971).

36. P.C. ii.29–31, v.31 (test. 1); Françis, *Vie*, p. 22.

37. P.C. ii.12–17; François, *Vie*, pp. 6–8.

38. V.P. i.7f.; P.C. ii.30f. (esp. test. 11 and 13), ii.14f. (test. 1), iii.17f.; François, *Vie*, pp. 13f.

39. P.C. v.32 (esp. test. 12); Bibliothèque Calvet, MS 207.

40. P.C. ii.1 (esp. test. 1), ii.15, ii.31, iv.31, iv.35, v.32–34.

41. P.C. v.34 (test. 13), ix.55–58.

42. V.P. iii.19, v.29; P.C. vi.20–25; François, *Vie*, pp. 15f., 44f.

43. V.P. v.27f.; P.C. iii.32 (test. 9), iv.46–48, xi.79 (test. 13).

44. P.C. ii.30f., ii.44f.

45. P.C. x.38–42; François, *Vie*, pp. 19–25; J. F. Huguenin, *Les Chroniques de la ville de Metz* (Metz: Lamort, 1838), p. 10.

46. P.C. viii.64, viii.68, viii.71, ix.59, ix.61f., ix.65–73; François, *Vie*, pp. 48f. Vauchez, *La Sainteté*, pp. 354–58, shows how Peter exemplifies a general crisis in the notion of episcopal sanctity.

47. P.C. viii.64, viii.68, viii.71, ix.59, ix.61f., ix.65–73; François, *Vie*, pp. 49–52.

48. V.P. ii.13, iv.21; P.C., iv.21, iv.23, iv.53f.; François, *Vie*, pp. 40f.

49. V.P. iv.21f.; François, *Vie*, pp. 29, 38–40.

50. P.C. iv.50, iv.75; François, *Vie*, pp. 29, 41f.

51. P.C., xi.79–84, xi.87–93; François, *Vie*, pp. 53–60.

52. P.C. xii.94–97; François, *Vie*, pp. 60f.

53. P.C. xii.98–105; François, *Vie*, pp. 61–63.

54. See the sources listed in the Guide to Primary Sources for these figures. On France and French saints, see Vauchez, *La Sainteté*, passim, and Weinstein and Bell, *Saints and Society*, pp. 181f. Vauchez, p. 419, cites Franciscan themes in the life of Elzear, but they are vague ones.

55. See André Vauchez, "Canonisation et politique au XIVe siècle: Documents inédits des Archives du Vatican relatifs au procès de canonisation de Charles de Blois, duc de Bretagne (+1364)," *Miscellanea in onore di Monsignor Martino Guisti, Prefetto dell'Archivio Segreto Vaticano* (=Collectanea Archivi Vaticani, no. 6) (Vatican City: Archivio Vaticano, 1978), pp. 381–404.

56. See M.-C. de Ganay, *Les bienheureuses Dominicaines (1190–1577), d'après des documents inédits*, 4th ed. (Paris: Perrin, 1924), pp. 193–237, 532–43.

57. Clare Gambacorta, i.5, ii.20.

58. Clare Gambacorta, i.4, ii.18, ii.22, iii.28.

59. Clare Gambacorta, ii.16.

60. Clare Gambacorta, i.4, i.6, i.8, ii.15, iii.29f., iv.31.

61. For general background, see William A. Hinnebusch, *The History of the Dominican Order*, vol. 1 (Staten Island, N.Y.: Alba House, 1966). On John Domenici, see *Acta sanctorum*, June, vol. 2, pp. 388–412, and *Giovanni Dominici (+1419): Saggi e inediti* (=Memorie Domenicane, n.s., no. 1) (Pistoia: "Centro Riviste" Padri Domenicani, 1970). Catherine's role as exemplar of the reform is discussed in John Wayland Coakley, "The Representation of Sanctity in Late Medieval Hagiography: Evidence

from Lives of Saints of the Dominican Order" (Ph.D. diss., Harvard University, 1980), pp. 86–89.

62. Clare Gambacorta, iii.23–28.

63. For the early history of the Franciscan order, see Raphael M. Huber, *A Documented History of the Franciscan Order*, vol. 1 (Milwaukee: Nowiny, 1944), and John Moorman, *A History of the Franciscan Order from Its Origins to the Year 1517* (Oxford: Clarendon Press, 1968). See also R. Manselli, "Agiografia francescana tra interpretazione teologica e religiosità popolare," in *Agiografia nell'Occidente cristiano, secoli XIII–XV: Atti dei Convegni Lincei* (Rome: Accademia Nazionale dei Lincei, 1980), pp. 45–56. For the fourteenth-century roots of the Observantine movement, see Duncan Nimmo, "Poverty and Politics: The Motivation of Fourteenth-Century Franciscan Reform in Italy," in Derek Baker, ed., *Religious Motivation: Biographical and Sociological Problems for the Church Historian* (= *Studies in Church History*, no. 15) (Oxford: Blackwell, 1978), pp. 161–78. Thomas Merton, *Contemplation in a World of Action* (paperback ed., Garden City, N.Y.: Doubleday, 1973), pp. 273–81, discusses the Franciscan eremitic tradition.

64. Materials for the mendicant orders other than the Dominicans and Franciscans are relatively sparse, but relevant background information can be obtained in P. R. McCaffrey, *The White Friars: An Outline of Carmelite History, with Special Reference to the English-Speaking Provinces* (Dublin: Gill, 1926), and Alessio Maria Rossi, *Manuale di storia dell'Ordine dei Servi di Maria (MCXXXIII–MCMLIV)* (Rome: Typis Pontificiae Universitatis Gregorianae, 1956). On the role of the mendicants generally in later medieval hagiography, see Vauchez, *La Sainteté*, pp. 388–410, and on mendicant hagiography as propaganda, ibid., pp. 131–42.

65. Vauchez, *La Sainteté*, passim, esp. pp. 215–56, and Weinstein and Bell, *Saints and Society*, pp. 175–79.

3. Patience

1. Henry Suso, i.20.

2. William James, *The Varieties of Religious Experience: A Study in Human Nature* (London: Longmans, 1902), pp. 297f.

3. Sister Thekla, ed., *Mother Maria: Her Life in Letters* (London: Darton, Longman & Todd, 1979), especially pp. 100–17. For this reference I am grateful to Carolyn Gifford.

4. Peter Olafsson, pp. 11, 13; Bridget of Sweden, pp. 18, 65f., 313–15, 318, 492–97, 583; Urban V, c. 82; Luitgard of Wittichen, c. 4; Dorothy of Montau, V.Lin. i.20, i.29; Christina Ebner, pp. 26f. See also Henry Suso, i.23, ii.34; Dalmatius Moner, c. 13; Ursulina of Parma, iv.42 (where patience is listed among other virtues); Robert of Salentino, v.50 (cf. iv.46); Joan of Castres, c. 3f. (source is from sixteenth century); Elzear of Sabran, V.Occ. pp. 89–97, 112f.

5. Peter of Luxembourg, V.P. v.32; François, *Vie*, p. 46.

6. Venturino of Bergamo, pp. 47–49.

7. Charles of Blois, especially pp. 27–29, 56f., 60, 67f., 73, 84f., 111, 114, 127, 134, 139, 146, 170, 188.

8. PL, vol. 76, col. 1264; cited by Ralph Hanna III, "Some Commonplaces of Late Medieval Patience Discussions: An Introduction," in Gerald J. Schiffhorst, ed., *The Triumph of Patience: Medieval and Renaissance Studies* (Orlando, Fla.: University of Presses of Florida, 1978), p. 72.

9. Roy J. Defferrari, ed., *Early Christian Biographies* (n.p.: Fathers of the Church, 1952), esp. pp. 138–45.

10. Gertrude of Delft, ii.10; Urban V, c. 83.

11. Jacopo Passavanti, *Lo specchio della vera penitenzia*, vol. I (Milan: Classici Italiani, 1808), pp. 98–119. For one example, see Elizabeth Achler, p. 99.

12. Peter Olafsson, p. 12; Elizabeth of Portugal, iv.24–26; Elzear of Sabran, V.Lat. iv.44–48.

13. Jane Mary of Maillé, Vit. i.5f., iii.19, v.36.

14. Elizabeth of Portugal, v.40f.; cf. Walter Nigg, ed., *Elisabeth von Thüringen* (Düsseldorf: Patmos, 1963).

15. Dorothy of Montau, V.Lin. ii.39, iii.63f. (cf. iii.66).

16. Andrew Corsini, ii.7 (cf. iii.11); Urban V, c. 84 (cf. c. 83); Peter Olafsson, p. 11; Elizabeth of Portugal, x.88; Jane Mary of Maillé, especially Vit. v.35.

17. Catherine of Sweden, iv.40f.

18. Nicholas Hermansson, Vit. pp. 34f.

19. James Oldo, iii.21f.; Nicholas Hermansson, Vit. pp. 34, 36; Jane Mary of Maillé, Vit. v.34; Clare Gambacorta, v.37; Villana de'Botti, c. 11f.; Delphina of Puimichel, P.C. art. 33. See also John of Alverna, p. 446; Bridget of Sweden, pp. 20f., 318–20, 442f., 583; Andrew Corsini, v.26; Peter Olafsson, p. 12; Elzear of Sabran, V.Lat. v.69; Francis Patrizzi, c. 12; Catherine of Sweden, vii.61; Brynolph, pp. 142, 148, 150, 155, 160, 166f.; Ursulina of Parma, iv.38.

20. Peter of Luxembourg, V.P. v.34, and P.C. xi.78f.; François, *Vie*, p. 58.

21. Francis Patrizzi, c. 5.

22. Elzear of Sabran, V.Lat. iv.48, V.Occ. 120f.; Jane Mary of Maillé, iii.22; Urban V, c. 82. See also Charles of Blois, p. 39; Bridget of Sweden, pp. 229, 249, 261, 314, 496, 583, Margaret Ebner, p. 14.

23. Richard Rolle, Vit.; Dorothy of Montau, V.Lin. ii.42; James Oldo, i.2.

24. Johannes von Saaz, *Der Ackermann aus Böhmen*, ed. Günther Jungbluth (Heidelberg: Winter, 1969–); *Death and the Plowman, or The Bohemian Plowman*, tr. Ernest N. Kirrmann (Chapel Hill, N.C.: University of North Carolina Press, 1958). On the *ars moriendi* literature, see Rainer Rudolf, *Ars moriendi: Von der Kunst des heilsamen Lebens und Sterbens* (Cologne: Böhlau, 1957). The pertinent material from Thomas More is cited in Bernard Basset, *Born for Friendship: The Spirit of Sir Thomas More* (London: Burns & Oates, 1965), pp. 30–38.

25. Peter Olafsson, p. 12; Clare Gambacorta, iv.35; Charles of Blois, p. 115 (see also pp. 56, 60, 84, 111, 170).

26. Catherine of Sweden, vii.61; Peter Olafsson, pp. 5, 12f.; Urban V, c. 64; Rulman Merswin, p. 41.

27. Jane Mary of Maillé, Vit. v.37; Catherine of Sweden, iv.41; Gertrude of Delft, ii.10; Villana de' Botti, c. 12.

28. Henry Suso, i.25.

29. Henry Suso, ii.38.

30. Henry Suso, ii.40.

31. Henry Suso, epil., i.28.

32. See Coakley, "Sanctity in Late Medieval Hagiography," pp. 98–102, for discussion of this theme in both saints' vitae.

33. Catherine of Siena, i.4.50f., ii.11.310, iii.5.394, iii.6.395–430.

34. *The Dialogue of Saint Catherine of Siena*, tr. Algar Thorald (reprint, Rockford, Ill.: TAN, 1974), pp. 335–44.

35. Catherine of Siena, *Dialogue*, trans. Suzanne Noffke (New York: Paulist, 1980), pp. 33, 141, 143. See Kenelm Foster and Mary John Ronayne, eds., *I, Catherine: Selected Writings of St Catherine of Siena* (London: Collins, 1980), esp. pp. 57–59, 60, 62, 119, 131, 140, 152, 169f., 177, 180, 196f., 231.

36. Henry Suso, i.3.

37. Catherine of Siena, ii.11.310; Urban V, c. 64; Francis Patrizzi, c. 5f.; Jane Mary of Maillé, Vit., i.3, iii.19; Clare Gambacorta, iv.36; Catherine of Sweden, iv.40; Andrew

Corsini, ii.7; Catherine of Siena, ii.4.143–46 (cf. ii.4.155–58); Dorothy of Montau, V.Lin. ii.31. Cf. Ecclus. 2:4.

38. Clare Gambacorta, ii.21; Nicholas Hermansson, Vit. p. 34; Charles of Blois, especially p. 160. On the overlapping of patience, humility, meekness, etc., see Hanna, "Some Commonplaces," p. 71.

39. Flora of Beaulieu, iii.37.

40. Nicholas Hermansson, Vit. p. 26, and P.C. art. 8–12, 20f.; Elzear of Sabran, V.Lat., i.5, ii.15, v.61; Catherine of Siena, i.9.80 (cf. iii.6.430); Christina Ebner, p. 11; Rulman Merswin, p. 49. See also Ursulina of Parma, iv.40.

41. V.P. iv.36; P.C., xi.78; François, *Vie*, p. 54.

42. Jane Mary of Maillé, Vit. vi.46; Villana de' Botti, c. 12.

43. John of Alverna, pp. 440f.; Henry Suso, ii.38.

44. Georg Schreiber, *Die Vierzehn Nothelfer in Volksfrömmigkeit und Sakralkultur: Symbolkraft und Herrschaftsbereich der Wallfahrtskapelle, vorab in Franken und Tirol* (Innsbruck: Wagner, 1959). Vauchez, *La Sainteté*, p. 484, remarks that the identification of sainthood with martyrdom was merely a memory, in that few late medieval martyrs attained canonization; yet the old ones remained important.

45. Henry Suso, i.23, ii.42; Catherine of Sweden, iii.22; Elzear of Sabran, V.Lat., iv.47, v.69; Andrew Corsini, iii.11; Jane Mary of Maillé, Vit. v.35, v.37. Clare Gambacorta's patience won acclaim for her as a "true lover of the cross" (ii.17).

46. Rulman Merswin, p. 42; Catherine of Siena, i.11.109.

47. Mary Felicitas Madigan, *The Passio Domini Theme in the Works of Richard Rolle: His Personal Contribution in Its Religious, Cultural, and Literary Context* (Salzburg: Institut für Englische Sprache und Literatur, 1978), pp. 245f., 248, 258, 261 (cf. pp. 256f.).

48. John Ruysbroeck, c. 10.

49. John Ruysbroeck, c. 11.

50. On this general problem, from a strictly orthodox perspective, see Heinrich Denifle, *Die deutsche Mystik des 14. Jahrhunderts: Beitrag zur Deutung ihrer Lehre*, ed. Otwin Spiess (Freiburg in der Schweiz: Paulusverlag, 1951).

51. Richard Kieckhefer, "The Notion of Passivity in the Sermons of John Tauler," *Recherches de théologie ancienne et médiévale*, vol. 48 (1981), pp. 198–211.

52. Honoré Bonet, *The Tree of Battles: An English Version*, ed. G. W. Coopland (Cambridge, Mass.: Harvard University Press, 1949), pp. 119–21.

53. I have substituted the word "trials" for the translator's "temptations."

54. In the *Nicomachaean Ethics* (iii.6–9), Aristotle is of course mainly interested in defining this virtue as a mean between extremes; it is in contrast to rashness that fortitude entails the ability to delay action. The scriptural reference is Acts 20:35.

55. Alcuin Blamires, "Chaucer's Revaluation of Chivalric Honor," *Mediaevalia*, vol. 5 (1979), pp. 245–69. For another example of the link, though with reference to women, see Thomas Wright, ed., *The Book of the Knight of La Tour-Landry, Compiled for the Instruction of His Daughters*, rev. ed. (London: Kegan Paul, 1906), pp. 102–4 (Tobias, Job, and St. Eustatius rewarded for patience; duty of grateful patience; power of patience, humility, and hope) and 151f. (Virgin as model of compassion and patience). Patience is not a traditional chivalric virtue; see Gustav Ehrismann, "Die Grundlagen des ritterlichen Tugendsystems," *Zeitschrift für deutsches Altertum und deutsche Literature*, vol. 56 (1918), pp. 137–216. Nor does it loom large in fourteenth-century chivalric biography, though this is often merely adapted from earlier texts; on this topic see J. A. Burrow, *Medieval Writers and Their Work: Middle English Literature and Its Background 1100–1500* (Oxford: Oxford University Press, 1982), p. 70: "There are in Middle English two main types of Life: the Vita Sancti or Saint's Life, and the Life of the chivalric hero. These have much in common; and it is not surprising to find the romance of Havelok recorded, under the title 'Vita Havlok', in a manuscript devoted chiefly to Saints' Lives. Romances, in fact, commonly keep company in the chief manu-

script collections . . . with hagiographical and other pious pieces. . . . Both deal with exemplary lives, marvellous events, and heroic deaths." Yet both genres deal mainly with long-deceased figures: the saints in question here are not figures of the fourteenth century.

56. Peter Olafsson, p. 12.

57. Henry Suso, i.20.

58. Henry Suso, ii.44.

59. Ulrich von Lichtenstein, *Frauendienst, oder: Geschichte und Liebe des Ritters und Sängers*, ed. Ludwig Tieck (Vienna: Grund, 1818); Ulrich von Liechtenstein, *Service of Ladies, translated in condensed form into English verse*, trans. J. W. Thomas (Chapel Hill: University of North Carolina Press, 1969); Ursula Peters, *Frauendienst: Untersuchungen zu Ulrich von Lichtenstein und zum Wirklichkeitsgehalt der Minnedichtung* (Göppingen: Kümmerle, 1971).

60. Quoted here from James Harvey Robinson and Henry Winchester Rolfe, *Petrarch: The First Modern Scholar and Man of Letters*, 2d ed. (New York: Putnam, 1914), pp. 318f.

61. Meister Eckhart, *Die deutschen Werke*, ed. Josef Quint, vol. 5 (Stuttgart: Kohlhammer, 1963), pp. 1–105 and 471–97. For the earlier history of the genre, see Peter von Moos, *Consolatio: Studien zur mittelalterlichen Trostliteratur über den Tod und zum Problem der christlichen Trauer* (Munich: Fink, 1971–72).

62. Hanna, "Some Commonplaces," p. 84, n. 24: "Specifically consolatory materials lie somewhat outside the scope of normal Christian discussions, in that Boethius and other writers in the genre presuppose that reason easily triumphs over pain, an attitude foreign to most religious discussions."

63. There were several early editions of the *Consolation;* I have used Johannes de Tambaco, *Liber de consolatione theologiae* (Speyer: Georgius de Spira, c. 1478). For analysis, see especially Albert Auer, *Johannes von Dambach und die Tröstbücher vom 11. bis zum 16. Jahrhundert* (Münster i.W.: Aschendorff, 1928); the relationship with Nominalism is discussed on p. 158. The treatise on the uses of tribulation is given in Albert Auer, *Leidenstheologie im Spätmittelalter* (St. Ottilien: Eos, 1952), pp. 1–18.

64. Lawrence L. Besserman, *The Legend of Job in the Middle Ages* (Cambridge, Mass.: Harvard University Press, 1979), pp. 75–113. Besserman generalizes: "in the fourteenth and fifteenth centuries, Job's popularity increased" (p. 75).

65. Eckart Greifenstein, *Der Hiob-Traktat des Marquard von Lindau* (Zurich: Artemis, 1979).

66. Hanna, "Some Commonplaces," pp. 65–87.

67. Charles of Blois, passim, esp. pp. 27f.

68. Hanna, "Some Commonplaces," pp. 67–71.

69. Ibid., pp. 71–77.

70. Ibid., pp. 77f. On the Stoics and their Christian opponents, see the forthcoming work of Marcia L. Colish, *The Stoic Tradition from Antiquity to the Early Middle Ages* (Leiden: Brill, 1984–).

71. Ludolphus de Saxonia, *Vita Jesu Christi ex Evangelio et approbatis Ecclesia Catholica Doctoribus sedule collecta*, ed. L. M. Rigollot (Paris: Palme; Brussels: Lebrocquy, 1878), i.35. The text and a somewhat different translation also appear in Sister Mary Immaculate Bodenstedt, *Praying the Life of Christ: First English Translation of the Prayers Concerning the 181 Chapters of the Vita Christi of Ludolphus the Carthusian: The Quintessence of His Devout Meditations on the Life of Christ* (Salzburg: Institut für Englische Sprache und Literatur, 1973), pp. 35f.

72. Ludolphus, *Vita Jesu Christi*, PL, vol. 76, col. 1264.

73. Ibid., ii.20.3.

74. Cf. Col. 1:24, where Paul speaks of his mission to "fill up those things that are wanting of the sufferings of Christ, in my flesh."

75. Ludolphus, *Vita Jesu Christi,* ii.52.6 and oratio.

76. *Thomae Hemerken a Kempis Opera omnia,* ed. Michael Iosephus Pohl, vol. 1 (Freiburg i.Br.: Herder, 1910), pp. 3–62 ("De paupertate, humilitate, et patientia, sive de tribus tabernaculis"). Thomas à Kempis: *The Imitation of Christ,* trans. Leo Sherley-Price (Harmondsworth: Penguin, 1952).

77. *Imitation,* iii.46 (importance of patience); i.13, iii.18 (growth in virtue); ii.3, ii.12 (sense of peace); iii.35f. (shield); i.16, i.24 (purgation); ii.12, iii.12, iii.16, iii.19, iii.47, iii.57f. (afterlife); i.16, iii.7, iii.13, iii.36, iii.57, iv.15 (humility); ii.9f. (consolations); iii.18, iii.56 (imitation of Christ's patience). There are numerous further examples.

78. Willelmus Mulder, ed., *Gerardi Magni Epistolae* (Nijmegen: Dekker, 1933), pp. 232–43.

79. Ibid., pp. 54, 57, 195; cf. p. 202.

80. Ibid., pp. 270, 278, 282–93; cf. pp. 294–303.

81. Guilielmus Paraldus, *Summa de virtutibus et vitiis* (Brescia: Britannicus, 1494), sig. 06^{r-v}.

82. Giovanni Boccaccio, *The Decameron: A New Translation,* ed. & trans. Mark Musa and Peter E. Bondanella (New York: Norton, 1977), pp. 134–42 (the story is the last one in the collection); Robinson and Wolfe, *Petrarch,* pp. 191–96; Geoffrey Chaucer, *The Complete Works,* ed. Walter W. Skeat, vol. 4, 2d ed. (Oxford: Clarendon Press, 1900), pp. 391–425.

83. Robinson and Wolfe, *Petrarch,* pp. 191–96.

84. For the general problem of historicity in saints' lives, see two articles by Klaus Schreiner: "'Discrimen veri ac falsi': Ansätze und Formen der Kritik in der Heiligen- und Reliquienverehrung des Mittelalters," *Archiv für Kulturgeschichte,* vol. 48 (1966), pp. 1–53; and "Zum Wahrheitsverständnis im Heiligen- und Reliquienwesen des Mittelalters," *Saeculum,* vol. 17 (1966), pp. 131–69.

85. The translation is from *The Canterbury Tales,* trans. Nevill Coghill, rev. ed. (Harmondsworth: Penguin, 1958), pp. 337 (reference to Petrarch), 354 ("married men . . ."), 369 (moral force; cf. 350, 355f., 360, 366, 370f.), and 363 (Job).

86. See Elie Golenistcheff-Koutouzoff, *L'histoire de Griseldis en France au XIVe et au XVe siècle* (Paris: Droz, 1933).

87. E.g., Dorothy of Montau, V.Lin. ii.39, iii.63f.

88. Charles Moorman, ed., *The Works of the* Gawain-*Poet* (Jackson, Miss.: University Press of Mississippi, 1977), pp. 67–100; William Langland, *Piers the Ploughman,* trans. J. F. Goodridge (Harmondsworth: Penguin, 1959), esp. pp. 189–215, 299–308; Elizabeth D. Kirk, "'Who Suffreth More Than God?': Narrative Redefinition of Patience in *Patience* and *Piers Plowman,*" in Schiffhorst, *Triumph of Patience,* pp. 88–104.

89. Timothy Fry, ed., *The Rule of St. Benedict in Latin and English with Notes* (Collegeville, Minn.: Liturgical Press, 1981), pp. 166f. The translation is adapted.

90. Aldegundis Führkötter, ed. and trans., *Das Leben der heiligen Hildegard von Bingen* (Dusseldorf: Patmos, 1968), p. 48; Richard of Chichester, i.4.46 (*Acta sanctorum,* April, vol. 1, p. 294). For Franciscan examples, see Marion A. Habig, ed., *St. Francis of Assisi: Writings and Early Biographies* (Chicago: Franciscan Herald, 1973), pp. 311–13 and 737–40, and Giovanni di Coppo, *The Legend of Holy Fina, Virgin of Santo Giminiano,* trans. M. Mansfield (reprint New York: Cooper Square, 1966), esp. pp. 10–15.

91. Most of these developments are summarized in Robert E. Lerner, *The Age of Adversity: The Fourteenth Century* (Ithaca, N.Y.: Cornell University Press, 1968), pp. 12f.; the quotes are from this passage. An author writing around 1336 suggested that the turn of the century had brought decline and disaster because thirteen is an unlucky number; see Robert E. Lerner, *The Heresy of the Free Spirit in the Later Middle Ages* (Berkeley: University of California Press, 1972), p. 235.

92. Christina Ebner, p. 11.

93. J. N. D. Kelly, *Jerome: His Life, Writings, and Controversies* (London: Duckworth, 1975), esp. pp. 104–15.

94. Quoted from article on Henry Suso in Butler, *Lives of the Saints* (as above, chap. 1, n. 10).

4. Devotion to the Passion

1. Catherine of Siena, *Dialogue*, esp. p. 29; see also the vita, i.11.110.

2. Flora of Beaulieu, iii.40.

3. Ludolphus, *Vita Jesu Christi*, lviii.1.

4. The development of this devotion is traced in Carl Richstaetter, *Christusfrömmigkeit in ihrer historischen Entfaltung: Ein quellenmässiger Beitrag zur Geschichte des Gebetes und des mystischen Innenlebens der Kirche* (Cologne: Bächem, 1949). For the general shift in spirituality, see R. W. Southern, *The Making of the Middle Ages* (New Haven: Yale University Press, 1959), pp. 231–40.

5. Phyllis Hodgson, ed., *The Cloud of Unknowing and Related Treatises on Contemplative Prayer* (Salzburg: Institut für Anglistik und Amerikanistik, 1982), c. 35 (pp. 39f.).

6. Nicholas Hermansson, p. 35; Catherine of Sweden, iv.31, iii.22; Bridget of Sweden, p. 76. See also Clare of Rimini, c.4.

7. Ademar of Felsinio, p. 467; Catherine of Siena, ii.6.187, ii.6.191. See also Clare of Rimini, c.12.

8. John of Alverna, p. 446; Jane Mary of Maillé, Vit. i.6; P.C., v.50, ii.11, v.53f., v.56 (cf. i.2).

9. Flora of Beaulieu, i.12; Jane Mary of Maillé, Vit. i.6; P.C., v.50, ii.11, v.53f., v.56.

10. Henry Suso, ii.42; Jane Mary of Maillé, P.C. v.56.

11. Peter of Luxembourg, P.C. ix.59 (test. 2), xi.74; François, *Vie*, pp. 14, 43. See Louis Reau, *Iconographie de l'art chrétien*, vol. 3 (Paris: Presses Universitaires, 1959), pp. 1108f.

12. Habig, *St. Francis*, especially pp. 308f.; Catherine of Siena, ii.6.193; Margaret of Faenza, Vit. ii.13; Flora of Beaulieu, i.13 (cf. ii.35), iii.49; Gertrude of Delft, iv.15–19 (cf. i.1). For an extensive compilation of material, see Antoine Imbert-Gourbeyre, *La stigmatisation: L'extase divine et les miracles de Lourdes: Réponse aux Libres-Penseurs*, vol. 1 (Paris: Bellet, 1898), especially pp. 31–93. Imbert-Gourbeye defines the phenomenon rather broadly. Elizabeth Achler, pp. 102f., is a graphic example.

13. Henry Suso, i.23; Rulman Merswin, pp. 42–44; Villana de' Botti, c.12.

14. Margaret of Faenza, Vit. ii.14. See also the passing reference in Catherine of Siena, i.9.111.

15. Bridget of Sweden, p. 76.

16. See Marcolino of Forli, p. 191, and Margaret of Faenza, Vit. ii.10f., Rev. i.5.

17. On this development see Vauchez, *La Sainteté*, p. 456.

18. August Closs, ed., *Weltlohn, Teufelsbeichte, Waldbruder: Beitrag zur Bearbeitung lateinischer Exempla in Mhd Gewande, nebst einem Anhang: de eo qui duas volebat uxores* (Heidelberg: Winters, 1934), pp. 114–19.

19. Ibid., p. 108. For Emmaus see Lk. 24:13–35.

20. F. P. Pickering, ed., *Christi Leiden in einer Vision geschaut: A German Mystical Text of the Fourteenth Century: A Critical Account of the Published and Unpublished Manuscripts, with an Edition Based on the Text of Ms. Bernkastel-Cues 115* (Manchester: Manchester University Press, 1952).

21. Edgar Hennecke, *New Testament Apocrypha*, ed. Wilhelm Schneemelcher, trans. R. McL. Wilson, vol. 1 (Philadelphia: Westminster, 1963), pp. 444–81. See also Sister John Sullivan, *A Study of the Themes of the Sacred Passion in the Medieval Cycle Plays* (Washington, D.C.: Catholic University of America Press, 1943), pp. 8–21.

22. On the general phenomenon, see Kurt Ruh, "Zur Theologie des mittelalterlichen Passionstraktats," *Theologische Zeitschrift* (Basel), vol. 6 (1970), esp. pp. 17f., and Sullivan, *A Study of the Themes*, pp. 35–49. The version of Pseudo-Bonaventure used here is Isa Ragusa and Rosalie B. Green, eds., *Meditations on the Life of Christ: An Illustrated Manuscript of the Fourteenth Century: Paris, Bibliothèque Nationale, Ms. Ital. 115* (Princeton: Princeton University Press, 1961). Ludolphus, *Vita*, has been cited previously. See Charles Abbott Conway, Jr., *The Vita Christi of Ludolph of Saxony and Late Medieval Devotion Centered on the Incarnation: A Descriptive Analysis* (Salzburg: Institut für Englische Sprache und Literatur, 1976); and Walter Baier, *Untersuchungen zu den Passionsbetrachtungen in der Vita Christi des Ludolf von Sachsen* (Salzburg: Institut für Englische Sprache und Literatur, 1977).

23. Ragusa and Green ed., pp. 5 (hypothetical method); 317f. (introduction); 323 (Gethsemane); 325f., 328f., 331, 336 (patience); 328f. (scourging); 333f. (nailing to cross).

24. Ludolphus, *Vita*, lviii.4, lxiii.13, lxiii.16, lxiii.23, lxvi.5 (mystical interpretations); lxii.18 (mockers); lxi.10, lxiii.1, lxiii.9, lxiii.11, lxiii.20, lxiv.17 (problems); lxiii.2, lxvi.6 (geographical information); lviii.6, lix.5, lxvi.10 (lists); lviii.3 (forest brother).

25. Sullivan, *A Study of the Themes*, pp. 8–21.

26. Pickering, *Christi Leiden*, pp. 65 (cf. 67, 74), 71f. James Marrow, "*Circumdederunt me canes multi*: Christ's Tormentors in Northern European Art of the Late Middle Ages and Early Renaissance," *Art Bulletin*, vol. 59 (1977), pp. 167–81, traces the artistic representation of such material. F. P. Pickering, *Essays on Medieval German Literature and Iconography* (Cambridge: Cambridge University Press, 1980), pp. 3–30, begins his discussion of the passion with reference to this work.

27. Madigan, *The Passio Domini Theme*, pp. 257, 248. Ruh, "Zur Theologie," pp. 19–31, emphasizes the biblical foundations for such detail.

28. *The Monk of Farne: The Meditations of a Fourteenth Century Monk*, ed. & intro. Hugh Farmer, trans. by a Benedictine of Stanbrook (London: Darton, 1961), pp. 43–45, 76f.

29. Madigan, *The Passio Domini Theme*, pp. 257f. (carrying of cross), 275f. (body after death), 248–52 (allegories).

30. Henry Suso, *Little Book of Eternal Wisdom* and *Little Book of Truth*, trans. James M. Clark (New York: Faber & Faber, n.d.), pp. 51f.

31. Madigan, *The Passio Domini Theme*, p. 100; Louis Gougaud, *Devotional and Ascetic Practices in the Middle Ages*, trans. by the author and G. C. Bateman (London: Burns, Oates & Washbourne, 1927), p. 76.

32. Closs, *Weltlohn*, pp. 117–19; Madigan, *The Passio Domini Theme*, pp. 257, 271f.

33. On these themes see Martin Elze, "Das Verständnis der Passion Jesu im ausgehenden Mittelalter und bei Luther," in Heinz Liebing and Klaus Scholder, eds., *Geist und Geschichte der Reformation: Festgabe Hanns Rückert zum 65. Geburtstag dargebracht von Freunden, Kollegen und Schüllern* (Berlin: de Gruyter, 1966), pp. 127–51.

34. Ragusa and Green ed., p. 331 (cf. pp. 318, 320f., 326–28, 330); Suso, *Little Book*, c. 3.

35. Ludolphus, *Vita*, lviii.3, lviii.5.

36. Ragusa and Green, *Meditations*, pp. 335, 338f., 344; Pickering, *Christi Leiden*, p. 80; Madigan, *The Passio Domini Theme*, pp. 260f. (cf. p. 277); see also Gerold Hayer, "Aggsbacher Marienklage aus dem Mittelhochdeutschen übersetzt," in *Die Kartäuser in Österreich*, vol. 2 (Salzburg: Institut für Anglistik und Amerikanistik, 1981), pp. 88–94, and Walter Baier, "Quellenkritische und theologische Anmerkungen zur Aggsbacher Marienklage," ibid., pp. 95–109. For the general theme of the Mother of Sorrows, see Theo Meier, *Die Gestalt Marias im geistlichen Schauspiel des deutschen Mittelalters* (Berlin: Erich Schmidt, 1959), pp. 145–20, and for the broader theological context see Jaroslav

Pelikan, *The Growth of Medieval Theology (600–1300)* (Chicago: University of Chicago Press, 1978), pp. 160–74.

37. Gertrud Schiller, *Iconography of Christian Art*, trans. Janet Seligman, vol. 1 (London: Humphries, 1971), pp. 29, 74, 81–83, 109 (cf. 45, 51, 88–90).

38. Sancta Birgitta, *Opera minora*, vol. 2 (= Sermo angelicus), ed. Sten Eklund (Uppsala: Almqvist & Wiksells, 1972), pp. 121–23; Bridget of Sweden, *Revelations and Prayers of St. Bridget of Sweden, Being the "Sermo Angelicus," or Angelic Discourse Concerning the Excellence of the Virgin Mary, Revealed to the Saint, with Certain Prayers*, trans. Ernest Graf (New York: Benziger, 1928). See Sister John Sullivan, *A Study of the Themes*, pp. 63–65, where Bridget's revelations concerning the passion are referred to as "by far the most beautiful" of her revelations.

39. E.g., George Henderson, *Gothic* (Harmondsworth: Penguin, 1967), pp. 160–68; Sister John Sullivan, *A Study of the Themes*, pp. 50–69.

40. Bernard of Clairvaux, *Sermons on the Canticle of Canticles*, vol. 1 (Shannon: Cistercian Fathers Series, 1971), pp. 147–55; see also the references in *The Exemplar: Life and Writings of Blessed Henry Suso, O.P.*, ed. Nicholas Heller, trans. Sister M. Ann Edward (Dubuque: Priory Press, 1962), vol. 2, p. 358, n. 9.

41. Suso, *Little Book*, c. 2.

42. Richard Kieckhefer, "The Role of Christ in Tauler's Spirituality," *Downside Review*, vol. 96 (1978), pp. 176–91.

43. On prayers, see Gougaud, *Devotional and Ascetic Practices*, pp. 83–87, and André Wilmart, *Auteurs spirituels et textes dévots du moyen âge latin: Etudes d'histoire littéraire* (reprint Paris: *Etudes Augustiniennes*, 1971), pp. 505–36. The lyric quoted is from Brian Stone, trans., *Medieval English Verse*, rev. ed. (Harmondsworth: Penguin, 1971), p. 41; there are several specimens in Frances M. M. Comper, *Spiritual Songs from English Manuscripts of the Fourteenth Century* (London: Macmillan, 1936); see David L. Jeffrey, *The Early English Lyric and Franciscan Spirituality* (Lincoln: University of Nebraska Press, 1975). For a narrative poem, see Grace Frank, ed., *Le Livre de la Passion: Poème narratif du XIVe siècle* (Paris: Champion, 1930); the genre is discussed in Sullivan, *A Study of the Themes*, pp. 70–85, and in J. A. W. Bennett, *Poetry of the Passion: Studis in Twelve Centuries of English Verse* (Oxford: Clarendon Press, 1982). The literature on passion drama is rich. On the French passion plays, see Sandro Sticca, *The Latin Passion Play: Its Origins and Development* (Albany: State University of New York Press, 1970), pp. 154–56; Grace Frank, ed., *La Passion du Palatinus: Mystère du XIVe siècle* (Paris: Champion, 1922); Grace Frank, "French Literature in the Fourteenth Century," in Francis Lee Utley, ed., *The Forward Movement of the Fourteenth Century* (Columbus: Ohio State University Press, 1961), pp. 73–75. On the German plays, see Sticca, *Latin Passion Play*, pp. 157–60; Rolf Steinbach, *Die deutschen Oster- und Passionsspiele des Mittelalters: Versuch einer Darstellung und Wesensbestimmung nebst einer Bibliographie zum deutschen geistlichen Spiel des Mittelalters* (Cologne & Vienna: Böhlau, 1970); Rolf Bergmann, *Studien zu Entstehung und Geschichte der deutschen Passionsspiele des 13. und 14. Jahrhunderts* (Munich: Fink, 1972).

44. Foster and Ronayne, *I, Catherine*: the themes of Christ crucified and Christ's blood occur throughout; for the cross, see pp. 57, 96, 108f., 113, 130, 145, 156, 177, 202, 204, 242; on the wounds, see pp. 72, 172, 223.

45. Ibid., p. 120 (paragraphs conflated).

46. Ibid., p. 79.

47. These points are aptly summarized by Gougaud, *Devotional and Ascetic Practices*, p. 76: "the fourteenth and fifteenth centuries . . . were those in which more than in any other the faithful received spiritual refreshment from the contemplation of their Saviour's sufferings. A number of objects of piety of that period representing the tortures of Christ in the most realistic manner and under the most varied forms were particularly suited to make vivid impressions on feelings which were already stirred by the calamities of the time."

48. Southern, *Making*, pp. 237f.; for general information see Schiller, *Iconography*. For the English examples, see Madigan, *The Passio Domini Theme*, p. 18.

49. Schiller, *Iconography*, pp. 146f.

50. Bruce Cole, *Sienese Painting: From its Origins to the Fifteenth Century* (New York: Harper & Row, 1980), p. 72.

51. Ibid., p. 117.

52. Schiller, *Iconography*, pp. 179—81.

53. Ibid., pp. 184—97 (and figs. 654, 657f.).

54. Ibid., pp. 197—229.

55. Ibid., pp. 151—58; Elisabeth Roth, *Der volkreiche Kalvarienberg in Literatur und Bildkunst des Spätmittelalters*, 2d ed. (Berlin: Schmidt, 1967).

56. There were, of course, exceptions; see Grace Frank, "Popular Iconography of the Passion," *Publications of the Modern Language Association*, vol. 46 (1931), pp. 333—40, for an example.

57. Bibliothèque Calvet (Avignon), MS 207, fol. 144r—147v. Peter of Luxembourg, V.P. i.7, iv.24, iv.26; P.C. ix.59 (test. 2), xi.74; Jane Mary of Maillé, Vit. v.34. On the link between art and visions, see Schiller, *Iconography*, p. 147.

58. Catherine of Siena, iii.6.403; Clare Gambacorta, i.4; Andrew Corsini, iv.15; James Oldo, i.3; Robert of Salentino, vi.54; Jane Mary of Maillé, Vit. i.2, v.34, iv.28; Henry Suso, i.23; Peter of Fulgineo, suppl., p. 368. For further indications of the power held by the sign of the cross, see Robert of Salentino, v.50, v.52—54, v.56, v.58. For further examples of prayer before a crucifix, see Venturino of Bergamo, p. 51; Ursulina of Parma, iv.40; Margaret of Faenza, Rev. i.10. There are poignant examples of such devotion in Margaret Ebner (p. 19) and Adelheid Langmann (e.g., p. 115).

59. Clare Gambacorta, app. 2.

60. Schiller, *Iconography*, pp. 189—91. For the shroud in the fourteenth century, see especially Ian Wilson, *The Shroud of Turin: The Burial Cloth of Jesus Christ?* (Garden City, N.Y.: Doubleday, 1978), pp. 165—83. M. G. Dickson, "Patterns of European Sanctity: The Saints in the Later Middle Ages (with Special Reference to Perugia)" (Diss., Edinburgh University, 1975), vol. 1, p. 225, cites veneration of blood-relics.

61. Jane Mary of Maillé, Vit. iv.31, P.C. iii.24.

62. Henry Suso, i.13. See Herbert Thurston, "The Stations of the Cross," *The Month*, vol. 46 (1900), pp. 1—12, 153—66, 282—93.

63. Jane Mary of Maillé, P.C. v.53; Peter of Luxembourg, P.C. ix.59 (test. 13); James Oldo, i.2f. See also Bridget of Sweden, p. 14.

64. Rulman Merswin, pp. 43f.; Jane Mary of Maillé, Vit. v.34, iii.23; Elzear of Sabran, V.Lat. v.69 (cf. V.Occ. p. 120f.); Delphina of Puimichel, P.C. art. 46; Villana de' Botti, c. 14; Henry Suso, ii.42. See also Elizabeth Achler, p. 105.

65. Ludolphus, *Vita*, lx.3, lix.18; Bridget of Sweden, pp. 14, 99, 228, 308, 439, 579 (see also 15, 310, 580 for other practices); Clare of Rimini, c.9.

66. Robert of Salentino, ii.20f., vi.64f.

67. V.Lat. ii.5. The term here rendered as "devotion" is *venia*, which can mean more strictly "prostration," though that translation seems narrow for all the exercises here recounted.

68. Ibid.

69. Huizinga, *The Waning of the Middle Ages*, pp. 136—59.

70. Jane Mary of Maillé, Vit. v.34; Catherine of Siena, ii.4.158 (cf. ii.6.212); James Oldo, ii.13; Villana de' Botti, c. 8; Henry Suso, i.16, i.4, i.18.

71. Peter Olafsson, pp. 3—5.

72. William K. Powers is working on an anthropological study of self-mutilation. (For this information I am grateful to Mary Douglas.)

73. Phyllis McGinley, *Saint-Watching* (New York: Viking, 1969), p. 19 ("The saints

differ from us in their exuberance, the excess of our human talents. Moderation is not their secret. It is in the wildness of their dreams, the desperate vitality of their ambitions, that they stand apart from ordinary men of good will").

74. V.Lat. ii.25.

75. P.C., p. 260 ("perfectius esset Christum imitari in passionibus quam in actionibus").

5. Penitence

1. John of Caramola, c. 2; Mary of Oignies, i.1.17 (*Acta sanctorum*, June, vol. 5, p. 551); Catherine of Siena, i.4.43.

2. PL, vol. 49, col. 1254.

3. See, for example, Jean Gerson, *Oeuvres complète*, ed. Mgr. Glorieux, vol. 7 (Paris: Desclée, 1966), pp. 140–42.

4. Catherine of Siena, i.2.30, ii.6.200, i.4.43f., i.7, ii.5.

5. *Confessions*, ii.4–ii.10 (pp. 31–37).

6. Peter of Luxembourg, V.P. v.27f.; P.C. v.44 (test. 17), vii.51f., viii.44 (test. 9); François, *Vie*, pp. 29f., 36f. This is a dimension of his spirituality which Johan Huizinga focuses on, in *The Waning of the Middle Ages*, pp. 167f., and following him Barbara W. Tuchman, *A Distant Mirror: The Calamitous 14th Century* (New York: Knopf, 1978), pp. 465–67.

7. P.C. ix.57f.; François, *Vie*, pp. 47f.

8. François, *Vie*, pp. 47f. The full text is in Henry Albi, *Le Voyage spirituel du b. Pierre de Luxembourg, cardinal, evesque de Mets, et protecteur de la ville d'Avignon* (Lyon: La Botiere, 1632).

9. Ibid., pp. 46f. Venturino of Bergamo, pp. 60f., refused to accept such donations.

10. Andrew Corsini, v.21; Francis Patrizzi, c. 6, 8; Henry Suso, i.16; Elzear of Sabran, V.Lat. v.65f.; Delphina of Puimichel, P.C., art. 47; Bridget of Sweden, p. 78. See also Bridget of Sweden, pp. 19, 312, 586.

11. V.Lin. i.16, ii.36, iii.46 (cf. iii.53, iii.74, iv.98).

12. V.Lin. iii.72f.

13. Flora of Beaulieu, iii.45f.; Catherine of Siena, iii.4.364; Elizabeth of Portugal, vi.54, xi.103; Elzear of Sabran, V.Lat. i.8, iii.30, v.62; Urban V, c. 33, 90; Catherine of Sweden, vii.63. See also Bridget of Sweden, pp. 17, 65, 312, 487, 582.

14. James Oldo, i.4; Henry Suso, ii.37; Urban V, c. 167; Elzear of Sabran, V.Lat., v.69; Catherine of Siena, V.P. iii.4.

15. *The Dialogue of Saint Catherine of Siena*, tr. Algar Thorald (reprint Rockford, Ill.: TAN, 1974), pp. 335–44.

16. Huizinga, *The Waning of the Middle Ages*, p. 21.

17. Umberto Eco, *The Name of the Rose*, trans. William Weaver (New York: Harcourt Brace Jovanovich, 1983), p. 119.

18. Henry Suso, i.3; Elzear of Sabran, V.Lat. ii.14, iv.52, v.65, v.67; Gertrude of Delft, ii.7, v.23.

19. Rulman Merswin, pp. 42f.

20. Catherine of Siena, ii.6.202f.; Jane Mary of Maillé, Vit. iii.23; Henry Suso, ii.36; Elzear of Sabran, V.Lat. v.67, V.Occ. pp. 114–19 (the statue is in the Lapidary Museum at Avignon); Catherine of Sweden, ii.16, ii.18. See also Clare of Rimini, c. 2.

21. Catherine of Sweden, i.2; Villana de' Botti, c. 4–6. For a parallel to the latter story—a tale of a woman who saw the devil in a mirror when she took too long preparing for mass—see Wright, *The Book of the Knight*, p. 46.

22. Andrew Corsini, i.1f.; Gonsalvo Sancii, pp. 549, 551. Cf. Silvester, c.1f.

23. Erhard Dorn, *Der sündige Heilige in der Legende des Mittelalters* (Munich: Fink, 1967).

24. *Confessions*, pp. 237–53 (bk. 10, chaps. 30–39). Cf. John Colombini ii.13–25.

25. James Oldo, ii.12; Dalmatius Moner, c.14, Catherine of Siena, i.4.45, i.6.64, ii.6.183–85 (See note to ii.6.183 in Kearns translation); Dorothy of Montau, V.Lat.v.30.

26. See Roland H. Bainton, *Here I Stand: A Life of Martin Luther* (New York & Nashville: Abingdon, 1950), pp. 54–56; Erik H. Erikson, *Young Man Luther: A Study in Psychoanalysis and History* (New York: Norton, 1958), esp. pp. 115f., speaks of Luther's scruples as "clasically compulsive"; Richard Friedenthal, *Luther, His Life and Times*, trans. John Nowell (New York: Harcourt Brace Jovanovich, 1970), pp. 44–47, emphasizes that Luther was healthy enough to be entrusted with positions of responsibility, and suggests that it is for polemical reasons that the later Luther portrays himself as having been tormented in earlier years; H. G. Haile, *Luther: An Experiment in Biography* (Garden City: Doubleday, 1980), esp. pp. 1–3, is generally skeptical regarding Luther's reports about his youth. What is of concern to us, however, is the legend about Luther more than the historical fact.

27. See Thomas N. Tentler, *Sin and Confession on the Eve of the Reformation* (Princeton, N.J.: Princeton University Press, 1977), pp. 21–23.

28. Henry Charles Lea, *A History of Auricular Confession and Indulgences in the Latin Church* (Philadelphia: Lea, 1896), vol. 1, p. 230.

29. Pierre Michaud-Quantin, *Sommes de casuistique et manuels de confession au moyen age: XIIe-XVIe siècles* (Louvain: Editions Nauwelaerts, 1962), pp. 7f.

30. In addition to Michaud-Quantin, see Mary Flowers Braswell, *The Medieval Sinner: Characterization and Confession in the Literature of the English Middle Ages* (Rutherford, N. J.:Fairleigh Dickinson University Press, 1983), pp. 19–60.

31. Ibid., p. 40.

32. This is the analysis of Braswell, ibid., pp. 40f.

33. Michaud-Quantin, *Sommes*, pp. 56, 66f.; on Passavanti, see Millard Meiss, *Painting in Florence and Siena after the Black Death: The Arts, Religion and Society in the Mid-Fourteenth Century*, pb. ed. (New York: Harper, 1964), pp. 83f. Cf. also Richard Rolle's *Judica me Deus*, ed. J. P. Daly (forthcoming).

34. W. A. Pantin, *The English Church in the Fourteenth Century* (Cambridge: Cambridge University Press, 1955), p. 192 (cited in Braswell, *The Medieval Sinner*, p. 7).

35. William Langland, *Piers the Ploughman*, trans. J. F. Goodridge (Harmondsworth: Penguin, 1959), pp. 99–118; Rodney Delasanta, "Penance and Poetry in the *Canterbury Tales*," *Publications of the Modern Language Association*, vol. 93 (1978), pp. 240–47; Lea W. Patterson, "Chaucerian Confession: Penitential Literature and the Pardoner," in Paul Maurice Clogan, ed., *Medievalia et Humanistica*, n.s., vol. 7 (Cambridge: Cambridge University Press, 1976), pp. 153–73.

36. Adapted from Braswell, *The Medieval Sinner*, pp. 102f.

37. Ibid., pp. 97–111; John Gower, *Confessio Amantis*, ed. Russell A. Peck (New York: Holt, 1966); John J. McNally, "The Penitential and Courtly Traditions in Gower's *Confessio Amantis*," in John R. Somerfeldt, ed., *Studies in Medieval Culture* (Kalamazoo: Western Michigan University Press, 1964).

38. Quoted in Tentler, *Sin and Confession*, p. 77.

39. See W. Werbeck, "Voraussetzungen und Wesen der 'scrupulositas' im Spätmittelalter," *Zeitschrift für Theologie und Kirche*, vol. 68 (1971), pp. 327–50, for references to the sources.

40. Lea, *Auricular Confession*, vol. 3.

41. See Richard Kieckhefer, "Radical Tendencies in the Flagellant Movement of the Mid-Fourteenth Century," *Journal of Medieval and Renaissance Studies*, vol. 4 (1974), pp. 157–76, and the sources there cited.

42. Francis Patrizzi, c. 20, 22; Catherine of Siena ii.6.215; Urban V, c. 167; Rulman

Merswin, p. 42; Cicco of Pesaro, c. 2f.; Catherine of Sweden, iv.36. See also Dalmatius Moner, c. 7.

43. Francis Patrizzi, c. 16.

44. PL vol. 49, col. 201–66.

45. Andrew Corsini, v.24; Clare Gambacorta, i.5(cf. i.3); Catherine of Sweden, i.4. See also Catherine of Sienna, i.4.44; Villana de' Botti, c. 8; Henry Suso, i.18; Bernard Tolomeo, iv.44; Robert of Salentino, i.13, ii.18; Peter of Fulgineo, ii.10; Dalmatius Moner, c. 9f.; Delphina of Puimichel, P.C., art. 39; John Domenici, ii.23.

46. Elizabeth of Portugal, x.91. See also Clare of Rimini, c.3. For abstinence from meat, see Catherine of Siena, i.6.58. For going without wine, James Oldo, ii.13, ii.15; Andrew Corsini, v.25; Catherine of Siena, R.C. i.6. For following the liturgical seasons, see e.g. Urban V, c. 58; James of Alverna, p. 440; Bridget of Sweden, pp. 16f.

47. Gertrude of Delft, ii.9; Clare Gambacorta, ii.21 (one of her sisters was accustomed to prepare "baccas Persicas" between two pieces of bread for her). See also Francis of Fabriano, i.6; Urban V, c. 59; Jane Mary of Maillé, Vit. iii.26, iv.28; John of Caramola, c. 30; James Oldo, ii.13f.

48. Catherine of Siena, i.2.31, i.3.44, i.6.59, ii.5.167, ii.5.170 (buf cf. ii.12.311); James Oldo, ii.14f.

49. Cicco of Pesaro, c. 6f.; Henry Suso, i.20. See also Conrad of Piacenza, ii.13f. (a sixteenth-century account).

50. Clare Gambacorta, i.4; Catherine of Siena, i.3.35; Andrew Corsini, v.23, v.25. See also Urban V, c. 24; Flora of Beaulieu, i.2f. (and her temptations, i.7–9). For virginity and chastity generally, see also Francis Patrizzi, c. 6; Dalmatius Moner, c. 8; Bernard Tolomeo, iv.47.

51. Jane Mary of Maillé, Vit. i.5, ii.15 (and P.C. i.6); James Oldo, i.4; Gonsalvo Sancii, pp. 549f.

52. Elzear of Sabran, V.Lat. i.6–12, iv.51–55 (and V.Occ. pp. 98–101); Delphina of Puimichel, P.C. arts. 1, 6–14 (and V.Occ. pp. 138–71). On their wedding night, Delphina cited the examples of Cecilia, Valerian, and Alexius in particular (P.C. art. 9); when she was sick, she told Elzear that if he did not promise never again to raise the question she would not recover (art. 10). The reference in the text to risking bodily death is obscure; presumably compulsion of some sort is what is intended.

53. Urban V, c. 63; Elzear of Sabran, V.Lat. iii.30; Henry Suso, i.17.

54. Urban V, c. 3; Catherine of Siena, i.6.61 (cf. i.4.51); Jane Mary of Maillé, Vit. iv.28 (cf. P.C. iii.15, iv.35, vi.70, vii.78); Gertrude of Delft, ii.10; Flora of Beaulieu, iii.50. See also Delphina of Puimichel, P.C. art. 17; Robert of Salentino, ii.19; Clare of Rimini, c.3; Bridget of Sweden, p. 13; Nicholas Hermansson, P.C. art. 2f.

55. John of Caramola, c. 5; Catherine of Siena, i.6.61, i.6.68; Andrew Corsini, iii.12, v.27; Nicholas Hermansson, Vit. p. 30, P.C. art.2; Urban V, c. 3. See also Richard Rolle, c. 5; Gerard Cagnoli, p. 491; Ademar of Felsinio, p. 464; Francis Patrizzi, c. 13; Catherine of Sweden, i.4, iv.38; Gonsalvo Sancii, p. 551; Henry Suso, i.17; Jane Mary of Maillé, Vit. ii.15; Dalmatius Moner, c. 12f.; Peter of Fulgineo, ii.11.

56. Andrew Corsini, iii.10, iii.14; Elzear of Sabran, V.Lat. v.66.

57. For passing references see Ademar of Felsinio, p. 464; Francis of Fabriano, i.6; Cicco of Pesaro, c. 1; Henry Suso, i.13, i.16; Villana de' Botti, c. 10; Gertrude of Delft, ii.7f.; Rulman Merswin, p. 40. Vauchez, La Sainteté, p. 457, comments on this decline of the ideal.

58. Jane Mary of Maillé, Vit. i.1, i.6, i.8, ii.14, iii.18, iii.25, iv.30; P.C. i.6, iv.35, vi.61, vi.67, vii.73, vii.74. See also Clare Gambacorta, i.8, ii.16, ii.20; Catherine of Sweden, iv.36, iv.38f.; Urban V, c.65–72, 166; Delphina of Puimichel, P.C. art. 20–25 (esp. vow of poverty, art. 22), V.Occ. pp. 184–93.

59. Clare Gambacorta, ii.20; Urban V, c. 65; Flora of Beaulieu, i.5f.

60. Jane Mary of Maillé, Vit. ii.16; Nicholas Hermansson, Vit. p. 30 (cf. p. 23);

Urban V, c. 86–88. See also Clare Gambacorta, i.6, ii.20; Gerard Cagnoli, p. 491; Villana de' Botti, c. 6; Richard Rolle, c. 1; Dalmatius Moner, c. 11; Delphina of Puimichel, P.C. art. 21.

61. Clare Gambacorta, iii.26; Villana de' Botti, c. 7. See also Catherine of Siena, i.9.83; Rulman Merswin, p. 42; Andrew Corsini, iii.12; Francis Patrizzi, c. 5; Jane Mary of Maillé, Vit. i.3, iii.25; Robert of Salentino, ii.17 (who spent twelve years in solitude).

62. Henry Suso, i.1; Flora of Beaulieu, i.1; Urban V, c. 70; Nicholas Hermansson, Vit. pp. 33f. See also Jane Mary of Maillé, Vit. ii.15; Delphina of Puimichel, P.C. art. 31.

63. Elzear of Sabran, ii.22.

64. John of Caramola, c. 5; Nicholas Hermansson, Vit. p. 34; Andrew Corsini, iii.12. See also Henry Suso, i.14; Richard Rolle, c. 3; Catherine of Siena, i.2.31, i.9.82; Jane Mary of Maillé, P.C. i.6; Catherine of Sweden, iii.21.

65. On mortification generally, see Bernard Tolomeo, iv.45; Sybillina Biscossi, ii.8–10; Brynolph, pp. 142, 148, 150, 152, 156, 162; Delphina of Puimichel, P.C. art. 34.

66. Andrew Corsini, v.27 (cf. iii.11); Francis of Fabriano, i.7f.; Francis Patrizzi, c. 19 (cf. c.6); Catherine of Siena, i.2.31, i.6.63, i.7.70; Francis of Fabriano, i.7. See also Elzear of Sabran, iii.35 (who recited Psalm 50 and, mindful of Christ's blows, beat himself hard on the back with an iron chain at each verse); Rulman Merswin, p. 42; Gonsalvo Sancii, p. 551; Ademar of Felsinio, p. 464; Urban V, c. 3; Delphina of Puimichel, P.C. art. 58; Peter of Fulgineo, ii.11; Bridget of Sweden, p. 14.

67. Clare Gambacorta, i.5; Henry Suso, i.15, i.5 (cf. i.18). On hairshirts see also Nicholas Hermansson, Vit. p. 30; P.C. art. 3, 30; Andrew Corsini, iii.12; Gerard Cagnoli, p. 491; Urban V, c. 3; Elzear of Sabran, V.Lat. iii.35; Ademar of Felsinio, p. 464; Jane Mary of Maillé, Vit. ii.14; Clare Gambacorta, i.5; Francis Patrizzi, c. 6; Gonsalvo Sancii, p. 551; Villana de' Botti, c. 6; Rulman Merswin, p. 47; Catherine of Siena, i.6.61; Iron chains: Catherine of Siena, i.6.61; Andrew Corsini, i.27; Jane Mary of Maillé, Vit. ii.14. Iron girdle or ring: Villana de' Botti, c. 6; John of Alverna, pp. 439f. Knotted cord: Elzear of Sabran, i.8; James Oldo, ii.13; Jane Mary of Maillé, Vit. vi.47, P.C. vii.82. Nettles: John of Alverna, p. 439.

68. Gerard Cagnoli, p. 491; Henry Suso, ii.35.

6. Rapture and Revelation

1. On mysticism generally, see Paul Szarmach, ed., *An Introduction to the Medieval Mystics of Europe* (Binghampton, N.Y.: State University of New York Press, 1984); Ray C. Petry, ed., *Late Medieval Mysticism* (Philadelphia: Westminster Press, 1957); May Ann Bowman, *Western Mystics: A Guide to the Basic Works* (Chicago: American Library Association, 1978); and Vauchez, *La Sainteté*, pp. 472–78.

2. Führkötter, *Das Leben der heiligen Hildegard;* F. W. E. Roth, ed., *Die Visionen der hl. Elisabeth und die Schriften der Aebte Ekbert und Emecho von Schönau* (Brunn: Verlag der "Studien aus dem Benedictiner- und Cistercienser-Orden," 1884).

3. Peter of Luxembourg, P.C. xi.74.

4. John Ruysbroeck, c. 17; Richard Rolle, vi.4; Flora of Beaulieu, ii.27, ii.32; Villana de' Botti, c. 6; Clare Gambacorta, ii.19; Elzear of Sabran, V.Lat. iii.36, iv.50 (and V.Occ. pp. 51–69); Robert of Salentino, ii.25. See also Elizabeth Achler, p. 104.

5. Henry Suso, i.12.

6. Vit. ii.2, ili.6 (cf. n.). Cf. Dan. 3:19–50.

7. See especially the prologue to *The Incendium amoris of Richard Rolle of Hampole*, ed. Margaret Deanesley (Manchester: Manchester University Press, 1915), p. 145; Elzear of Sabran, V.Lat. i.9, iv.50; Flora of Beaulieu, i.15 (cf. iii.43); Gertrude of Delft, i.3; Clare Gambacorta, iii.18; Jane Mary of Maillé, Vit. ii.10.

8. Elzear of Sabran, V.Lat. ii.16; Flora of Beaulieu, iii.42 (cf. iii.46 and iii.53); Peter

of Luxembourg, P.C. xi.74; John Ruysbroeck, c. 15. See also Venturino of Bergamo, pp. 54–56, 60; Robert of Salentino, iv.42; Delphina of Puimichel, P.C. art. 40.

9. Jane Mary of Maillé, P.C. i.6, ii.9; Flora of Beaulieu, iii.41; Gonsalvo Sancii, p. 492; Catherine of Siena, i.2.32f., ii.6.184, ii.6.192. See also Dalmatius Moner, c. 15; Robert of Salentino, iv.41; Bridget of Sweden, pp. 24, 203. For background, see Herbert Thurston, *The Physical Phenomena of Mysticism*, ed. J. H. Crehan (London: Burns & Oates, 1952).

10. Clare Gambacorta, iii.18; Flora of Beaulieu, ii.21, iii.50, iii.45, iii.53.

11. Catherine of Siena, ii.6.213–16.

12. "Septililium B. Dorotheae," *Analecta Bollandiana*, vol. 4 (1884), p. 216.

13. Catherine of Sweden, i.7, ii.18, iii.24 (for Bridget and Catherine); Jane Mary of Maillé, Vit. i.2, i.6, ii.16; P.C. v.51, v.56, vii.80; Henry Suso, ii.42f. See also Catherine of Sweden, iv.33; Elzear of Sabran, V.Lat. iv.55; Elizabeth of Portugal, iii.17–22.

14. Jane Mary of Maillé, P.C. iii.25; Elzear of Sabran, V.Lat. ii.23.

15. Christina Ebner, pp. 15f.

16. Bridget of Sweden, p. 202; Flora of Beaulieu, ii.27, ii.21f., ii.33f.

17. Christina Ebner, pp. 21f., 28.

18. Henry Suso, ii.34–37; Catherine of Siena, i.12.114–16.

19. Flora of Beaulieu, ii.32.

20. Henry Suso, i.32; Catherine of Siena, i.10.100. See Richard Kieckhefer, "Meister Eckhart's Conception of Union with God," *Harvard Theological Review*, vol. 71 (1978), pp. 203–25, for the notion of habitual or ongoing union.

21. Elzear of Sabran, V.Lat. ii.17–20, v.61f. On the canonists, see Brian Tierney, *Foundations of the Conciliar Theory: The Contributions of the Medieval Canonists from Gratian to the Great Schism* (Cambridge: Cambridge University Press, 1955).

22. John of Caramola, c. 4; Gerard Cagnoli, pp. 492f.; Nicholas Hermansson, p. 22; Gertrude of Delft, v.23, vi.27; Andrew Corsini, iv.18; Villana de' Botti, c. 10; Francis Patrizzi, c. 17; Peter Olafsson, pp. 15f.; Gertrude of Delft, vi.26; John of Caramola, p. 493; James Oldo, iii.21. See also Bridget of Sweden, pp. 22, 201f.

23. James Oldo, i.1, i.7; Clare Gambacorta, v.38; Catherine of Sweden, v.42 (for Bridget).

24. Gertrude of Delft, v.22; Gerard Cagnoli, pp. 492f.; Catherine of Sweden, ii.12. See also Villana de' Botti, c. 10; Catherine of Sweden, ii.12; Sybillina Biscossi, iii.18, iii.20; Delphina of Puimichel, P.C. art. 18, 42. The sixteenth-century life of Conrad of Piacenza tells how he was invited to a dinner but declined, partly because he knew that a cat had taken the fish that was to be served (ii.16).

25. Peter Olafsson, p. 16; Jane Mary of Maillé, P.C. vii.77. See also Bernard Tolomeo, iv.51f.; Venturino of Bergamo, p. 61; Conrad of Piacenza, iii.25; Bridget of Sweden, pp. 22, 202.

26. Ursulina of Parma, ii.11–iii.29.

27. Catherine of Siena, ii.4.150–52, ii.10.277–97. For another case of detecting sins by odor, see Bridget of Sweden, pp. 24, 274.

28. See Robert E. Lerner, "Medieval Prophecy and Religious Dissent," *Past & Present*, no. 72 (August 1976), especially pp. 17f.

29. Robinson and Rolfe, *Petrarch*, pp. 384–96.

30. Stephen Beissel, *Geschichte der Verehrung Marias in Deutschland während des Mittelalters: Ein Beitrag zur Religionswissenschaft und Kunstgeschichte* (Freiburg i.Br. Herder, 1909); Peter Meinhold, "Die Marienverehrung in der deutschen Mystik," *Saeculum*, vol. 27 (1976), pp. 180–96; Leo Scheffczyk, "Zur Geschichte der Marienlehre und Marienverehrung, in *Marienbild in Rheinland und Westfalen (14. Juni bis 22. September 1968 in Villa Hügel, Essen)*, pp. 15–42; Leonard Küppers, "Zur Geschichte der Mariendarstellung in der bildenden Kunst," ibid., pp. 43–54; Beverly Boyd, *The Middle English*

Miracles of the Virgin (San Marino, Calif.: Huntington Library, 1964); Grace Frank, "French Literature in the Fourteenth Century," pp. 71–73.

31. Andrew Corsini, iii.14; Gerard Cagnoli, p. 493; Bridget of Sweden, p. 79; James of Porta, p. 617. See also Delphina of Puimichel, P.C. art. 7; Robert of Salentino, i.11.

32. Catherine of Sweden, ii.18, i.7.

33. Francis Patrizzi, c. 24.

34. Vit. i.2, i.6, ii.16; P.C. v.51, v.56, vii.80.

35. Sancta Birgitta, *Opera minora*, vol. 2, ed. Sten Eklund (Uppsala: Almqvist & Wiksells, 1972), pp. 121–23.

36. Dickson, "Patterns of European Sanctity," vol. 1, discusses all aspects of the cult of saints. For James of Voragine, see the forthcoming study by Sherry Reames.

37. Catherine of Siena, i.5.53; Catherine of Sweden, iii.28 (for Bridget). See also Margaret of Faenza, Vit. i.6f. and Rev. ii.14; Ursulina of Parma, ii.13–15; and D. M. Faloci Pulignani, ed., "La Visione del Beato Tommasuccio," *Miscellanea Francescana di storia, di lettere, di arti*, vol. 8 (1893), pp. 148–58.

38. P.C. iv.40, v.55, v.57.

39. Flora of Beaulieu, ii.24, i.16.

40. Henry Suso, i.5, i.23.

41. Dorothy of Montau, V.Lin, iv.84; Cf. Kieckhefer, "Meister Eckhart's Conception," pp. 214f.

42. Flora of Beaulieu, ii.25, iii.47f. See also Elizabeth Achler, p. 108; Imelda Lambertini, c.7f. (The latter died, presumably in ecstasy, on receiving communion.)

43. Christina Ebner, p. 32; Jane Mary of Maillé, P.C. v.54. See also Catherine of Siena, ii.6.181; Bridget of Sweden, p. 202.

44. Jane Mary of Maillé, P.C. v.54; Flora of Beaulieu, iii.48. See also Elzear of Sabran, V.Lat. ii.28 (for story of Bertranda Carmata of Carpentras); Catherine of Siena, ii.12.323.

45. Caroline Bynum, *Jesus as Mother: Studies in the Spirituality of the High Middle Ages* (Berkeley: University of California Press, 1982), esp. pp. 256–58, suggests this along with other factors.

46. V.Lat. ii.21, v.65f.

47. Christina Ebner, p. 42; John Ruysbroeck, c. 28.

48. Flora of Beaulieu, ii.27, ii.21f., ii.33f.

49. Jane Mary of Maillé, Vit. 24 (cf. P.C. v.50, v.58); Flora of Beaulieu, iii.39, iii.41. See also Bridget of Sweden, p. 23.

50. Christina Ebner, pp. 26f.

51. Bridget of Sweden, pp. 80f.

52. Catherine of Siena, i.2.33, i.9.84f.; Peter Olafsson, p. 3; Catherine of Siena, ii.2.129; John Ruysbroeck, c. 24. See also William Gnoffi, i.5, ii.12.

53. Catherine of Siena, i.11.105–11.

54. Jane Mary of Maillé, Vit. iii.24; Rulman Merswin, p. 40; Flora of Beaulieu, ii.29 (which comes before 28), ii.32; Dorothy of Montau, V.Lat. iv.1.

55. Flora of Beaulieu, ii.23; John of Alverna, p. 444.

56. Elzear of Sabran, V.Lat. ii.21. Elizabeth Achler, p. 104, recovered painfully.

57. Flora of Beaulieu, iii.53. See also Margaret of Faenza, Vit. i.6 (cf. Rev. i.6).

7. Unquiet Souls

1. V.Lin. iii.47, iv.85, iv.95, iv.100. There are many parallels in the V.Lat., especially books 4–5.

2. *Confessions,* p. 3 (bk. 1, chap. 1).

3. Gerhart B. Ladner, *"Homo Viator*: Mediaeval Ideas on Alienation and Order," *Speculum,* vol. 42 (1967):233–59.

4. See E. I. Watkin, *Poets and Mystics* (London & New York: Sheed and Ward, 1953), p. 122.

5. Francis Patrizzi, c. 12; Clare Gambacorta, i.4, ii.18; Gonsalvo Sancii, p. 551; Catherine of Sweden, iv.31; Ademar of Felsinio, p. 464; Dorothy of Montau, V.Lat., passim; Dalmatius Moner, c. 5 ("cepit . . . continuis orationibus crebrisque fletibus insistere, multis gemitibus et pectorum tunsionibus se affligere"). See also Delphina of Puimichel, P.C., art. 27.

6. F. W. Faber, *The Lives of St. Rose of Lima, the Blessed Colomba of Rieti, and of St. Juliana Falconieri* (London: Richardson, 1847), pp. 15f., (cf. 3, 18–20, 28, 31, 44f., 81, 77, 84, 91, 100).

7. The source for her life is *The Book of Margery Kempe,* ed. Sanford Brown Meech (London: Milford, 1940); there is an edition in modern English, by the same title, edited by W. Butler-Bowdon (London: Cape, 1936). For the most recent literature, see Clarissa W. Atkinson, *Mystic and Pilgrim: The Book and the World of Margery Kempe* (Ithaca, N.Y.: Cornell University Press, 1983). The correspondence of events in 1373 is noted by Edmund Colledge, in James Walsh, ed., *Pre-Reformation English Spirituality* (London: Burns & Oates, n.d.), p. 211.

8. The similarities were first observed by Hope Emily Allen, in Meech's edition of the *Book,* pp. liii–lxii. They have been explored by Ute Stargardt, in "The Influence of Dorothea von Montau on the Mysticism of Margery Kempe" (Ph.D. diss., University of Tennessee, 1981).

9. *Book,* i.58 (cf. i.17).

10. Ibid., i.28. On weeping, see Atkinson, *Mystic and Pilgrim,* pp. 58–65.

11. Ibid., i.54, i.34, i.52, i.54; on the theme of patience see also i.18, i.50.

12. Ibid., i.14.

13. Ibid., proem, i.3, i.57, i.86.

14. Ibid., i.14, i.4, i.22, i.28, i.46, i.60, i.79–81, i.28, i.30. The vision of the passion ends with an account of the resurrection, but because of Christ's *Noli me tangere* Margery is left disconsolate rather than rejoicing (i.81).

15. See Walsh, *Pre-Reformation English Spirituality,* p. 212, 220.

16. *Book,* i.35f., i.89.

17. Ibid., i.89. See Atkinson, *Mystic and Pilgrim,* pp. 120–28.

18. The reference to Mary of Oignies is in ibid., i.62.

19. Ibid., i.72.

20. Ibid. i.52. Atkinson, *Mystic and Pilgrim,* pp. 116–20, discusses Margery's relations with the clergy.

21. This is a central thrust of Atkinson's book, and the essence of Stargardt's dissertation.

22. Drew E. Hinderer, "On Rehabilitating Margery Kempe," *Studia Mystica,* vol. 5 (1982), pp. 27–43; the quote is on p. 35.

23. George D. Bond and I are coeditors of a volume on sainthood in world religions (forthcoming), which will endeavor to show how this tension is manifested in different religious traditions. It is a main theme also for Weinstein and Bell, *Saints and Society.*

24. See Peter Dinzelbacher, *Visionen und Visionliteratur im Mittelalter* (Stuttgart: Hiersemann, 1981). Dinzelbacher includes religious and secular visions in his survey, and establishes a typology to cover both.

25. G. R. Potter, "Some Characteristics of the Fourteenth Century," in R. W. Seton-Watson, ed., *Prague Essays, Presented by a Group of British Historians to the Caroline University of Prague on the Occasion of Its Six-hundredth Anniversary* (Oxford: Clarendon Press,

1949), p. 27; Robert E. Lerner, *The Heresy of the Free Spirit in the Later Middle Ages* (Berkeley & Los Angeles: University of California Press, 1972), esp. p. 243.

26. Johannes Tauler, *Die Predigten Taulers,* ed. Ferdinand Vetter (Berlin: Weidmann, 1910), no. 6, 8.

27. *Butler's Lives,* ed. Thurston and Attwater, September, p. 334.

28. See Janet Coleman, *Medieval Readers and Writers, 1350–1400* (New York: Columbia; London: Hutchinson, 1981). I intend to examine the manifestations in saints' lives in a separate context.

29. Catherine of Siena, i.2.31.

30. Watkin, "In Defence of Margery Kempe," in his *Poets and Mystics,* 104–35.

31. Hinderer, "On Rehabilitating," p. 37.

32. Ibid., pp. 37f.

33. Gilbert K. Chesterton, *Orthodoxy* (London: John Lane, 1909), pp. 148–87.

34. Michelle Murray, "The Jagged Edge: A Biographical Essay on Simone Weil," in George Abbott White, ed., *Simone Weil: Interpretations of a Life* (Amherst: University of Massachusetts Press, 1980), pp. 13–28.

35. Lawrence S. Cunningham, *The Meaning of Saints* (San Francisco: Harper, 1980), pp. 80–82.

36. One thinks perhaps of antinuclear or environmental groups that have rallied support from less adventuresome followers by taking dramatic and often illegal measures of protest.

37. See Huizinga, *The Waning of the Middle Ages,* esp. pp. 22–45. Lawrence Stone, reviewing Tuchman's *Distant Mirror* in the *New York Review of Books,* vol. 25 (September 28, 1978), p. 4, says, "her basic theme . . . is the very convincing one that the fourteenth century suffered from a severe case of what we now call 'cognitive dissonance.' Rarely has the gap between the ideal and the real been so large." See also Marjorie Reeves and Stephen Medcalf, "The Ideal, the Real and the Quest for Perfection," in Stephen Medcalf, ed., *The Later Middle Ages* (New York: Holmes and Meier, 1981), pp. 56–107.

38. Schiller, *Iconography,* p. 222.

Index

DATE DUE

OCT 1 2 2005		
FEB 2 1 2006		